SPECIAL EDUCATIONAL NEEDS AND DISABILITY

THE BASICS

Special Educational Needs and Disability: The Basics has been fully updated in light of the 2014 Children and Families Act in England and now also includes a focus and discussion of legislation across the whole UK. Providing an engaging and complete overview, it examines the fundamental principles of the subject from policy to practice. This book covers the historical development of special provision and key legislation, policy-making, the identification and assessment of young people's special or additional learning and behaviour needs, and ways to address barriers to learning associated with various kinds of difficulty.

Essential revisions to this second edition include:

- discussion of the implications of the 2014 *Special Educational Needs and Disability Code of Practice: 0 to 25 years* for heads, governors, SENCOs, staff, students and families in schools in England
- a focus on the law relating to special or additional support needs in Wales, Scotland and Northern Ireland, and its implications
- an update on statutory assessment requirements and advice on compiling them, including the new Education Health and Care Plans in England.

This book is an ideal starting point for all those with questions about what constitutes special educational needs and disability and how individuals can be supported in practice. It is essential reading for policy-makers, trainees, teachers and all those working with young people who experience difficulties and their families.

Janice Wearmouth is Professor of Education at the University of Bedfordshire, UK.

The Basics

ACTING
BELLA MERLIN

AMERICAN PHILOSOPHY
NANCY STANLICK

ANCIENT NEAR EAST
DANIEL C. SNELL

ANIMAL ETHICS
TONY MILLIGAN

ANTHROPOLOGY
PETER METCALF

ARCHAEOLOGY (SECOND EDITION)
CLIVE GAMBLE

ART HISTORY
GRANT POOKE AND DIANA NEWALL

ARTIFICIAL INTELLIGENCE
KEVIN WARWICK

THE BIBLE
JOHN BARTON

BIOETHICS
ALASTAIR V. CAMPBELL

BODY STUDIES
NIALL RICHARDSON AND ADAM LOCKS

BUDDHISM
CATHY CANTWELL

CAPITALISM
DAVID COATES

CHRISTIANITY
BRUCE CHILTON

THE CITY
KEVIN ARCHER

CONTEMPORARY LITERATURE
SUMAN GUPTA

CRIMINAL LAW
JONATHAN HERRING

CRIMINOLOGY (SECOND EDITION)
SANDRA WALKLATE

DANCE STUDIES
JO BUTTERWORTH

EASTERN PHILOSOPHY
VICTORIA S. HARRISON

ECONOMICS (THIRD EDITION)
TONY CLEAVER

EDUCATION
KAY WOOD

ENERGY
MICHAEL SCHOBERT

EUROPEAN UNION (SECOND EDITION)
ALEX WARLEIGH-LACK

EVOLUTION
SHERRIE LYONS

FILM STUDIES (SECOND EDITION)
AMY VILLAREJO

FINANCE (THIRD EDITION)
ERIK BANKS

FOOD ETHICS
RONALD SANDLER

FREE WILL
MEGHAN GRIFFITH

GENDER
HILARY LIPS

GENOCIDE
PAUL R. BARTROP

GLOBAL MIGRATION
*BERNADETTE HANLON AND
THOMAS VICINIO*

GREEK HISTORY
ROBIN OSBORNE

HUMAN GENETICS
RICKI LEWIS

HUMAN GEOGRAPHY
ANDREW JONES

SPECIAL EDUCATIONAL NEEDS AND DISABILITY

THE BASICS

Second Edition

Janice Wearmouth

LONDON AND NEW YORK

Second edition published 2016
by Routledge
2 Park Square, Milton Park, Abingdon, Oxon OX14 4RN

and by Routledge
711 Third Avenue, New York, NY 10017

Routledge is an imprint of the Taylor & Francis Group, an informa business

First edition published 2012 by Routledge

British Library Cataloguing-in-Publication Data
A catalogue record for this book is available from the British Library

Library of Congress Cataloging in Publication Data
A catalog record for this book has been requested

ISBN: 978-1-138-93876-2 (hbk)
ISBN: 978-1-138-93877-9 (pbk)
ISBN: 978-1-315-67546-6 (ebk)

Typeset in Bembo
by Saxon Graphics Ltd, Derby

DEDICATION

This book is for Chris and Hannah, with lots of love and all good wishes for the future.

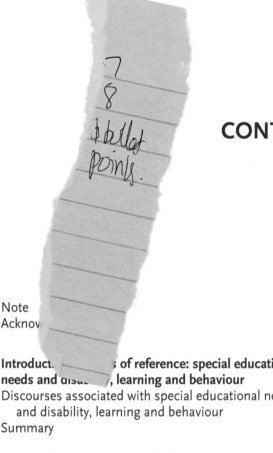

7
8
+ bullet
points.

CONTENTS

NOTE

Whilst every effort has been made to ensure that details associated with legislation in relation to SEND/additional needs across the UK are accurate at the time of writing, as is noted at appropriate points in the text some changes in the law are envisaged and may well be put into place shortly.

ACKNOWLEDGEMENTS

I would like to thank Widgit for their kind permission to reproduce examples of their Symbol Set.

I would also like to thank the following colleagues very much for their assistance and advice in relation to legislation associated with special educational needs, additional support needs and inclusion in Scotland, Northern Ireland and Wales: Mike Gibson, Cathy McGee, Sharon McMurray, Rosemary Kilpatrick and Eileen Taylor.

I would also like to acknowledge Martha Smith's contribution in the area of autism.

INTRODUCTION

Frames of reference: special educational needs and disability, learning and behaviour

Over time, a number of frames of reference – that is, ways of looking at and interpreting what is around us – have been developed and become important in the world of special educational needs and disability (SEND). It is important to recognise these and have a grasp of how they are used in order to understand SEND policy, practice and provision. This Introduction includes a discussion of frames of reference that are very commonly used in schools in relation to children's SEND, learning and behaviour. It also includes a brief discussion of different ways in which the 'needs' of each child can be viewed in relation to the difficulty that is experienced and what they imply about the individual learners so described.

A number of pen portraits of young people who experience different kinds of disabilities and difficulties in learning and behaviour serve to illustrate some of these frames of reference. A problem-solving approach to addressing needs that can be very effective in overcoming barriers to learning is discussed.

DISCOURSES ASSOCIATED WITH SPECIAL EDUCATIONAL NEEDS AND DISABILITY, LEARNING AND BEHAVIOUR

In schools, the expression 'special educational needs and disability' is used in relation to students' learning. We might ask ourselves whether the frame of reference we use to judge the learning and behaviour of children identified as having 'special educational needs and/or a disability' enables us to understand these children in the same way as others. These days, with inclusion in schools and society in such high focus, the practical consequences of our answer to this question are very important for us all. We might illustrate this point with reference to 'James', whose dyslexic difficulties were misinterpreted at one point in his education as slowness in learning for which an appropriate response was withdrawal from the mainstream classroom and tuition with other 'slow learners'. Fortunately for him other teachers later on took a different view. They recognised that here was a young man who, in circumstances where people listened to him, could be articulate and, apart from difficulties in literacy acquisition, very able.

Discourses around difficulties in literacy, and their consequences

A few years ago, 'James', aged 21, graduated with an Upper Second Honours degree from a well-known English university. He went on to study for his Master's degree. He had clearly become academically very successful with very high expectations of himself. High expectations of him by others was not always the case, however.

In his primary school, aged 9, 'James' was placed in the lowest ability groups for reading and writing in his class and withdrawn for special lessons on account of serious difficulties in literacy acquisition:

> First of all, when I went to the lessons, I was called out in front of the class, and they were referred to as special lessons, and politically correct as the teacher thought that was, it really wasn't. Kids are cruel, and I felt really targeted and singled out.

He was clearly dyslexic, as later assessment by an educational psychologist confirmed. Dyslexia was not a label that was recognised in James' local education authority at that time, however. Separation from competent literacy learners in the classroom and tuition in low-level 'remedial' literacy activities that he felt were irrelevant and meaningless resulted in feelings of hopelessness, helplessness and frustration. Great feelings of defiance and frustration resulted from the conflict between the provision made by the school and what he felt he needed, and from his own impotence in the situation:

> The lessons that they gave seemed very simple. They were like obvious repetitive stuff, going over stuff that I found simple ... I think the type of work that it was, was perhaps, writing out a page of like, a hundred, you know a full page worth of say a letter at a time, say D, repeating it over and over again. and although my handwriting wasn't fantastic, I could write the letter D, but then that seemed to bear no relation to me writing a word.

The category of 'slow learner' had been created in that school in order to manage special literacy provision, and hovered in the air ready to 'gobble up' likely candidates such as James (Mehan, 1996).

James' experiences in secondary school were very different, however. There he was encouraged to see himself as capable of making sense of his own world. Teachers responded to his difficulties in a way that suited his individual learning needs and they engaged in two-way discussion with him about the best ways to address his learning needs. With the added motivation of teachers expecting that he could learn, despite extreme tiredness every day, James began to look for ways to achieve and overcome his difficulties:

> I became very strategic ... it was a strategy I worked out for myself [that] seemed blatantly obvious. If the course provides a syllabus, and the examiners can only ask you on that syllabus, then why

> not learn everything in the syllabus, and keep to that? Basically for the sciences, I could get a book, and just work through each point of the syllabus, and if I knew it then ... I didn't almost need the lessons. ... I basically listed each point of the syllabus, and found the relevant piece of information and picked it out.

Self-taught study skills, supported by sensitive, aware teachers who responded to James' initiatives and a growing sense of personal agency enabled James to achieve success at the General Certificate of Secondary Education level (GCSE):

> before then it was blips ... But when I did my GCSEs, I think all told I took thirteen, I got two A stars, six As five Bs. By then people were like, 'Bloody hell!' and then it got to my A-levels, and in the three sciences I got three B grades which was quite good.

These skills, refined for study at degree level, enabled James to extend responsibility for his own learning until his graduation.

(Adapted from Wearmouth, 2004a, pp. 60–67)

Interestingly enough, and as discussed in Chapter 5 (see pp. 125–8), in recent years greater understanding of the effects of dyslexia on individual learning and achievement has led to a severely dyslexic individual potentially being classed as 'disabled', giving him/her an entitlement to 'reasonable adjustments' in the educational or work context under the terms of the Equality Act, 2010. Hence, for example, a dyslexic university student may be offered use of a laptop computer as a 'reasonable adjustment' to enable access to the academic curriculum.

WHAT DOES THE LABEL 'SPECIAL EDUCATIONAL NEEDS AND/OR DISABILITY' TELL US ABOUT CHILDREN?

Of course some young people experience sensory and/or physical difficulties, multiple and profound difficulties in learning, language issues, and so on. However, as we shall see in Chapter 2, giving a child the label 'special educational needs and/or disability' (SEND), such as a 'SEND child', tells us nothing specific enough about a student and his or her learning to begin to conceptualise what might be done to ensure that s/he can access the curriculum on offer, because the term covers a whole range of areas – learning, social, emotional and health, sensory, and so on. In addition, labelling pupils as 'special needs' children, or children 'with SEND', is highly problematic for other reasons.

In schools, as Fulcher (1989) points out, staff may react to children's difficulties in a number of ways. Some might use a frame of reference concerned with what is 'wrong' with children and how this 'problem' can be dealt with. Focusing on what is wrong with a person means emphasising ways in which s/he is different or deficient, where 'deficiencies' can be 'treated' like an illness. It can often be experienced, especially by the learners themselves, as a very negative way of meeting needs. Where use of the label 'special educational needs and/or disability' depends on the sense of deficiency in children, it is often seen as reflecting a 'medical' or 'deficit model' of difficulties in learning and/or behaviour. This model has a sense of being in some way inferior or distant from the norm, for example, *dis-, un-, -challenged, difficulty*. This way of looking at students' difficulties may in itself prevent a positive approach to diversity and difference.

Other people's frames of reference might be more concerned with children's well-being and their own moral duty to help them. They may worry about the child and feel sympathy for the child's struggles. In some situations, the difficulties that children experience may be seen as a tragedy for the individual and/or the family, and the children treated like 'charity cases'.

Another frame of reference for understanding difficulties is viewing the social context in which learning takes place as a potential barrier. An examination of the physical environment, including the resources, teaching approaches, the difficulty and/or interest level of the task or activity, may show how they can act as facilitators for, or constraints on, learning. Social factors can turn some differences into disabilities. In a broader context, one might ask, for example, what part economic deprivation and poverty contribute to creating difficulties in learning experienced by children. We might then think about the extent to which 'learning difficulties' might be seen as 'obstacles to learning' arising from the society in which those students live. It might be economic factors, government policy, institutional practices, broader social attitudes or inappropriate physical surroundings that stop people from doing things.

Within school or college settings we often see some of these views of the difficulties experienced by children.

Connotations of the SEND label

Frames of reference associated with the SEND label may carry positive or negative connotations in relation to individual children. On the surface, the notion of fulfilling a 'need' conveys a sense of kindliness. In practice, however, the kind of special or additional provision that is made may imply a value placed on pupils (Salmon, 1995). There may be an assumption of agreement between all the interested parties about what is 'needed' which often (but not always, of course) ignores 'crucial issues' of the lack of power that may be allowed to pupils and parents in the decision-making process. Sometimes, as discussed below, this is associated with a view that interventions should be planned by experts and 'done to' the child with SEND. Cole (2005) reports her own study of the views of teachers who were mothers of children with special educational needs and notes how the perspectives of the mother-teachers changed when their own children were identified as experiencing difficulties. What they came to value as 'inclusion' emerged as a result of their own individual experiences. They valued the small things that professionals did to make their children and themselves feel included, who tried hard and demonstrated good faith. The specifics of what they wanted for their children in terms of provision differed, but, in the end, they wanted to see their children included in the community. These mother-teachers are reported as taking their role as advocates for their own children and the children with whom they worked very seriously.

Sometimes personal experiences with students can open our eyes to some of the issues related to the labels we give to students.

Discourses around challenging behaviour

Eleven-year-old 'Jamie S' was another boy identified as 'having problems', but this time categorised as both disruptive and lazy. He was placed in the 'remedial' band, along with students who experienced difficulty in conceptual development: language, problem-solving, communication and abstract thinking. I taught his group Classical Studies, which Jamie loved. He was the first with the answer to everything and was very articulate. At the end of one year, he corrected my version of a tale from Greek mythology that I had related many months before. He was right; I was wrong. There was a clear disjunction between the label 'remedial' and my observation of him as articulate, interested and engaged in his learning. He loudly resisted writing tasks because, as I later (but much too late for Jamie) realised, like James above he was dyslexic – and, like James, was educated in a local authority where dyslexia was not recognised. In some lessons he expressed his feelings of frustration with the lack of cognitive challenge and pressure to write with obviously hostile behaviour. In my lessons I was relying largely on narrative so pressure to cope with text did not apply. In the hierarchy of power and influence in schools, those with a professional responsibility for sustaining existing organisational structures may well experience the rejection of school provision by students such as Jamie as challenging to the existing order as well as to themselves. They may then go on to interpret the behaviour of these students, and the students themselves, as deviant and as 'needing' to be cured by a special intervention programme.

(Wearmouth, 2003)

The use of the word 'need' is extremely sensitive in the context of education. In some parts of the UK 'need' in education is seen to arise as the result of some kind of deficiency in an individual. In the same way that a starving person 'needs' sustenance, for example, a young person with special educational needs 'needs' special provision to access the school or college curriculum. It is not simply the word itself that is at issue, however, but the question about who has the power to decide which children have needs, what those needs are and how these should be met (Armstrong, 1994). There is also a question about appropriate expectations of children identified as 'having' SEN. There is a strong relationship between teachers' expectations and student achievement, self esteem and development that has been well documented since the seminal work of Rosenthal and Jacobson (1968). Salmon (1995) comments on her perception that the term SEN (now SEND) is too often associated with a sense of failure to come up to the mark. Instead of signifying belonging and entitlement, she sees the terms *special* and *need* as 'weasel words' with connotations of helplessness and inadequacy. They are used to justify relegating the problem to a specialist, whilst at the same time leaving teachers 'feeling helpless and deskilled' (Salmon, 1995, pp. 73–74). In a similar vein, Corbett (1996) comments that students with the special needs label can become marginalised by schools. She asks, 'What does "special" mean? If we detach this word from its anchor in "educational" we can see that "special" does not mean especially good and valued unless we use a phrase like, "you are a special person".' She notes that 'special' 'is linked to needs, implying dependency, inadequacy and unworthiness' (Corbett, 1996, p. 3).

Not all educators take the same view, however. Some, for example, Cole (1990), argue that identifying children's 'special educational needs' has a very humanitarian aim. This is to provide additional resources, develop specialist methods to address particular difficulties in learning, or overcome the effects of a disability in order that children can benefit from their education. Without identification of individual needs it is impossible to justify individual attention.

Interpretations of 'need'

'Melvin', aged 13, was small, thin, frequently hungry and dirty. He had the reputation of being an incorrigible kleptomaniac. Several times he was found stealing from peers, staff, the local shops and people queuing at the bus stop near the school. Whilst still only 12, he had stolen a local bus and driven it along the high street. He was caught because he was so small that he could only see through the spokes of the steering wheel and passers-by reported a bus travelling along with no driver. Some of his teachers saw him as intrinsically bad and wanted him to be excluded permanently because they thought he was a threat to his peers and to the school. What he 'needed' was expulsion from mainstream and treatment in a special school. The educational psychologist thought he 'needed' hypnotherapy, to 'treat' and 'cure' him. Others took a more charitable view. His problem was not badness within himself, but neglect by his family. They felt that what he really 'needed' was food and clean clothes and that then he would be 'sorted out'.

(Adapted from Wearmouth, 2009)

SUMMARY

In this Introduction we have seen how important it is to recognise the frame of reference within which the special educational needs of children are understood. In my own experience of teaching in eight different schools, it is very clear that this strongly affects how we treat them and the kind of provision that is made.

Chapter 1 sets the scene for understanding frames of reference commonly used in the area of special educational needs and disabilities by discussing a variety of psychological models of human learning and behaviour that have been dominant in educational circles at different times. Chapter 2 then outlines the history of provision for children seen as 'different' from peers on account of learning, physical or behaviour difficulties, and the changes in thinking about such difficulties over time. Chapter 3 focuses on children's difficulties in communication and interaction, common indicators of these difficulties, their relationship with learning, and some of the ways that such difficulties might be addressed. Chapter 4 is concerned with understanding and addressing difficulties in cognition and learning, with particular attention given to moderate and specific learning difficulties. Chapter 5 turns to issues of social, emotional and mental health, and Chapter 6 to understanding and addressing sensory and/or physical difficulties and needs. Chapter 7 relates to the challenges of assessing young people's special educational needs and disabilities, and Chapter 8 to the range of people who might be expected to have an interest in supporting children who experience some sort of difficulty, and their likely role, and to some of the challenges in relation to this kind of partnership work – with examples of what can happen in practice.

MODELS OF HUMAN LEARNING
Behaviourist, constructivist and eco-systemic approaches

INTRODUCTION

Crucial to understanding difficulties in learning and behaviour and ways to address these is familiarity with common frames of reference within which that learning and behaviour is viewed. There is an important, though in some ways simplistic, distinction that we can make between the view that the mind is a passive recipient of knowledge and merely reacts to outside influence, and the view that it is pro-active in interpreting and constructing the world. In terms of frames of reference from educational psychology, a passive view of the human mind is most commonly reflected in the behaviourist model. Here all behaviour is assumed to be learned. Underlying behavioural principles is a basic concern with observed events, that is what people actually do, not on assumptions about intentions or statements *about* behaviour and its effects. In the world of special needs provision individual education plans have often been drawn up with interventions designed to shape learning and behaviour that are 'done to' the child. The opposite view of the human mind, that it is active in reaching out and constructing meaning, is reflected in frames of reference most commonly associated with constructivist and socio-cultural views of learning.

UNDERSTANDING LEARNING FROM A BEHAVIOURIST VIEW

Principles linked to behaviourist psychology (Skinner, 1938, 1953; Baer *et al.*, 1968) have often dominated thinking about how to intervene when things are seen to have gone wrong in terms of learning and behaviour in educational institutions (Dwivedi & Gupta, 2000). It is particularly important, therefore, to be familiar with the frame of reference associated with this approach.

UNDERSTANDING PRINCIPLES OF BEHAVIOURISM

Almost all the principles of behaviourist approaches were derived from work with laboratory animals, for example, Skinner (1938). Early experiments with animals assumed that all behaviour is learned through a process of conditioning. In a famous sequence of trial-and-error learning tasks, rats learned to press levers in order to find food (Skinner, 1938). Learning involved the formation of a stimulus–response association, that is, pressing the lever and finding food, in the rats' memory. Reinforcement through a reinforcer, in this case food, strengthened the association between stimulus and response. If the association between stimulus and response was broken by removing the reward, the rats' behaviour would gradually cease through 'extinction'. The opposite of positive reinforcement is negative reinforcement. Undesirable behaviour is discouraged and desired behaviour encouraged through putting a stop to something unpleasant. Where something unpleasant occurred as a result of an action it is viewed as 'punishment'.

The same behavioural principles have been applied to attempts to modify interactions between teachers and pupils in school contexts. The behavioural model works on the principle that behaviour is learned, and that responses (or behaviours) are strengthened or weakened by their consequences.

When behavioural principles are applied in school settings, the reinforcing conditions or consequences of behaviour as well as the physical and social context in which the behaviour occurs are systematically modified in order to improve students' behaviour. When viewed against the behaviourist frame of reference, behaviour experienced as disturbing is seen as having been learned through positive reinforcement in some way. Most work in response to issues of individual students' behaviour that is perceived as disturbing by teachers has been based 'on behavioural management approaches (which employ strategies such as positive reinforcement, response cost, extinction and so on) where the reinforcing conditions or consequences of a behaviour are adjusted in order to moderate its frequency' (Dwivedi & Gupta, 2000, p. 76). Operant conditioning – reinforcing what teachers want their students to do again, ignoring or punishing what they want students to stop doing – has been widely applied in teaching in UK classrooms since the 1970s (Merrett, 1985). One way to address undesirable behaviour is therefore to ensure that whatever is rewarding and reinforcing is removed so that the behaviour is extinguished. In addition, whenever individuals behave in ways that are seen as more appropriate, they should be rewarded in a way that clearly recognises the greater acceptability of the new behaviour within contexts where that behaviour is clearly acceptable. Another way is to identify and alter the stimulus context or setting (the 'setting conditions') in which that behaviour occurs.

In addition to classroom management, behavioural approaches have often been used in the SEND area for programmed instruction where tasks requiring repetitive practice, like learning multiplication tables, spelling, phonic work and word recognition can be broken down into small stages, and where correct responses by students can be rewarded and reinforced.

Applying behavioural principles to difficulties in behaviour and learning

Behavioural principles can be applied to changing behaviour at individual or group level. Rogers (1994a and 1994b), for example, encourages adopting a behavioural approach towards teaching primary school pupils whom he describes as 'behaviourally-disordered' (BD) to take responsibility for their own behaviour. He notes: 'While most students respond to the normal socialisation into rights-respecting behaviour, some will need to be *specifically taught*'. He goes on to comment, '…. learning targets can be developed as specific *behaviour* plans that involve teacher modelling, student-rehearsal and feedback and encouragement in the natural setting of the classroom (Rogers, 1994, pp. 166–167).

Effective behaviour management is not simply about increasing and decreasing behaviours, but also about teaching students to discriminate between settings (times and places) where certain behaviours are appropriate and acceptable, and other settings where they are not. In Rogers' view, we should not excuse students from 'taking ownership for their disruptive behaviour', or 'facing accountability for such behaviour by facing appropriate consequences' or 'learning that behaviour is not an accident of birth or location', and that 'one can learn to make better and more conscious choices about behaviour' (Rogers, 1994, p. 167).

Individual student behaviour

Individualised behaviour management strategies should make clear to pupils what behaviours are unacceptable and also provide opportunities for modelling, rehearsing and reinforcing behaviours that are acceptable (Rogers, 1994, pp. 167–169). Behavioural methodology is a scientifically based technology, so the first requirement is a clear definition of the target behaviour. For instance, if a child is thought to be 'hyperactive' Merrett (1985) suggests an operational definition of behaviours such as 'out of seat' will be required. Once the behaviour has been operationally defined, there should be systematic observational sampling across times of day, situations, nature of activity, person in charge and so on. Such observations need to be taken over a period of about five days to establish the baseline level of responding. Once the baseline can be clearly seen an analysis detailing the following three stages should be carried out:

A – the antecedent event(s), that is, whatever starts off or prompts
B – the behaviour, which is followed in turn by
C – the consequence(s).

(Merrett, 1985, p. 8)

Merrett advises that where a consequence of a behaviour 'is shown to be maintaining [the] behaviour at a high level then that consequence is, by definition, and regardless of its nature, reinforcing it positively'. Telling children off can temporarily choke off certain behaviours, but these may recur after a very short time. This can be 'very frustrating for the teacher'. However, it may be the teacher's scolding that is maintaining the child's behaviour. 'By definition "ticking off" is positively reinforcing the child's "attention-seeking" behaviour. If that positive reinforcement is removed then the rate of occurrence of the behaviour will be reduced. It will eventually become extinguished' (Merrett, 1985, p. 9).

Strategies to maximise students' learning of new behaviours include 'shaping', which breaks complex tasks down into a series of steps and ensures that each step is reinforced in a particular sequence. Other procedures include modelling, where students are rewarded for matching the behaviour being displayed for them.

From a behaviourist perspective, then, and as Rogers (2013) comments, a child's background is no excuse for poor behaviour. Socially acceptable behaviour is learned and can, therefore, be taught. Key to motivating pupils to choose appropriate behaviour are 'positive reinforcers': teacher praise, rewards of various sorts and positive communications with parents. If children disrupt the lesson they should take ownership of this and be given a reminder what the rules are: 'Jayson … you're calling out … Remember our class rules for asking questions, thanks' (Rogers, 2013, p. 238). In classrooms, younger children can be given a non-verbal cue to appropriate behaviour and shown clearly what is expected.

Adults' behaviour is very important in modelling and reinforcing specific ways of behaving in particular situations. In doing so it is really important not to allow oneself to be drawn into a power struggle that some young people find rewarding and that is likely to reinforce the way they are behaving. Students may imitate negative as well as positive behaviour however, so, for example, the use of abusive or sarcastic language should be avoided at all costs. This might entail modelling ways of resolving conflict which respect the rights of students to learn and feel safe, and

- meet the needs of both parties, that is, provide win–win outcomes wherever possible
- bring an end to the conflict, or at least reduce it
- do not leave either party 'wounded'.

(Sproson, 2004, p. 319)

There are a number of techniques that can enable teachers to avoid power struggles with students:

- Some young people may take pleasure in not doing what they are asked immediately, especially if there is an audience of peers. In this situation Rogers (2013, p. 240) among others advocates that, in the classroom, teachers build in a brief 'take-up' period for pupils to respond: '"Craig … Deon … you're chatting – it's whole-class teaching time." Make the request, walk away so as to imply compliance, and acknowledge compliance when it happens.'
- The 'broken record' approach (Rogers, 2013) also allows teachers to repeat a request calmly without being drawn into an argument. For example, as Sproson (2004, p. 320) exemplifies:

> Teacher: John, start your work, thanks.
> John: It's boring.
> Teacher: John, start your work, thanks.
> John: Didn't you hear what I said?
> Teacher: Start your work, thanks.
> John: This lesson's just so boring … (picking pen up – if you're lucky!)
> Teacher: Pleased to see you getting down to work – well done.

- Pupils bringing inappropriate objects into classrooms, or engaging in inappropriate activities might be given what Rogers (2013, p. 242) calls 'directed choices'. As a newly appointed teacher, my own sister was once in a situation where teenage girls brought long sticks into her mathematics lesson in a class where every student had been suspended the previous term – to test her out, as they later admitted. She simply responded by directing their choices: 'Shall I put them in this cupboard or that one? I'll keep them safe for you till the end of the day.' They never asked for them back.

Group behaviour

One very well-known framework for classroom management that has been based on behavioural principles is that of 'Assertive

Discipline' (Canter & Canter, 1992). 'Assertive teachers' communicate expectations to students clearly and confidently, and reinforce words with actions in order to 'manage' students' behaviour in schools. Canter and Canter (1992, p. 12) assert that students need to know 'without doubt' what teachers expect of them, what will happen if they choose not to comply, and that appropriate behaviour will be overtly reorganised. They also need to be taught 'how to choose responsible behavior' (1992, p. 13).

Canter and Canter (1992, p. 17) see teacher's 'own negative expectations about her [or his] ability to deal with disruptive student behavior' as major factors preventing teachers from asserting themselves in the classroom. Key to successfully managing classroom behaviour, therefore, are teachers' positive expectations of their own ability to do this. Clear rules derived from a behaviourist approach enable teachers to do this. They advocate setting up a classroom discipline plan with three parts: rules, positive recognition and consequences. Rules should be limited in number, focus on observable events, be applicable throughout the time period, apply to behaviour only, and may involve students in their compilation. Key to motivating students to choose appropriate behaviour are 'positive reinforcers' which include teacher praise, rewards of various sorts and positive communications with parents. Teachers are exhorted to teach the classroom discipline plan. They are advised to 'explain why you have consequences', to 'teach the consequences', and 'immediately begin reinforcing students who follow the rules'. Rules should be reviewed frequently, at the start of the year and as needed later on. The discipline plan should be posted up in the classroom and sent home to parents (Canter & Canter, 1992, p. 115).

Canter and Canter recommend that teachers should take the time to 'identify the academic activities, routine procedures and special procedures for which [he or she needs to determine] specific directions' (1992, p. 123) at the beginning of every year. By 'specific directions' they mean 'identify the classroom situations for which specific directions are needed. Then determine those directions.' Subsequently, 'teach your specific directions immediately prior to the first time the activity takes place.' It is often also helpful to put posters and other illustrations around the classroom 'to help remind students of appropriate behavior [sic] during different activities and procedures' (Canter & Canter, 1992, p. 139).

After implementing the stated consequences of a rule-breaking misdemeanour, teachers should look for every opportunity to recognise, and thus 'shape', appropriate behaviour.

Critiques of behavioural techniques for controlling and shaping behaviour

A number of criticisms of behaviourist techniques for controlling and changing behaviour have been commonly expressed. For example, behavioural approaches might serve teachers' wishes to manage students rather than responding to individual needs (Hanko, 1994) and engaging students' interests. These approaches might also lead children into becoming overly dependent on praise. In any case, inappropriate use of praise can be damaging to some students for two reasons. If it is not sincere students may well see through it. Also, students who have learned from previous experiences that they are likely to find learning activities in school difficult will be very discouraged by teachers' obvious lack of understanding of their situation. Consequently, 'a praise-refusing student's determination not to be lured into the risks of failing yet again may be further reinforced' (Hanko, 1994, p. 166). In every school I taught at, I met praise-refusing students who have, seemingly, shut themselves off from teachers. Many have been socially isolated and, to judge by body language, feel appalled at their own loneliness yet cannot do anything about it. I well remember the case of Paul, undernourished, dirty, smelly, and always alone, but hovering as close to the entrance of the school building as he could manage. No amount of attempts by me to 'shape' his behaviour through praise would have enabled him to socialise more with peers.

Behavioural approaches might also encourage students into unthinking conformity to authority (Milgram, 1974). There is an assumption that the school curriculum to which students are expected to comply is appropriate and relevant and that school and teacher processes and practices are equitable and reasonable for all students, but we all know that this is not necessarily the case. Further, these approaches tend to ignore the importance of cultural and community contexts, together with the traditional values, in which behaviour is defined and understood (Glynn & Bishop, 1995; Macfarlane, 1997, 2000a, 2000b). There is an assumption that teachers know which types of rewards and sanctions are 'meaningful' to individual students as positive or negative reinforcers. Where teachers do not understand the cultural norms of their students, they may 'mis-cue' in their application of behaviour management strategies. Gee (2000) illustrates this point vividly with an example of a small girl who told a story at the class 'sharing time'. The story was full of rhythm, pattern and repetition and would have been highly valued in the child's family and local community, where oral performance was prized according to its entertainment value. The teacher, however, was anticipating a different (unarticulated) style of oral performance, that of being informative, linear and succinct, and did not appreciate the child's form of story-telling. Subsequently this child was referred to the school psychologist for telling tall stories.

Sometimes, too, behavioural approaches fail to take adequate account of the emotions. As Hanko (1994) comments, 'emotional factors affect learning, especially if we see only their provocative or withdrawn facade which usually hides children in constant misery, loneliness, self-loathing and fear ... teachers are frequently baffled by children who 'don't respond even to praise', 'spoil their work the moment I praise it', 'just shrug it off' and 'don't seem to care' (Hanko, 1994, p. 166).

Applications of a behaviourist approach to new learning

Behaviourist principles can be applied when devising programmes for learning new material. A learning sequence using behaviourist principles might be structured by, first, breaking down the new information into a series of small steps, then teaching this information separately and sequentially. The difficulty level of the questions has to be graded so the learner's response is always correct. The learner responds to every question and receives immediate feedback and reinforcement of positive learning behaviour and the correctness of the response. Good performance in the lesson, in other words, the desired behaviour of effort and achievement, is reinforced by verbal praise, prizes and good grades.

Thinking clearly about the next steps in learning can be very useful where a child experiences difficulties in conceptual understanding. Behaviourist approaches to learning in what we might call the basic skills can be very powerful in their effectiveness. Numbers of spelling programmes and basic numeracy programmes using the four rules of number have been devised along these lines, reinforcing the learning through repetitive drill and practice with rewards (reinforcers) for correct responses. However, these approaches cannot apply to all new learning. For example, the requirement for information to be broken down into small steps and for each response to be reinforced immediately restricts what can be learned through this approach. Not everything can be broken down into a clear sequence of stages that are the same for all learners. There is criticism of these approaches that they can be rigid and mechanical. Although it is useful in learning repetitive tasks like multiplication tables and those word skills that require a great deal of practice, higher order learning is another matter. Further, it is not possible, or desirable, that all new learning should be pre-programmed and that the outcomes should be known in advance because that would deny the importance of, for example, individual critical thinking, personal research and analysis and individual responses to art, drama, music and so on. Also, some educators, for example, Hanko (1994), feel that behavioural approaches also fail to address students' ability to reflect on their own learning and achievement adequately.

Even so, behaviourist approaches have been very commonly adopted in schools and can still be identified in many software programmes intended, for example, to encourage awareness of the four rules of number in mathematics, phonics in decoding text and reading, and designed to provide immediate feedback and reinforcement of learning.

COGNITIVE-BEHAVIOURAL APPROACHES

Recent years have seen a move away from strict behaviourist approaches towards alternative ways of understanding learning that take greater account of how individuals construct reality for themselves. Cognitive-behavioural approaches have emerged from behavioural psychology and have a number of additional key characteristics, one of which relates to a focus on the way the mind processes information. Cognitive-behavioural approaches can incorporate a wide range of cognitive processes, including the use of perception, language, problem solving, memory, decision-making and imagery. For example, in the school situation when students begin to pay attention to 'the stream of automatic thoughts which accompany and guide their behaviour, they can learn to make choices about the appropriateness of these self-statements, and if necessary introduce new thoughts and ideas' (McLeod, 1998, p. 72). This can result in behaviour more appropriate to the school context and lead to a higher level of academic achievement.

Techniques to encourage meta-cognitive awareness of behaviour

In the area of student behaviour in schools, a number of researchers have employed the concept of meta-cognitive awareness (that is, awareness of one's own thinking, feelings and emotions) in the area of emotional regulation, or self-management in order to cope with feelings such as violence, bullying, disaffection or isolation (Meichenbaum & Turk, 1976; Shapiro & Cole, 1994). A common application of this approach is to the management of feelings of anger (Harris, 1976; Wilde, 1994, 1995). As Wilde (2001, pp. 192–193) notes, the first step is to encourage students to recognise bodily sensations that precede displays of anger.

> One of the simplest ways to teach children to identify their internal body cues is to ask them to respond to the query, 'What do you notice in your body just before you get angry?' Students often reply that they 'feel warm all over', or that they 'notice their pulse is racing', or 'make fists with their hands'. They might clench their teeth, or 'start shaking all over, or 'feel their muscles get tight, especially in their arms.
>
> (Wilde, 2001, pp. 192–193).

The intention is to give them the chance 'to distract themselves or walk away before they react' (p. 192). Distraction involves persuading students to think about something other than the focus of their anger. It can be done through helping them to remember positive events in detail such as the happiest or funniest experience they can remember (p. 193).

The assumption behind this is that it is almost impossible for a student to imagine a happy, funny or relaxing scene and still be angry.

In another cognitive-behavioural approach, de Shazer's (1985) 'solution-focused brief therapy' (SFBT) continues to be employed in some places. This approach developed out of clinical practice at the Brief Family Therapy Center in Milwaukee, Wisconsin, USA in the 1980s (de Shazer 1985, 1988). SFBT is focused on solutions rather than problems, hence the main task is to help a student imagine how s/he would like things to be different, and what it would take for them to be so. The best known technique is that of the 'miracle question' (de Shazer, 1988). A paraphrase of this might be, 'If one night, while you were sleeping, a miracle happened and the problem that brought you here was solved but you didn't know that the miracle had happened because you were asleep, what would be different when you woke up in the morning that would tell you that the miracle had taken place?' As de Shazer *et al.* (2007, p. 40) comment: 'ultimately the miracle question is not so much about figuring out what would be a "dream come true" ... as it is about discovering ... and replicating the effects of it'.

Also important are the 'scaling questions':

On a scale of 1 to 10 where 1 is the worst it's ever been and 10 is after the miracle has happened, where are you now?

Where do you need to be?

What will help you move up one point?

How can you keep yourself at that point?

In the context of schools, students are invited to work out ways of reaching a positive outcome and to use their responses to learn ways of behaving more appropriately in school and/or achieve more highly in academic terms.

CONSTRUCTIVIST APPROACHES

In recent years there has been an increasing interest in constructivist views of learning with a focus on ways in which individuals actively construct their understanding of the reality in which they live. There is a recognition here that 'the emotional and behavioural difficulties which people experience in their lives are not caused directly by events but by the way they interpret and make sense of these events' (McLeod, 1998, pp. 71–72). How young people think of themselves in school has an enormous impact on their learning and behaviour. Pollard comments that some might be 'highly anxious and continually under-value themselves'. Some can seem 'over-confident and extremely resilient'. Some may know their own strengths and weaknesses whilst others 'may seem to have relatively naïve views of themselves. Children may be gregarious, or loners, or they may be lonely' (Pollard, 2002, pp. 97–98). Learning is highly dependent on both the context, what the learner makes of the situation in which s/he finds himself and the interaction between them (Lave & Wenger, 1998; Greeno, 1998).

From this view, difficulties in learning and behaviour 'problems' in schools are also situated in the interaction between the context and the perceptions of students (Mehan, 1996; McDermott, 1999; Lave & Wenger, 1998). It is important therefore for adults to understand how children make sense of their own circumstances and what impression is conveyed to students of others' views of them. Adults in schools have to be concerned all the time with the sense that children are making of their worlds, their experiences, tasks in classrooms, and so on. Being open to this demands careful and sensitive listening, observation and reflection. It appears obvious that taking the young person's view seriously is essential to any consideration of how we might reduce obstacles to students' learning (Hart, 1995). Learning programmes are likely to be more effective when students have some sense of ownership over them.

Children, like the rest of us, come to decisions about what learning is worth investing in. They judge whether the benefits of any given learning situation outweigh the time, effort and (in some classrooms) the risk of being wrong and exposing themselves to public humiliation in being thought stupid. Questions of value-to-oneself are at the heart of the learning process. Young people may not make the effort if they do not perceive it as worthwhile in relation to the effort that is required. All learners are active, all learners think about their learning, all have views about it and all have feelings about it, no matter what the context. All learners have some power and control. They may enthusiastically comply with the demands set for them or may outwardly comply but inwardly be resentful. They may be unco-operative or disruptive and resist the demands made on them. For young people in schools, feeling that they have some control over their learning, understanding why they are learning something, choosing how to do it and when to do it, may be important. Allowing learners some degree of choice in, or power over, what they learn and how they learn invites them to take control over their learning. This is not always easy in busy classrooms. However, offering some choices that can be accommodated within the school day gives learners responsibility and acknowledges that they have preferences, dislikes and ideas.

Not just literacy!

Arnold was another student about whom I had many concerns. Over the two years I worked with him in a comprehensive upper (13–18) school his written work showed just how little progress he seemed to have made in literacy skills. He just did not seem to care. He came to school in a shirt that was always dirty. He smelled of body odour and nicotine. I never knew what Arnold was thinking. I never knew what he felt about his own lack of literacy. If we had known, it might have made a difference either to our approach or to the outcome educationally. Arnold left school functionally illiterate.

(Adapted from Wearmouth, 2009)

CONSTRUCTING UNDERSTANDING

Whilst Skinner's work was seminal to advances in understanding learning from a behaviourist perspective, a number of researchers have contributed to the way we often think about children's learning from a constructivist view. Two of the foremost theorists are Jean Piaget (1896–1980) and Lev Vygotsky (1896–1934). Other leading educationalists, for example, Jerome Bruner, have picked up and developed Vygotsky's ideas.

Jean Piaget

Jean Piaget, a Swiss psychologist, was one of the theorists who contributed a lot to the thinking that children learn by doing. From his work with his own children Piaget (1954, 1964, 1969) concluded that there were four universal stages of learning:

- Sensorimotor (0–2 years);
- Preoperational (2–7 years);
- Concrete operational (7–11 years);
- Formal operational (11+ years).

At the first stage, sensorimotor, the child is born with a set of reflex movements and perceptual systems, learning is, in general, through trial and error and there is quick development of direct knowledge of the world as the child relates physical actions to perceived results of those actions.

At the next stage, preoperational, the child develops the ability mentally to represent events and objects (the semiotic function) and to engage in symbolic play but is not yet able to see others' point of view, which is characteristic of 'egocentrism'.

At the stage of concrete operations the child develops the ability to use logical thought or operations (rules) but can only apply logic to physical objects, hence the term **concrete** operational. The child also becomes less egocentric and begins to be able to see things from the viewpoint of others. S/he starts to develop an understanding of conservation of number, area, volume, orientation and reversibility, but is not yet able to think abstractly or hypothetically.

Finally, from the age of around 11 years, and at the stage of formal operations, the child acquires the ability to use abstract reasoning and manipulate ideas in his/her head, without being dependent on concrete objects to, for example, combine and classify items, do mathematical calculations, think creatively, and imagine the outcome of particular actions.

There have been a number of criticisms of Piaget's work. For example, in basing his research on his own children he was using a skewed sample of the child population from which to draw his conclusions. He also appears to have underestimated children's abilities at different ages (Wood *et al.*, 2001). In addition, there is insufficient consideration of different social or cultural contexts in which children in general live and grow. Further, some of the methods for the research on which these conclusions were based have been questioned (Donaldson, 1984). Also, Piaget's work implies that child development occurs in discrete stages, but actually, of course, it is uninterrupted with some stages continuing throughout adulthood.

Despite the criticisms, this particular frame of reference, implying that children's direct experience with their environment is vitally important to their learning, has made a strong contribution to primary schools organising their classrooms with the children in mind and providing a rich learning environment with concrete materials and resources. Piaget's research evidence led him to conclude that learners construct knowledge by interacting with their environment and what is in it and that they re-construct their thoughts in the light of new experiences. As they grow older, learners develop more detailed and accurate understandings or constructions of the things they experience.

Lev Vygotsky

Akin to Piaget's model of constructivism but developed in a very different context, that of Soviet Russia, is the social constructivist model of Lev Vygotsky. As Vygotsky (1962), suggested, language is also important to the sense-making process in addition to a carefully organised rich learning environment. Vygotsky concluded that it is through interacting with others, especially a more knowledgeable other, that learning mainly occurs and is developed. This means that relationships among learners themselves and between learners and adults that are bound up with the learning environment are also important.

The next steps in learning of which a child is capable and the range of knowledge and skills that learners are not yet ready to learn on their own but can learn with support from, and in interaction with, more informed and experienced others, for example, adults, is called the 'zone of proximal development' or ZPD in this model. Within the zone the more experienced other is central. Learning involves practice below the zone, for example, to encourage the development of skills to automatic level. One important reason why Vygotsky's views have become popular in education circles in recent years is that they give a clear role for the teacher in the person of this more experienced, informed other.

The view of learning just described emphasises the social and cultural context of learning and the role that adults play in supporting that learning, and is often called 'socio-constructivism' (the construction of knowledge in a social context), or referred to as taking a socio-cultural perspective on learning. The ideas from this view of learning underpin much of the current work on formative assessment – 'assessment for learning' – that is discussed in Chapter 7 of this book.

Jerome Bruner

Bruner (1966) outlines three modes of representation of reality used by humans as they develop their conceptual understanding of the world which, like Piaget's model above, move from the concrete 'learn by doing' to the abstract:

- enactive
- iconic
- symbolic.

The 'enactive' mode of representation works through action. We 'do' and then we understand and know. In their very early years, young children rely on enactive modes to learn. As they learn to move, they learn to do so through their own actions without the need for verbal and/or written and/or physical symbols. Children unable to experience their world by sight, hearing, taste, touch or smell, or unable to move easily will be less able to understand and know through 'doing' unless special efforts are made to enable them to access their world otherwise.

The 'iconic' mode is a visual representation of the real object. Images therefore stand for the physical object. Using this mode of representation, children learn to understand what pictures and diagrams are and how to do mathematical calculations using numbers and without counting objects.

The 'symbolic' mode is an abstract representation of something else. Abstract symbols are 'arbitrary' meaning that they do not necessarily bear any resemblance to whatever it is that they represent. For example, commonly in spoken language the sound of a word bears no resemblance to reality, unless it is onomatopoeic.

Children's learning involves becoming proficient in each of these increasingly more complex modes, but they may experience difficulty at any point in their development. A common feature in children who experience cognitive difficulties is weakness in understanding and remembering that a symbol can 'stand for' something else, for example, something concrete or an action. As discussed in Chapter 4, teachers might need to build in strategies to classroom teaching which facilitate access to the curriculum in ways that address these difficulties, for example, much more time to acquire concepts through experience of using and manipulating concrete objects.

SCAFFOLDING LEARNING

One of the ideas that has been developed from a socio-cultural view is that of 'scaffolding' to support learning (Wood *et al.*, 1976). Rogoff (1990) identifies six elements in scaffolding learning. Firstly, engage the learners' interest in the task, and then demonstrate how to do it. Next, if possible, reduce the number of steps needed for the task so learners can recognise their own progress. Then, control frustration and offer feedback so that learners can see their own progress. Finally, find a way to motivate the learners so they continue with the task.

To be successful, the interaction must be collaborative between student and the more knowledgeable other. The scaffolding must operate within the learner's zone of proximal development. The scaffolder must access the learner's current level of understanding and then work at slightly beyond that level, drawing the learner into new areas of learning. The scaffold should be withdrawn in stages as the learner becomes more competent. In schools, the final goal is for the learner to become autonomous, secure enough in the knowledge required to complete the task.

Not all learning requires the physical presence of an adult. Learners need scaffolding from more knowledgeable others, but not too much. Learning is also about participating, for example, having the chance to behave as a reader, writer and so on, alongside other readers and writers. Learning is often highly charged with emotion. Feelings accompanying success can be very pleasant and/or exciting. The sense of failure can be very upsetting and/or disturbing, especially when it is a frequent occurrence. Feelings are therefore very powerful in supporting, or preventing, learning. Getting the balance right is crucial. This is often especially difficult in school where there is a tendency in most classrooms for the adults to talk too much and for the learners to talk too little. Other resources, apart from adults, can scaffold learning also: information technologies, peers, books, materials, pop music and so on.

UNDERSTANDING DIFFICULTIES IN LEARNING

We can only make sense of new ideas and information in terms of what we already know. It is hard to learn unless what we are reading about, listening to or looking at makes sense to us. If we think about reading a novel – or children reading a story book – without a way of relating to the words and the ideas in a passage we are not likely to be interested in it. Children can make sense of new ideas only by relating them to what they already know.

Teachers and other adults in schools are responsible for finding ways to support learners to make connections with what they already know. One straightforward way to do this is to talk with learners of any age about what they do or do not know and encourage them not to be embarrassed to discuss difficulties they might be experiencing. Young people have a right to be heard (Council of Europe, 1966). At the same time listening to what they say is an important part of the process of supporting learning. Misconceptions may be very common and not noticed unless we listen to the learner. Many students in schools experience difficulties in learning in the area of mathematics. 'Karen', aged 14 repeatedly made subtraction errors of the following kind:

```
 9842
-1357
 8515
```

She thought that the subtraction rule was always to subtract the smaller from the larger figure, whether the figure appeared in the upper or lower line. She had made the same mistake for years and had never understood why her mathematical attainment was so poor until, one day, she was asked to do a 'think-aloud' in the classroom. The challenge for those with an interest in mathematics education is to understand how to break this pattern. Those teachers who are effective in teaching mathematics to the whole range of student learners are those who take very seriously, and are committed to, developing students' mathematical thinking (Anthony & Walshaw, 2007, p. 1). This commitment is characterised by a number of principles, among which are a recognition that all students can become mathematical learners and a 'commitment to maximise access to mathematics'. Other factors are important also: good mathematical knowledge, relationships student to student and teacher to student, the 'connectedness of both people and ideas', 'interpersonal respect and sensitivity', and 'fairness and consistency'.

Teachers' beliefs, expectations and understandings of all students as active agents in their own learning are as important in the area of mathematics as in any other area of the school curriculum. Effective teachers neither embarrass students nor ignore wrong answers. They use mistakes to enhance the teaching. There is now a large body of evidence that demonstrates the beneficial effects of students being encouraged to articulate their mathematical thinking (Fraivillig *et al.*, 1999; Lampert, 1990; O'Connor, 1998). By expressing their ideas, students provide their teachers with information about what they know and what they need to learn. Hiebert and colleagues (1997) have found that teacher talk that is effective in supporting mathematical understanding and competence involves drawing out the specific mathematical ideas that students are using to work out the answers to problems, supporting students' understanding of the accepted conventions in mathematics, and sharing other methods and ways of working through mathematical problems.

Effective mathematics teachers often listen to what students have to say and re-frame student talk in mathematically appropriate language. This provides teachers with the chance to highlight connections between mathematical language and conceptual understanding. Many students who experience difficulty in mathematics lack the confidence to speak out in the classroom, however. I well remember the occasion when teaching mathematics to a bottom set of 14-year-old students in a secondary school I was asked by one boy: "ere, Miss, why do you bother with us when you can teach them clever kids?' As noted already, for students to be prepared to volunteer their answers in mathematics lessons they need to feel safe and know that they will not be humiliated by either the teacher or their peers if they are wrong. The first step for the teacher in all this is probably to ensure this sense of safety for all the students in the classroom.

As a teacher in a secondary school, I frequently noticed a number of pupils who experienced difficulties in literacy acquisition and expression, using capital 'b's' and 'd's' in the middle of words, for example, 'aBle'; 'saiD'. For a long time I simply corrected these errors. However, after a long time when they persisted I asked the pupils to write the words and talk through what they were doing. They all said that they knew the difference between 'B' and 'D' in upper case, but could not remember them in lower case. When I looked to see how they were writing these letters they made no difference between lower case b's and d's, starting them both at the top and running down to the curve, left or right, at the bottom. It is no wonder that they could not remember the difference. They tried to show that they knew the correct spellings by using upper case letters, which they could clearly distinguish.

What these examples illustrate is how learners try to make sense of a new experience or a new problem by trying to fit them to similar experiences of problems they have met before. If there is a good fit then it is more likely that the learner will understand the current experience or solve the problem correctly. If the gap between the existing knowledge or experience and what is needed to understand the current problem or experience is too large, however, this is unlikely to happen.

Karen (see above) had gone on making the same subtraction errors because, as she later explained, she was 'useless' at mathematics and was too embarrassed to explain her reasoning. I had simply never thought to ask the boys why they used upper case letters in the middle of words because it did not occur to me that they might have chosen to do this deliberately. Concentrating only on the right answer can mean losing the chance to gain insights into learners' understandings and misunderstandings and, therefore, the opportunities to support learning at the right moment.

AN ECO-SYSTEMIC POSITION

The final frame of reference in relation to learning and behaviour that is taken from psychology and discussed here is the view that the behaviour and learning of individuals can be viewed as part of an eco-system. The school and the home are seen as being two separate systems with their own individual ways of operating. The eco-systemic approach understands school behaviour and learning problems in terms of dysfunctions in the family system, in the school system, or in the family–school relationship system (Campion, 1985; Dowling & Osbourne, 1985). Cooper and Upton (1991), for example, describe the case of 11-year-old John, a student at a special school for students identified as experiencing emotional and behavioural difficulties. At home he reported he was bullied by staff at school, but never complained about this at school. His complaints to his mother meant that she was repeatedly involved in his school life, where she acted as his advocate, and elicited protective behaviour from her. Her protection in the school situation was in contrast to the role she played at home, where she slept most of the day because she worked in a club at night. 'If the suggestion of bullying by staff was eliminated, it is likely that John would find some other way to elicit positive behaviour towards himself by his mother' (Cooper & Upton, 1991, p. 24). From an eco-systemic approach, there would be an analysis of the system operating in John's home and the roles played by the various members to explain both John's and his mother's repeated behaviours. There would also be an analysis of the roles played by the various members of staff at school in relation to the home situation. An appropriate intervention would need to aim to involve John and his mother in a collaborative relationship usually organised by a consultant family therapist. 'Such consultations may result in the adjustment of systemic structure (Minuchin, 1974), in the form of an adjustment in the roles performed by members of one or other of the systems involved, or in the adjustment of systemic boundaries, whereby weakened boundaries are strengthened, or overstrong boundaries are relaxed'. In the situation of John and his mother, perhaps the home-based relationship between John and his mother was lacking in warmth, 'to the extent that John has to engineer the type of situation described above, in which his mother plays a protective role'. A possible solution for this might be actively to look for a situation where John's mother took a protective role. 'The precise nature of this remedy would be dependent upon the outcome of meetings between the family and the therapist' (Cooper & Upton, 1991, p. 24).

PROBLEM-SOLVING SPECIAL NEEDS PROVISION

There is no golden formula for addressing the special learning needs of all students who experience difficulties in schools. There are some general principles, however. Every student is different and every situation is different. Addressing difficulties is a question of problem-solving. Firstly, find out about the learner and the difficulties s/he experiences. Then think about the requirements of the particular curriculum area and barriers to learning in the classroom environment and in the particular curriculum area. Finally, reflect on and implement what will best address those barriers to help the learner achieve in the classroom.

SUMMARY

How we understand learning and what lies at the root of a 'learning difficulty' in school has a very strong influence on how we respond. Over the years, different social or psychological understandings have given rise to different interventions.

Research confirms that strategies recommended for particular special educational needs are useful for most students. Lewis and Norwich (2000), for example, point out that there is little evidence that staff should use entirely different teaching approaches for most students with SEND. Instead they suggest that staff should give students more time to solve problems, more chances to practise their skills, more examples to learn from and more experience of using knowledge and skills in different situations. They should also provide more strategies to help learn information and skills, more preparation for the next stage of their learning, and more frequent assessment of what is and what is not being learned and why.

The extent to which children qualify under the legal definition as children 'with special educational needs and/or disabilities' depends to a large extent on the policies and resources within their Local Authorities (LAs) and educational settings as well as the wording of particular Education Acts. In the next chapter we will look at teachers' current legal responsibilities in teaching children identified as having SEND, set against the context of a historical perspective on special education.

SPECIAL EDUCATIONAL NEEDS AND DISABILITY
Evolution of the field

INTRODUCTION

In Chapter 1 we saw how our own experiences and values as human beings and professional educators influence the way in which we interpret difficulties experienced by students in schools (Fulcher, 1989; Wearmouth, 2009). Chapter 2 begins with an overview of the history of provision for children seen as 'different' from peers on account of the learning or physical difficulties they experienced or the behaviour they displayed, and continues with a discussion of the way that schools' thinking about learning, behaviour and children's rights has changed over time.

DEVELOPMENT OF THE 'SPECIAL' EDUCATION SECTOR FOR THE FEW: A HISTORICAL PERSPECTIVE

The way in which educational provision is currently organised is a product both of its own history and of the values, beliefs and political ideology of our society (Wearmouth, 2009). Over the years, special education provision has been characterised by a number of recurring themes. For example, there is the question of whether to separate off children who experience difficulties of various kinds into special segregated provision, or integrate them into mainstream. Then there is an issue of what kind of curriculum should be offered: whether it should be the same for all children, or different for some groups. Echoing down the years, for instance, has been discussion around the academic–vocational/manual divide. There has also been discussion about whether, and how, to classify children into the various groupings of difficulties. As a corollary of this, if classification is seen as appropriate, what characterises the differences both between the groupings themselves and between the children so classified and others? How children in the various groups should be and/or are valued, and the value that can be deduced from the kind of provision that is deemed to be appropriate is also important. For many years, too, there was debate about whether some young people are capable of being educated in any form that is recognisable as 'education' at all.

Other on-going discussion and debate includes the question about why the special education sector was developed in the first place. Were special education systems created by caring professionals wishing to address the needs of children in difficulty more effectively? Is special education provision essentially benevolent? Did it evolve primarily to help children who were different in some way, or who experienced difficulties? Did special educational provision develop to serve the economic and commercial interests of society? Did these interests dictate that as many people as possible with difficulties should be productive and contribute to an industrial society? Certainly businessmen 'played a part in the founding of pioneer establishments for the deaf and for the blind, and ... throughout the 19th century trade training took up much of the lives of the handicapped attending them' (Cole, 1990, p. 101). Did it, perhaps, develop to provide a means to exclude troublesome pupils, or pupils who required a lot of the teacher's time, from mainstream classes? For example, when a new national system of secondary schools was designed in the 1944 Education Act, did the smooth running of those schools demand the exclusion of some pupils, for example, those categorised as 'educationally subnormal'? Are there vested interests from, for example, the medical profession and psychologists that support the existence of special provision?

SPECIAL EDUCATION PROVISION: THE EARLY YEARS

As Warnock (DES, 1978, ch. 2) notes, early institutions for children who experienced difficulties of various sorts were founded by individuals or by charities, rather than government agencies, and catered only for a few. Later, central government intervened, initially to support and supplement what was provided through voluntary agencies. Later still the government created a national framework for special education provision, but it was not until the 1970s that this framework included the entitlement of all children to an appropriate education.

The early institutions were very different from today's schools. They were designed to focus on moral improvement, training in work skills, and the Christian religion (Oliphant, 2006), often for adults as well as children. In Britain they began in the second half of the eighteenth century, firstly with schools for blind and deaf children. For instance, the School of Instruction for the Indigent Blind, established in 1791 in Liverpool, together with other private foundations that quickly followed it, including the School for the Indigent Blind in London, founded in 1800, and the Asylum and School for the Indigent Blind in Norwich in 1805, were solely concerned with instructing inmates in the Christian faith and in earning their living. They relied on adult and child labour to make a profit in their workshops. The inmates were obliged to spend several hours a day praying or listening to readings from the scriptures as they worked. Oliphant (2006, p. 55) notes that the School of Industry in Liverpool was, according to its founding plan, intended, along with religion, 'to furnish the blind with employment that may prevent them from being burdens to their family and community. ... The *Plan* required that 'habits of industry' be formed, with men making baskets, tablecloths and whips while the women spun yarn, made sail-cloths and picked oakum. As recipients of public charity, the inmates had little freedom of choice and this, together with a focus solely on religion and work, could provoke misdemeanours. As the Liverpool School Visitors' Books record, those who missed Sunday service or fell asleep in church might be punished through the use of a 'bread and water table'. There were also instances of 'miscreants being locked in the beer cellar for a week for offences such as refusing either to be washed or to wear shoes instead of clogs'. In 1825, two boys were flogged for insolence and another for 'making away with his yarns' (Oliphant, 2006, p. 58). It was not until other schools were founded thirty years later that educational aspects were introduced into the curriculum, for example, in the London Society for Teaching the Blind to Read in 1838.

Only a small proportion of blind children went to school. Most blind children's prospects were 'pretty grim' (Cobham, Foreword to Bell, 1967, p. 11) and there were very few attempts to challenge the general attitude to the educability of the blind. One of the most significant, however, was the foundation of the 'College for the Blind Sons of Gentlemen' in 1866 in Worcester. Bell (1967, p. 16) notes that its aims, as published in its 1872 report, were 'to bestow a sound and liberal education upon persons of the male sex afflicted with total or partial blindness, and belonging by birth or kinship to upper, the professional or the middle classes of society'. (The equivalent for girls was not established until 1921, by the National Institute for the Blind (NIB) in Chorleywood.) Academic goals were very high and set towards the professions of the Church, law and education. Football, cricket, swimming and athletics were merged with the academic side of the curriculum. Foster, headmaster of the College, felt: 'If prosecuted steadily, systematic physical exercises will greatly diminish ... that ungracefulness of bearing which has helped to confirm the impression of the blind man's inferiority' (Bell, 1967, p. 22). Worcester College remained the only route for blind children to achieve higher qualifications and entry into the professions until after the Second World War, however.

The first schools for the deaf were also very limited in the education they offered. The first was founded in Edinburgh in the 1760s: Mr Braidwood's Academy for the Deaf and Dumb. It took in a small number of paying pupils, who were taught to speak and read. As Warnock (DES, 1978, p. 9) comments, although the education they provided was subordinated to training, 'many of their inmates failed to find employment on leaving and had recourse to begging'.

Attempts were made to teach a trade to girls with physical disabilities from poor homes in the Cripples' Home and Industrial School for Girls established in Marylebone in 1851, and to boys in the Training Home for Crippled Boys founded in Kensington in 1865. Again, the children were expected to work for their living and produce goods for sale.

For those children who experienced serious difficulties in learning, until the end of the nineteenth century there was little provision apart from workhouses and infirmaries for those who needed secure care. The first specific provision made for them was the Asylum for Idiots established at Highgate in 1847, which took people of all ages. By 1870 there were five asylums. Only three professed to offer any kind of education. For children to be admitted to these institutions parents had to agree to them being certified as 'idiots', a label that attracted much odium (Cole, 1989, p. 22).

School boards were established under the terms of the (1870) Forster Education Act in England and Wales, and the (1872) Education (Scotland) Act, and charged with ensuring provision of elementary education in places where there were insufficient places through voluntary enterprise. They did not specifically include disabled children, but a few school boards did admit blind and deaf children to ordinary elementary schools or to centres attached to these schools.

EDUCATION FOR (ALMOST) ALL

These Education Acts established the foundations of elementary education. The 1870 Education Act, Chapter 75, pp. 445–446 reads, for example:

> There shall be provided for every school district a sufficient amount of accommodation in public elementary schools (as herein-after defined) available for all the children resident in such district for whose elementary education efficient and suitable provision is not otherwise made, and where there is an insufficient amount of such accommodation, in this Act referred to as 'public school accommodation', the deficiency shall be supplied in manner provided by this Act.

Under the terms of this Act (p. 471) School Boards were empowered, with the approval of the Education Department, to make byelaws that required:

> (1) [...] the parents of children of such age, not less than five years nor more than thirteen years, as may be fixed by the byelaws, to cause such children (unless there is some reasonable excuse) to attend school.

In 1880 a further Education Act finally made school attendance compulsory between the ages of five and ten, although attendance until the age of 13 was compulsory for those who had not achieved the standard of education required by local byelaws. The 1880 Education Act (Chapter 23) reads, for example:

> Every person who takes into his employment a child of the age of ten and under the age of thirteen years, resident in a school district, before that child has obtained a certificate of having reached the standard of education fixed by a byelaw in force in the district for the total or partial exemption of children of the like age from the obligation to attend school, shall be deemed to take such child into his employment in contravention of the Elementary Education Act, 1876, and shall be liable to a penalty accordingly.
>
> (§ 4, p. 143)

However, not all areas took it up, and by the early 1890s attendance within this age group was falling short at 82 per cent . Fees were also payable until a change in the law in 1891. The government became increasingly involved and further legislation in 1893 extended the age of compulsory attendance to 11, and in 1899 to 12.

As a result of the introduction of compulsory schooling, large numbers of children came to school for the first time. Many appeared to have poor intellectual ability and made little or no progress. Up till now those children who experienced less serious learning difficulties had largely managed with day-to-day living in a society that was a lot less complex than ours. However, now that they were compelled to attend school their presence was felt to be holding others back in the large classes that existed in public elementary schools. The question was what to do with them, especially as national level funding for individual schools and, therefore, teachers' salaries, depended in part on the outcomes of examinations of pupils conducted by school inspectors, as, for example, in England between 1863 and 1890, when the policy was abandoned.

In 1889 a Royal Commission distinguished between three groups of children seen as experiencing varying degrees of learning difficulties: 'feeble-minded', 'imbeciles' and 'idiots'. Feeble-minded should be educated in 'auxiliary' schools away from other children; imbeciles should be sent to institutions where education should concentrate on sensory and physical development and improved speech. 'Idiots' were not thought to be educable. Cole (1989, p. 40) outlines evidence presented to the Sharpe Report (Education Department, 1898) of what might happen to these children. 'In London, before 1892, the feeble-minded over 11 years old had been mixed with 5-year-olds in Standard 1'. However, teachers were 'so concerned with getting their average children through the Standards and so conscious of HMI's [inspectors'] expectations that they would send the feeble-minded to play in a corner with a slate'. These days we would consider the use of these labels for children unacceptable. However, in the nineteenth century there was a big difference in status and respect given to those groups of students who had been identified as 'different' from the rest. In 1896 a Committee on Defective and Epileptic Children appointed to investigate the need for special provision for some pupils recommended that school authorities should make provision for all 'defective' children in their area and be able to make attendance compulsory. This included children with physical disabilities. The Sharpe Report comments that, by 1897, twenty-seven special schools had been founded in London for 'feeble-minded' children. Even at that time, however, there were parents who felt that there was a stigma attached to their child's placement in a special class, and resisted it. One witness to the Sharpe Committee said that parents 'will admit anything except that their children are defective in intellect' (Cole, 1989, p. 40). In any case, special provision is expensive, and the 1899 Elementary Education (Defective and Epileptic Children) Act merely gave permission for School Boards to make such provision.

The same 1889 Royal Commission mentioned above recom-mended compulsory education for the blind from age 5 to 16, and for the deaf from age 7 to 16. Deaf children, generally considered slower to learn on account of difficulties in communication, were to be taught separately by teachers who should be specially qualified to do so.[1] Legislation in Scotland followed in 1890 with the Education of the Blind and Deaf Mute Children (Scotland) Act, and in England and Wales in 1893 with the Elementary Education (Blind and Deaf Children) Act. It was not until 1938, when the (1937) Education (Deaf Children) Act came into effect, that deaf children were compelled to attend school from the age of 5.

In 1902 the old school boards were abolished and a two-tier system of local education authorities for elementary and secondary education was established. County and county borough councils were given powers to provide secondary education for blind, deaf, defective and epileptic children. The Mental Deficiency Act of 1913 required local education authorities in England and Wales to ascertain and certify which children aged 7 to 16 in their area were defective. Those judged by the authority to be incapable of being taught in special schools were to pass to the care of local mental deficiency committees. Interestingly, Cyril Burt, later Sir Cyril, was appointed to a part-time position of school psychologist for the London County Council in 1913, with the responsibility of picking out the 'feeble-minded' children, in accordance with the 1913 Act.

Two further Acts compelled authorities to provide for the education of 'mentally defective' children and physically defective and epileptic children: the Elementary Education (Defective and Epileptic) Act (1914), which required local authorities to make provision for 'mentally defective' children; and the Education Act (1918), which widened the scope of the 1914 Act to include physically defective as well as 'mentally defective' children (Section 20). However, the (1929) Wood Committee Report concluded that only one third of those children who were 'mentally defective' under the terms of the 1914 Act had actually been assessed and, of these, only one half were attending special schools.

In Scotland, the Education of Defective Children (Scotland) Act of 1906 empowered school boards to make provision in special schools or classes for the education of defective children between the ages of 5 and 16, whilst the Mental Deficiency (Scotland) Act of 1913 required school boards to identify children in their area who were 'defective'. Those children who were considered ineducable became the responsibility of parish councils for placement in an institution.

In 1921 an Education Act consolidated previous legislation, requiring children in the four categories of blind, deaf, mentally and physically defective (but not 'idiots' or 'imbeciles') and epileptic to be educated. 'Defective' and epileptic children should be certified by local education authorities and then educated in special provision, of which there was a whole range made by both voluntary bodies and LEAs. As Warnock (DES, 1978) comments, the statutory foundation of special provision continued broadly until the 1944 Act. Blindness and deafness were not defined and there was no provision for the identification and certification of these children. The parents of children in any of the four categories were required to see that their child attended a suitable special school from the age of 5 in the case of blind or deaf children, or 7 for other children, until the age of 16. Local education authorities had the duty to ensure the provision of such schools.

The rise and demise of open-air schools for delicate children

To understand the current form and organisation of special educational provision we have to be aware of the social, political and ideological context from which that provision derives (Wearmouth, 2009). The rise and demise of a particular form of special provision that no longer exists serves to illustrate this point: open-air schools for 'delicate' children.

The foundation of open-air schools in Britain at the beginning of the twentieth century has to be seen against a context of concern that had arisen around the physical well-being of large numbers of children, particularly in the cities where the air was often heavily polluted and living conditions for most people were wretched. As Cole (1989) notes, recruitment of soldiers to fight in the Boer War had highlighted the large proportion who were medically unfit to fight. As a result of this concern the government passed the Education (Provision of School Meals) Act in 1906 to enable local education authorities (LEAs) to provide school lunches and, in 1907, the Education (Administrative Provisions) Act to require LEAs to carry out medical checks on all their pupils. Gamlin (1935) notes how open-air schools were modelled on a German example. In the Berlin Education Authority a school doctor examining children observed that many of them were anaemic and debilitated. He strongly recommended open-air treatment, suitable surroundings, careful supervision, good feeding, and exercise and, as a result, the first open-air school was established in 1904 in pine woods in Charlottenburg. The first British open-air school was Bostall Woods, founded in Woolwich, in 1907. This was soon followed by others in which 'pupils with weak hearts, bronchial complaints or suffering from malnutrition were subjected to a somewhat Spartan regime'. Lessons were 'spent out of doors or in three-sided rooms, with meals provided and a compulsory rest period in the middle of the day'

(Cole, 1989, p. 51)

Classrooms in Aspen House open-air school in Streatham, London, had floors and roofs but no walls and were completely open to the elements. When it rained, children on the end of the rows might get wet. In winter if it had snowed, the children might have to clear snow off the tables and chairs before they could start the lesson. There was no heating but, however cold it became, lessons continued and pupils just had their clothes and blankets with which to keep warm. A medical official in Leicester noted that, among the characteristics of children admitted to these schools were 'Stunted growth, loss of muscular tone and dryness of hair [and] rings around the eyes, long silky eyelashes, inflammation of the eyelids, enlarged glands, anaemia, feeble circulation and shallow breathing' (Cathcart, 2005). Thousands of children in Britain matched this description, particularly in city slum areas. This, combined with the cheapness of schools that were effectively three-sided sheds with corrugated iron roofs, led to an expansion of their numbers. By the 1930s there were 4,000 children a year from London who were sent to open-air boarding schools. They might be funded by LEAs, charities or private philanthropists, for example, the Cadbury family in Birmingham.

The *Independent* newspaper (23 January, 2005) carried interviews with some of the ex-pupils of such schools.

George Cooke, 84, recalled the cold of a 1930s winter at Brent Knoll School, south London. As a 10-year-old he wore shorts like all other boys at the time and was given a blanket to keep warm. Others remembered more positive aspects of open-air schools. Norman Collier, aged 82, considered he and other children benefited academically. He, for example, became a company director later on in life. Frances Wilmot, an asthmatic who was a pupil at Uffculme in the 1950s, remembered small classes and caring teachers, a great contrast with some of the children's own homes.

Doubts about the value of open-air schools had crept in as early as 1930, when a report from the Industrial Research Board questioned the value of being out of doors in all weathers. These doubts were increased when medical officers surveying open-air schools for the Ministry of Education in 1949–50 commented: 'When the canvas curtains were drawn, rain drove in and above the curtains so that the floor and furniture were often wet. We saw children scraping frozen snow off the desks and chairs before they could be used' (Cole, 1989, p. 113). Even so, in 1955, 12,000 'delicate' children were still being educated in open-air schools in England and Wales. However, medical opinion was moving away from favouring Spartan conditions for 'delicate' children. In addition, improved standards of living, slum clearances, the advent of the National Health Service, the arrival of antibiotics, notably streptomycin, which reduced the incidence of tuberculosis, and the provision of milk and meals in schools meant that the open-air movement gradually became redundant.

DEVELOPMENTS IN DIFFERENTIATED CURRICULA FOR DIFFERENT LEARNERS

Towards the end of the Second World War, a coalition government reorganised the education system through the 1944 Education Act in England and Wales and sought to develop a common national framework for the education of a diverse student population. The statutory system of education was to be organised in three progressive stages to be known as primary education, secondary education, and further education.

(1944 Education Act, Part 11, § 7)

Local authorities were required to provide primary and secondary schools

sufficient in number, character, and equipment to afford for all pupils opportunities for education offering such variety of instruction and training as may be desirable in view of their different ages, abilities, and aptitudes.

(Part 11, § 8(1))

The government advised local education authorities to 'think in terms of three types' of state secondary schools in circular No. 73 (12 December 1945). A booklet, *The Nation's Schools*, explained that the new 'modern' schools would be for working-class children 'whose future employment will not demand any measure of technical skill or knowledge' (MoE 1945, quoted in Benn and Chitty 1996, p. 5). Although this booklet was withdrawn, the policy remained the same and was restated in *The New Secondary Education* two years later (Wilkinson, 1947).

The tripartite system of secondary education, as had been recommended in a Report by Sir William Spens in 1938, was quickly adopted by many local education authorities, with grammar schools for the most able, secondary modern schools for the majority, and secondary technical schools for those with a technical or scientific aptitude. In fact, the Act itself never mentioned the words 'tripartite', 'grammar schools' or 'secondary modern schools'. It simply required that education should be provided at three levels: primary, secondary and further. Indeed, the Parliamentary Secretary to the Board of Education, J Chuter Ede, commented in a speech reported in *The Times* of 14 April 1944:

I do not know where people get the idea about three types of school, because I have gone through the Bill with a small toothcomb, and I can find only one school for senior pupils – and that is a secondary school. What you like to make of it will depend on the way you serve the precise needs of the individual area in the country.

(quoted in Chitty & Dunford, 1999, p. 20)

Those who put the 1944 Act into effect formalised a system of selection based on the results of assessment techniques that, they believed, could differentiate different 'types' of learners. They thought it possible to design different curricula for different learning 'types' who could be educated in separate sectors of the system. In mainstream, students took an examination at the age of 11 and were selected into different types of secondary school: grammar, technical and secondary modern. Within individual mainstream schools students were selected into ability 'streams'. Students might be directed into academic or work-related programmes according to measured 'ability'. It seemed to many that the educational hierarchy that developed was fair. Students appeared to be able to rise to a level which reflected their ability. Also, it was based on psychometric testing which at that time was thought by many educators to be reliable and valid.

In the area of special education, the 1944 Education Act, Sections 33 and 34, set out the legal basis for subsequent provision. The duty of local education authorities to ascertain which children required special educational treatment, hitherto confined to defective and epileptic children, was extended to children with all types of disability, generally described in the Act as 'pupils who suffer from any disability of mind or body'. These days we might call this way of viewing difficulties in learning as the 'medical' or 'deficit model'. Certification of defective children within the education system was abolished. Any child considered educable would have access to schooling. Children seen as ineducable in school were to be reported to the local authority for the purposes of the Mental Deficiency Act 1913. Local authorities were empowered to require parents to submit their children for medical examination. In Scotland, the Education (Scotland) Act (1945) repeated much of the content of the Education Act 1944.

The Handicapped Students and School Health Service Regulations (1945) in England and Wales developed a new framework of eleven categories of students: blind, partially sighted, deaf, partially deaf, delicate, diabetic, educationally subnormal, epileptic, maladjusted, physically handicapped and those with speech defects. Maladjustment and speech defects were included for the first time. The College of Speech Therapists was founded in 1945. Between 1949 and 1954, the number of speech therapists employed by local education authorities increased from 205 to 341 and the number of children treated annually rose from 25,098 to 44,800. The regulations required blind, deaf, epileptic, physically handicapped and aphasic children to be educated in special schools. Children with other disabilities could attend mainstream if there was adequate provision (DES, 1978, 2.46).

Official guidance in 1946 estimated that the number of children who might be expected to require special educational treatment, not necessarily in special schools, would range from between 14 per cent and 17 per cent of the school population.

During the years which followed, the two groups which continually expanded in numbers were those students considered 'educationally sub-normal' (ESN) and those identified as 'mal-adjusted' (DES, 1978).

> The category of educationally sub-normal children was seen as consisting of children of limited ability and children retarded by 'other conditions' such as irregular attendance, ill-health, lack of continuity in their education or unsatisfactory school conditions. These children would be those who for any reason were retarded by more than 20 per cent for their age and who were not so low-graded as to be ineducable or to be detrimental to the education of other children. They would amount to approximately 10 per cent of the school population.
>
> (DES, 1978, 2.48)

As Warnock (DES, 1978) comments, post-war planners assumed that ordinary schools would have the major share in making provision for those young people with difficulties in learning and/or behaviour:

> Detailed suggestions were made for provision. In large urban areas about 1–2 per cent of the school population would need to be educated in special schools (including 0.2 per cent in boarding schools); the remaining 8–9 per cent of the school population would be provided for in ordinary schools.
>
> (DES, 1978, 2.48)

However, during the war a lot of accommodation in schools had been destroyed, many schools that survived were in a bad state, and raising the school leaving age meant that additional building was needed. Secondary modern schools in particular often had large classes, and suitably trained teachers were in short supply (DES, 1978, 33–40). The outcome for special educational provision was that the planners' intentions were not wholly fulfilled, and special education came to be interpreted much more narrowly than official guidance anticipated. Provision in ordinary schools failed to develop as expected.

The number of children in ESN special schools nearly doubled between 1947 and 1955 from 12,060 to 22,639. Even so, the number of children awaiting placement was over 12,000. Politicians increasingly looked to medicine and the growing profession of psychology for solutions to behaviour in schools that was construed as deviant (Ford *et al.*, 1982). Warnock (DES, 1978) notes that education authorities in Scotland were empowered in 1945 to provide a child guidance service which would advise teachers and parents on appropriate methods of education and training for these children. By 1966, twenty-five of the thirty-five education authorities had a child guidance service. In England, the number of child guidance clinics increased from 162 in 1950 to 367 some twenty years later. To keep pace with this kind of expansion in numbers, the Summerfield Working Party (1968) recommended new and expanded arrangements for training of educational psychologists and a doubling of numbers. In 1978, an HMI survey of behavioural units found that 239 special units for disruptive children had been established in sixty-nine of the ninety-six LEAs in England.

The Education (Handicapped Children) Act 1970 removed the power of health authorities to provide training for children who experienced the most serious difficulties in learning (deemed 'mentally handicapped') and required the staff and buildings of junior training centres to be transferred to the education service. Around 32,000 children in institutions of various sorts together with an unknown number at home now became entitled to special education. In future they were to be regarded as 'severely educationally sub-normal' (ESN(S)), as opposed to the moderately educationally sub-normal (ESN(M)) group who had previously made up the ESN category. In Scotland the 1974 Act also gave education authorities responsibility for the education of children who previously had been viewed as 'ineducable and untrainable'.

EDUCATION FOR ALL

The system established after 1944 and intended to make appropriate provision for the whole pupil population of the nation seemed stable. However, as Clark *et al.* (1997) note, many commentators in education began to see that the system of selection into grammar, technical and secondary modern schools was not as fair as was first thought. For example, differing proportions of students were selected for each type of school in different areas of the country. Considerable doubt was increasingly thrown on the reliability and validity of the psychometric tests that were used to discriminate between children, and there was obvious overlap between the learning needs of students in mainstream and special schools (Wearmouth, 1986). In addition, movement between school types was very difficult indeed, regardless of the amount of progress made by individual students. Further, a growing concern for equality of opportunity in society at large led some researchers in education to comment that the system was divisive and functioned to sustain the position of some already advantaged societal groups. For example, Douglas (1964) and Hargreaves (1967) found a disproportionate number of middle-class children in grammar schools.

The result of all this was, beginning in the 1960s and increasingly in the 1970s, the establishment of comprehensive schools, the introduction of special classes and 'remedial' provision in mainstream, and the integration of some children from special to mainstream schools.

INTRODUCTION OF THE CONCEPT OF SPECIAL EDUCATIONAL NEEDS

In 1978 a review of special educational provision in Great Britain for children and young people was published in the Warnock Report. It introduced a new concept of 'special educational needs' to replace previous categorisation 'by disabilities of body or mind'. Following Warnock teachers were advised to plan on the assumption that one in five children would have 'special educational needs' at some time in their school career. Official guidance in 1946 estimated that the number of children requiring special educational treatment might be up to 17 per cent of the school population. A study by Rutter, Tizard and Whitmore (1970) had enquired into the incidence of difficulties in learning in the school population. The report from this study showed teachers' perceptions that, on average, 20 per cent of their students were experiencing difficulty of some kind. Since that time, the figure of 20 per cent has been used to estimate the number of children nationally who might experience difficulties. Of the total number of students, approximately 2 per cent are seen by policy-makers as likely to have difficulties which require additional or extra resources to be provided. This figure of 2 per cent is clearly useful to resource-providers, for example, local education authorities, to estimate what proportion of their resources they are likely to have to set aside for individual students' educational needs. However, it is an arbitrary one, drawn from a count of students in special schools in 1944 (DES, 1978). The law, focusing as it does on individual need, gives no such figures for the incidence of children likely to need statutory assessment. However, LAs, whose duty it is to implement legislation, have used such DfEE guidance to establish general criteria for assessment.

The 1981 Education Act attempted to translate the Warnock Report into legislation. The eleven categories of handicap were replaced with the view that pupils' difficulties occur on a continuum, and that a 'special educational need' exists if a child has 'significantly greater difficulty in learning' than peers, or a disability that hinders him or her from using educational facilities normally available in the local school.

Local authorities were given responsibilities to identify needs which called for provision in addition to that normally available in the school. Parents should be consulted about provision for their child, and could appeal against a local authority's decisions. All children should be educated in mainstream schools but with certain provisos: that their needs should be met there, and that it was compatible with the education of other children and with the 'efficient use of resources'.

DIFFERENCES IN VIEWS

Locally and nationally different pressure groups pursue a wide variety of conflicting goals. For instance, many people within the Deaf community feel that it is vital to their culture that their children go to their own schools. They want them to be allowed to learn within a signing environment which draws upon a rich heritage and sense of self-identity. Some organisations, such as Barnados and Scope, run their own schools. In many local authorities, too, it is possible to find campaigns run by schools and parents to keep special schools open. Equally, organisations such as the Centre for Studies on Inclusive Education (CSIE), Parents for Inclusion, and the Alliance for Inclusion work hard to promote the closure of special school provision and the development of mainstream schools that are open to all. Similarly it is possible to find individual parents and children involved in comparable battles. The press and internet are full of stories of people fighting to get their child into (or back into) a mainstream setting or fighting for them to be removed from mainstream and placed in a special school.

Inclusive or special schools?

The tension between including children with difficulties and segregating them into special provision has surfaced repeatedly. 'In every age, many concerned professionals have been reluctant to segregate the handicapped' (Cole, 1990, p. 106). The Sharpe Report of 1898, for example, contains a report from Dr James Kerr of the Bradford Schools Board that teachers wished 'to get rid of these [so-called "feeble-minded"] children' so that they would have fewer problems in schools and classrooms (Education Department, 1898, p. 19). However, another contributor to the report stated that opinion was divided on the subject. 'There appears to be amongst the teachers … a general agreement that the children, where they are tractable, are as well, if not better, in the ordinary schools under ordinary arrangements' (Education Department, 1898, p. 216). Indeed many teachers were reported as wanting 'to exclude only the openly disruptive children and the severely handicapped' (Cole, 1990, p. 102).

Decisions about whether inclusive mainstream, or special schools, are more likely to meet children's learning needs are not always clear-cut. Two groups of students about who teachers often express very serious concerns are those who experience profound and complex difficulties in learning who may also have acute physical disabilities, and those whose behaviour is perceived as very threatening and disruptive. It may be that some students are so vulnerable that the overriding consideration for them is a protective environment where their individual care needs can be considered together with their education. Whether the actual location is a mainstream or special site may be of less relevance than other considerations. The quality of the specialist facilities to support children's physical requirements, the level of understanding between students and staff and the effectiveness of the system of communication between home and school are very important irrespective of location. In relation to the second, the proviso that students 'with special educational needs' should be educated in mainstream schools provided that this is compatible with the education of peers is often seen as the justification for placement in an alternative location.

In 1997 the government issued a Green Paper *Excellence for All Children* to which over 3,000 parents/carers responded. The ratio of parental responses favouring special as opposed to mainstream provision for students who have Statements of Special Educational Needs was 20:1. The sample of parents responding cannot be considered a cross-section of those whose children have a Statement. Mostly these Statements referred to educational needs arising from sensory impairments or multiple and complex difficulties in learning. One of the reasons given for supporting special provision was that physically disabled children were often perceived to suffer at the hands of non-disabled peers. 'Children can be treated like, and feel like, a freak if they are integrated as individual disabled children' (letter from parent). One parent wrote: 'The worry caused when your child is being bullied or feeling depressed affects the whole family. Taking an Asperger child out of that environment greatly increases the quality of the child's life as well as the family'. There was also a view that, although the same opportunities are often not available to students in special schools as those in mainstream, this does not mean these opportunities automatically become available if the child is moved into mainstream. These opportunities must be made available within the special schools rather than transferring the children to mainstream. In addition, there was a perception of intolerance by children and staff in mainstream, of gross dissatisfaction with levels of resourcing, staff training, awareness and understanding in mainstream, and a perception that special schools constitute a 'reservoir of shared knowledge and expertise in teaching' of students with specialist needs. The minority of parents wanting a mainstream education for their children had equally strong views on their children's rights to be respected as full members of society. In preparation for this they felt it most appropriate that they should be included in local mainstream schools with additional provision to meet their individual needs.

The Ofsted (2010) review in England found that no one model – such as special schools, full inclusion in mainstream settings, or specialist units co-located with mainstream settings – worked better than any other. The effective practice seen during the review encompassed a wide range of models of provision, often with significant flexibility in the way in which services were provided within any one local area. However, it became apparent during the review that the pattern of local services had often developed in an ad hoc way, based on what had been done in the past rather than from a strategic overview of what was needed locally.

The key implication of these findings is that any further changes to the system should focus not on tightening the processes of prescribing entitlement to services but, rather, on improving the quality of assessment and ensuring that where additional support is provided, it is effective. Ofsted felt that it was important to improve teaching and pastoral support early on so that additional provision is not needed later and to develop specialist provision and services strategically so that they are available to maintained and independent schools, academies and colleges. Legislation should be simplified so that the system is clearer for parents, schools and other education and training providers, ensuring that schools do not identify pupils as having special educational needs when they simply need better teaching. Those providing services for children should focus on the outcomes for the children and young people concerned.

LEARNING DIFFICULTIES, DISABILITIES AND THE LAW

Education law varies across the four countries of the UK. Having said that, until recently there have been strong similarities in England, Wales and Northern Ireland in some respects. This applies to the definition of what constitutes a special learning or behavioural need as well as the assessment of the need and the kind of provision that is made. Proposals by the National Assembly for Wales for revisions to legislation in Wales and by the Department for Education for revisions in Northern Ireland, and new legislation that was introduced in England in 2014, may increase the differences between them, however. Education law in Scotland is regulated by the Scottish Government in Edinburgh and continues to be different.

The same disability law, most recently legislation introduced by the Equality Act, 2010, operates across the countries of the UK. It does not, however apply to Northern Ireland where the relevant disability equality legislation is the Disability Discrimination (Northern Ireland) Order 2006.

SPECIAL EDUCATIONAL NEEDS IN ENGLAND, WALES AND NORTHERN IRELAND

In England, Wales and Northern Ireland, under the terms of the relevant legislation a child[2] has special educational needs if he or she has a learning difficulty[3] which calls for special educational provision to be made for him or her (Education Act, 1996, Part 1V, § 312(1), Education Order (Northern Ireland) 1996, Part 11, § 3(1); (Children and Families Act, 2014, Part 3, § 20 (1)). That is, a young person only has 'special educational needs' when special provision is required to meet them: learning difficulties do not in themselves constitute such a need.

In understanding the legal definition of SEN fully, we need to understand what is meant by 'learning difficulty'. Similar definitions of what constitutes such a difficulty apply in England, Wales and Northern Ireland. That is, a child or young person may be seen as having such a difficulty if s/he experiences

 a significantly greater difficulty in learning than the majority of same-age peers, or
 b s/he has a disability which prevents him (or her) from making use of (educational) facilities 'of a kind generally provided for' same-age peers in mainstream educational institutions.

> (Education Act 1996, Part 1V, § 312 (2);
> Education Order (Northern Ireland) 1996, Part 11, § 3(1);
> Children and Families Act 2014, Part 3, § 20 (2))

In law, a learning difficulty creates a need. The need is 'special' if the provision required to satisfy it is 'special'. A student might have a 'learning difficulty', for example, if s/he has a specific literacy difficulty which makes it hard to engage in the same learning activities as other students. This much is fairly obvious – but a child might also have a 'learning difficulty' if s/he has a physical disability that creates a barrier to moving around the school or classroom to participate in those activities with peers.

This way of defining a learning difficulty raises a number of questions. Included in them are how to measure 'significantly greater difficulty in learning' and how to compare one student to the majority. Comparing individuals against what we feel most people at that age should be learning and the way they should be learning it is bound to lead to mistakes, leaving some children without support and others with support that is unnecessary. Then there is a question of how to gauge the contexts in which a difficulty becomes significant, for example, whether remembering names is difficult only in examinations, or in everyday learning situations also. Finally, what is meant by a general level of provision? Some schools have space for particular sporting activities, others do not, for example. All teaching staff tend to adapt their classrooms to suit their way of working.

The majority of those who might be defined as having learning difficulties will experience difficulties of a mild nature. Whether they are identified as needing additional support is very variable in different parts of the country. It is not unusual for schools to use formal curriculum attainment levels as a general marker in an attempt to identify children with learning difficulties or disabilities. In England, for example, practitioners will often identify someone as having learning difficulties in relation to expected progress in the National Curriculum. The danger here is that this allows assessment designed for a different purpose to validate decisions which affect provision and children's learning. Inevitably, whatever system is used to define students' needs, the professional, resource and policy judgements involved in the decision-making process will always leave room for inequality.

The second part of the definition refers to a 'disability' as causing learning difficulties. This means that, by law, a person with a visual impairment has a learning difficulty if the individual cannot access the same facilities as peers. This aspect of the definition of learning difficulty means that, if LAs and schools provide appropriate learning opportunities, then no child would be hindered 'from making use of educational facilities generally provided' (Education Act 1996, § 312, DENI, 1998, para. 1.4 Children and Families Act 2014, Part 3, § 20 (2)(b))), and therefore no child would have special educational needs.

ADDITIONAL SUPPORT NEEDS IN SCOTLAND

In Scotland, the Education (Additional Support for Learning) (Scotland) Act (2004) (as amended – see below for discussion of this law) established the concept of 'additional support needs'. For the purposes of this Act a child or young person has such needs if 'for whatever reason', s/he is not likely to be able 'to benefit from school education provided or to be provided' for him/her 'without the provision of additional support' (Scottish Executive, 2004, p. 18, § 1). 'School education' here includes, in particular, such education that is directed to the development of the personality, talents and mental and physical abilities of the child or young person to their fullest potential (Scottish Executive, 2004 § 3).

'Additional support' in this context is defined as:

> provision which is additional to, or otherwise different from, the educational provision made generally for children or, as the case may be, young persons of the same age in schools (other than special schools) under the management of the education authority for the area to which the child or young person belongs.
>
> (Scottish Executive, 2004, p. 206)

A 'co-ordinated support plan' is seen as needed if the child or young person has additional support needs arising from

i   one or more complex factors, or
ii multiple factors,

and if the needs 'are likely to continue for more than a year' (p. 74, § 3), with the proviso that 'significant additional support' is required to address the needs. In this situation, a factor is defined as 'complex' if 'if it has or is likely to have a significant adverse effect on the school education of the child or young person.

THE LAW RELATING TO SPECIAL NEEDS IN ENGLAND, WALES AND NORTHERN IRELAND

In England and Wales the 1981 Act is seen by many as the key piece of legislation concerned with children and young people who experience difficulties or have disabilities in education. It introduced 'statements of special educational need', which set out an analysis of the difficulties students experience in schools and the curricular and human and material resources needed to address them.

The 1993 Education Act replaced the 1981 Education Act in all but a few minor details, although it covered much the same ground. This Act gave the responsibility for co-ordinating special education provision solely to local authorities irrespective of the type of school attended by the pupils concerned. It introduced a *Code of Practice for the Identification and Assessment of Special Educational Needs* (DfE, 1994), new procedures for assessing 'needs' and specifying resources in 'statements of special educational needs' and a new tribunal system to hear appeals against these formal assessment procedures. Parents were given legal remedies against decisions about their children in assessment and statementing. The old local educational authority appeals panels which heard complaints from parents were replaced by 'independent' tribunals chaired by lawyers, following the model of industrial tribunals. The introduction of the Code of Practice, with its status of statutory guidance, gave the tribunals a shared text to guide their practice in hearing appeals about formal assessments.

The 1993 Act was repealed and replaced by the 1996 Act in November 1996, with Part IV of the new Act incorporating all the provisions of Part III of the 1993 Act. The 1996 Act remains the basis for education-related law in Wales, but the law in England changed substantially in 2014 with the Children and Families Act.

Legislation in Wales

Education-related law in Wales, then, is still based on the 1996 Act. However, the National Assembly of Wales set out a proposal to amend legislation related to SEND policy and provision in 2012 in a consultation document *Forward in Partnership for Children and Young*

People with Additional Needs. In summary, the proposal in this consultation document was to:

- introduce the concept of 'additional needs' (AN), rather than 'special educational needs';
- replace statements of SEN with new integrated 'Individual Development Plans' (IDPs) that:
  - include assessment and provision involving agencies beyond education where appropriate for young people aged 0–25 years with the highest levels of need, and
  - require multi-agency panels, called 'Support Panels', to assess and agree the support services from education, social and health services that should be recorded in the IDP.
- require relevant bodies to collaborate in respect of provision for additional needs.
- set out the duties to be required of relevant bodies (such as LAs and health services);
- set out the resolution process for any disputes;
- require the Welsh Ministers to issue a Code of Practice related to the new statutory framework for AN.

At the time of writing the new legislation has not yet been approved by the National Assembly of Wales.

Legislation in Northern Ireland

The 1996 Act itself does not apply in Northern Ireland although Part 11 of the Education Order (Northern Ireland) (1996), which remains the basis of legislation related to special educational needs in the province, bears a close similarity to the 1996 Act in England and Wales. The 1996 Education Order was amended by the Special Educational Needs and Disability (Northern Ireland) Order (SENDO), (2005) Part II, Articles 3 to 12 and Schedule 1 to take account, specifically, of disability legislation that had been introduced across the UK in 2001. The new SEN provisions:

- strengthen the rights of children with SEN to be educated in ordinary schools where parents want this and the interests of other children can be protected;

- require Boards to make arrangements for services to provide parents of children with SEN with advice and information;
- require Boards to provide a means of resolving disputes with schools and Boards;
- require Boards to comply, within prescribed periods, with orders of the Tribunal and make other technical changes in support of the Tribunal appeals process and the statementing process;
- require schools to inform parents where they are making special educational provision for their child.

(DENI, 2005, p. 8, § 3)

Recently a proposition to amend the law related to SEND was introduced in the Northern Ireland Assembly on 2nd March 2015 through the Special Educational Needs and Disability Bill (Bill 46/11–16). Among the proposals in the Bill:

Clause 1 places a new duty on the Education Authority to have regard to the views of the child in relation to decisions affecting them;

Clause 3 extends the existing duties of Boards of Governors in relation to SEN, including a requirement to maintain a personal learning plan (PLP) for each pupil with SEN and ensuring that a teacher is designated as a learning support co-ordinator (LSC)

[...]

Clause 9 gives children with SEN who are over compulsory school age rights previously exercisable by parents, including the right to appeal and to request a statutory assessment.

(http://www.niassembly.gov.uk/globalassets/documents/raise/publications/2015/education/3815.pdf, accessed 30.03.15)

Children and Families Act (2014) in England

Since 1996 a further Act, the Children and Families Act (2014), has brought about a number of changes in the law in England. Much of the new law is still the same as in 1996. However, the new system of supporting children and young people with SEN now applies to young people from birth to 25 years as long as they stay in education or training. This issue of age is important. In law a child becomes a young person when s/he is no longer of compulsory school age (that is, s/he became 16 before the last day of the summer term (Section

83(2)). Once a child becomes a young person s/he can take decisions in relation to the Act on his/her own behalf, rather than the parents, subject to a young person 'having capacity' to take a decision under the Mental Capacity Act (2005). If young people do not have the mental capacity to make a decision on their own, their parents will automatically be assumed to be making the decision on their behalf unless the Court of Protection has appointed a Deputy. It can never be assumed by a school or college that a young person does or does not have the mental capacity to make a decision, however. The decision about whether young people have mental capacity to make a particular decision is something that they and their parents should make in the first instance.

This new system will not cover children or young people if they are disabled and have health and/or social care needs but no SEN.

Section 19 of Part 3 of the Act requires that the views, wishes and feelings of children, young people and their parents, and their participation, must be central to every decision the LA makes in regard to assessing a child or young person's SEN and how to support them.

It is the LA's duty to ensure they identify all children and young people who have or may have SEN and/or disabilities in their geographical area. A child or young person with SEN is entitled to support that enables them to achieve the 'best possible educational and other outcomes'. The school or college that a child or young person attends should put support in place to make sure this is happening. If it does not, the LA has the responsibility to ensure it does.

Statements of special education need[4] are being replaced by Education Health and Care Plans (EHCs). A young person in further education is now legally entitled to the special educational provision specified in their EHC plan, but EHC plans do not apply to higher education. Only the LA can carry out an EHC needs assessment to identify needs and provision to meet those needs. If an EHC plan is then issued, the LA has the legal duty to ensure that the educational provision is made. This duty can never be delegated to a school or college whatever funding arrangements are in place. Where there is health provision in an EHC plan, the local health commissioning body – usually the Clinical Commissioning Group – has the duty to provide. It is also the Local Authority's duty to provide the social care provision in an EHC plan if it results from an assessment under social care legislation.

Every LA must develop and publish a 'Local Offer' (§ 30) that sets out the services and provision it expects to be available both inside and outside the LA's area for children and young people with SEN and/or a disability. The Local Offer should make clear what special educational provision it expects the schools and colleges in its area to make from their existing budgets. LAs have a duty to publish comments about the Local Offer from children, young people and their parents, and the action they intend to take in response (§ 30(6)).

The LA is obliged to consider identifying a personal budget (§ 48) for educational provision for a child or young person if the parent requests it when they are carrying out an EHC needs assessment or when they are reviewing an EHC plan. The personal budget is the notional amount of money that would be needed to cover the cost of making the special educational provision specified in the EHC plan. A head teacher or principal has a veto if they do not agree to a direct payment being made for special educational provision which would need to be delivered in their school or college.

LEGISLATION IN SCOTLAND

The Education (Additional Support for Learning) (Scotland) Act 2004 provides the legal framework for local authorities and other agencies to support all children and young people who require it through the provision of additional support for learning. The Act places duties on education authorities (and in certain circumstances health, social work and Skills Development Scotland) to plan and make joint provision for all children and young people with additional support needs, including those with complex or multiple additional support needs. Where their needs are significant, requiring support from education and another appropriate agency, and would last more than one year, children and young people may require a statutory co-ordinated support plan to bring together all of the support necessary to meet their learning needs. This Act also sets out rights for parents, establishes mechanisms for resolving differences for families and authorities through mediation and dispute resolution, and established the Additional Support Needs Tribunals (Scotland).

The legislation was amended by the Education (Additional Support for Learning) (Scotland) Act 2009. The amendments related, among other issues, to increasing the rights of parents to make out-of-area placing requests and to expanding access to the Additional Support Needs Tribunals for Scotland (ASNTS), and to the provision of a new national advocacy service for parents and young people. In addition the 2009 Act automatically deemed that all looked after children and young people have additional support needs unless the education authority determined that they do not require additional support to benefit from school education.

CURRENT DEFINITIONS: AREAS OF 'NEED'

The 'need' which assessment and subsequent provision should address is conceptualised somewhat differently across the UK. The *Special Educational Needs Code of Practice for Wales* (2004, § 7.52), just as the previous Code of Practice in England (DfES, 2001, para. 7.52) did, recommends that assessment and provision should focus on four broad 'areas of need', described as communication and interaction, cognition and learning, behaviour, emotional and social development, and sensory and/or physical. More recently, however, the *Special Educational Needs and Disability Code of Practice: 0 to 25 Years* (DfE, 2014, § 5.32) in England has refined the conceptualisation of the third 'broad' area of need from 'behaviour, emotional and social development' to 'social, emotional and mental health'.

Clearly there is a lot of overlap between these areas, For example, in terms of communication and interaction, lack of facility with receptive and expressive language has important implications for cognition and learning. As the Code in Wales cautions:

> Although needs and requirements can usefully be organised into areas, individual pupils may well have needs which span two or more areas. For example, a pupil with general learning difficulties may also have behavioural difficulties or a sensory impairment. Where needs are complex in this sense it is important to carry out a detailed assessment of individual pupils and their situations.

> (NAW, 2004, § 7.53).

A number of teaching approaches that are identified in the Code in Wales as appropriate for addressing the learning needs of students who experience difficulties in communication and interaction may also be appropriate to those who experience difficulties in cognition and learning:

These children may require some, or all, of the following:

- flexible teaching arrangements
- help in acquiring, comprehending and using language
- help in articulation
- help in acquiring literacy skills
- help in using augmentative and alternative means of communication
- help to use different means of communication confidently and competently for a range of purposes including formal situations
- help in organising and co-ordinating oral and written language
- support to compensate for the impact of a communication difficulty on learning in English or Welsh as an additional language
- help in expressing, comprehending and using their own language, where English or Welsh is not the first language.

(NAW, 2004, § 7.56)

In Scotland the approach is rather different, however. The revised *Supporting Children's Learning Code of Practice* (Scottish Government, 2010, p. 13) offers a (non-exhaustive) list of children or young people who may require additional support for a variety of reasons. This includes those who:

- have motor or sensory impairments
- are being bullied
- are particularly able or talented
- have experienced a bereavement
- are interrupted learners
- have a learning disability
- are looked after by a local authority
- have a learning difficulty, such as dyslexia
- are living with parents who are abusing substances
- are living with parents who have mental health problems
- have English as an additional language

- are not attending school regularly
- have emotional or social difficulties
- are on the child protection register
- are young carers.

A wide range of factors broadly grouped into four overlapping areas are identified as potentially creating barriers that may lead to the need for additional support:

- learning environment
- family circumstances
- disability or health need
- social and emotional factors.

The definition of additional support provided in the Act is broad and inclusive to reflect the rather broader concept of who might require additional provision. Forms of additional support that are identified in the Code in Scotland relate to what is needed to help individual children and young people benefit from school education and are categorised under three broad headings (p. 21):

- approaches to learning and teaching
- support from personnel
- provision of resources.

RESPONDING TO INDIVIDUAL NEEDS

When a teacher is seriously concerned about the progress made by a child in a classroom, it is very important to be aware of the process that should be followed to maintain the child's access to education.

THE CODES OF PRACTICE

In the years following the 1981 Education Act a number of deficiencies in the procedures for assessing pupils thought to 'have special educational needs' had become apparent. The Audit Commission and Her Majesty's Inspectorate identified three key problems:

- lack of clarity about what constitutes special educational need and about the respective responsibilities of schools and LEAs;
- lack of systems to ensure that schools and LEAs are accountable for their work in the area of special needs;
- lack of incentives for LEAs to implement the 1981 Act.

(Audit Commission/HMI, 1992, para. 126).

In 1994, the government published a *Code of Practice for the Identification and Assessment of Special Educational Needs* (DfE, 1994) for use in England and Wales. The Code was designed to offer 'statutory guidance' to schools in England and Wales on how to interpret the law to address issues of ways to provide appropriate support to those with learning difficulties. It was designed on the model of industrial Codes of Practice, to provide a shared text for use at tribunals, should there be any dispute between parents/carers and the school and LEA (now LA) with regard to the appropriateness of provision. A similar publication was produced later in Northern Ireland (DENI, 1998). In Scotland the legal framework and associated advisory documents are different.

Since that time two further Codes have been published offering statutory guidance to LAs, governing bodies, schools and colleges. Their statutory nature is reflected in Part IV of the 1996 Education Act, § 313, in England and Wales, which reads, for example:

(1) The Secretary of State shall issue, and may from time to time revise, a code of practice giving practical guidance in respect of the discharge by [local authorities] and the governing bodies of [maintained schools] [and maintained nursery schools] of their functions under this Part.
[...]
On any appeal under this Part to the Tribunal, the Tribunal shall have regard to any provision of the code which appears to the Tribunal to be relevant to any question arising on the appeal.

These Codes reflect changes in the law, firstly in relation to the 1996 Education Act and, most recently, to the Children and Families Act 2014 (DfES, 2001; National Assembly of Wales, 2004; DfE, 2014).

In the section below the content and implications of the most recent Codes[5] in operation in the UK are reviewed in chronological order of their publication.

Code of Practice in Northern Ireland

As noted above, the law dealing with Special Education in Northern Ireland is contained in the Education (Northern Ireland) Order 1996 as amended by The Special Educational Needs and Disability (Northern Ireland) Order 2005 (SENDO). The Department of Education provided statutory guidance for Education and Library Boards and schools in a *Code of Practice on the Identification and Assessment of Special Educational Needs* (DENI, 1998) and also a Supplement to the Code of Practice (DENI, 2005), which was produced as a result of the SENDO. The fundamental principles outlined in the Code are based on those enshrined in the Education (Northern Ireland) Order 1996:

- the needs of all pupils who may experience learning difficulties during their school careers must be addressed; the Code recognises that there is a continuum of needs and a continuum of provision which may be made in a variety of forms;
- children with special educational needs require the greatest possible access to a broad and balanced education, including the Northern Ireland Curriculum;
- the needs of most pupils will be met in mainstream schools, and without a statutory assessment or a statement. Children with special educational needs, including those with statements, should, wherever appropriate and taking into account the wishes of their parents, be educated alongside their peers in mainstream schools;
- even before a child reaches compulsory school age, he or she may have special educational needs requiring the intervention of the Boards as well as the health services;
- the knowledge, views and experience of parents are vital. Effective assessment and provision will best be secured where there is partnership between parents and schools, Boards and other agencies.

(DENI, 1998, § 1.6)

The principal novel element in the original Code (DfE, 1994), compared to the law and the Regulations, and an element that is reflected in the Northern Ireland Code (DENI, 1998), was the introduction of a five-stage model of assessment. In paragraph 119 schools are enjoined to establish clear procedures to identify children whose 'academic, physical, social or emotional development' is giving cause for concern, in consultation with parents and the child, develop and review individual education plans designed to address individual needs, assess children's performance and make use of outside specialist advice particularly from Stage 3. This staged model reflects that set out in the Warnock Report (DES, 1978, pp. 60–63), versions of which some local education authorities subsequently adopted. The Code attempted to make the statementing process clearer, more useful to parents and teachers, and faster. It suggested that when the learning difficulties 'are significant and/or complex; have not responded to relevant and purposeful measures taken by the school and external specialists, and *may* call for special educational provision' outside resources normally available to mainstream schools, 'the LEA should consider very carefully the case for statutory assessment' (paras 3.59 to 3.94). The first three stages are based in the school, with the assistance of external specialists where needed; at stages 4 and 5 the Library Board shares responsibility with schools.

- Stage 1: teachers identify and register a child's special educational needs and, consulting the school's SEN co-ordinator, take initial action.
- Stage 2: the SEN co-ordinator takes lead responsibility for collecting and recording information and for co-ordinating the child's special educational provision, working with the child's teachers.
- Stage 3: teachers and the SEN co-ordinator are supported by specialists from outside the school.
- Stage 4: the Board considers the need for a statutory assessment and, if appropriate, makes a multi-disciplinary assessment.
- Stage 5: the Board considers the need for a statement of special educational needs; if appropriate, it makes a statement and arranges, monitors and reviews provision.

(DENI, 1998, § 1.7)

In this Code of Practice, an 'individual education plan' (IEP) is introduced at stage 2. This term individual education plan follows the American model outlined in the 1975 special education law in the USA, Public Law 94–142, where a plan for a child perceived as having difficulties had to be drawn up in order to attract additional federal funds. The IEP summarises action to be taken at home and at school to address difficulties in learning. It focuses on the nature of the child's learning difficulties rather than other elements of the school context which impact on learning.

To reflect the amendments to the 1996 Education (Northern Ireland) Order that were brought about by the SENDO in 2005, a supplement to the Code was published in September, 2005. The Supplement aimed to

> provide a clear understanding and consistency of approach for schools, Boards and others on the steps to be taken in carrying out their statutory functions as they relate to the special educational needs (SEN) aspects of the SENDO and to provide additional guidance in developing inclusive education in schools for children with SEN. It explains the new SEN duties and provides case studies in order to show responsible bodies what steps might be taken to meet these duties
>
> (§ 1.6)

Code of Practice in Wales

The fundamental principles of the *Special Educational Needs Code of Practice for Wales* (NAW, 2004) are linked to the 1996 Education Act that applied in both England and Wales when the Code was published. Strong similarities can be seen here with the principles of the Code in operation in Northern Ireland in relation to a young person's entitlement to having his/her needs met 'normally' in a mainstream setting with access to a broad balanced curriculum, and a focus on the need to listen to the views of the young person and his/her family(NAW, 2004, §1.5).

A number of 'critical success factors' are included in the Code in Wales to ensure the inclusion of children with special educational needs:

- the culture, practice, management and deployment of resources in a school or setting are designed to ensure all children's needs are met
- LEAs, schools and settings work together to ensure that any child's special educational needs are identified early

- LEAs, schools and settings exploit best practice when devising interventions
- those responsible for special educational provision take into account the wishes of the child concerned, in the light of their age and understanding
- special education professionals and parents work in partnership
- special education professionals take into account the views of individual parents in respect of their child's particular needs
- interventions for each child are reviewed regularly to assess their impact, the child's progress and the views of the child, their teachers and their parents
- there is close co-operation between all the agencies concerned and a multi-disciplinary approach to the resolution of issues
- LEAs make assessments in accordance with the prescribed time limits
- where an LEA determines a child's special educational needs, statements are clear and detailed, made within prescribed time limits, specify monitoring arrangements, and are reviewed annually.

(NAW, 2004, § 1.5)

The 2004 Code in Wales also acknowledges the idea of a continuum of needs, but, like the (2001) Code, in England,[6] moves away from the five-staged approach to recommend a graduated approach to individualised interventions through provision at 'School Action' or 'School Action Plus'. 'School Action' begins when a class teacher, special educational needs co–ordinator (SENCO) or teaching assistant identifies a child as having special educational needs that require individual provision additional to, or different from, a differentiated curriculum and strategies that are usually provided in the class. The school receives no additional funding for the child. 'School Action' is likely to involve consultation between the class teacher, the school's SENCO and the parents, collation of information already available about the child's progress, and closer attention to the child's programme of work in the classroom, and closer monitoring of progress. The individual education plan for the young person

should only record that which is additional to or different from the differentiated curriculum plan that is in place as part of normal provision. The IEP should be crisply written and may focus on three or four key targets. IEPs should be written in Welsh, English or bilingually if appropriate. IEPs, and the ways in which they can help, should be discussed with parents and the child.

(NAW, 2004, § 4.27)

'School Action Plus' is for children who are likely to need support from specialists outside the school, often a teacher from the LA's special needs support service, and an educational psychologist. Others might include therapists of various kinds: speech, physio- and/or occupational health professionals; nurses, health visitors, doctors, education welfare officers and social workers, member of the local child guidance or family guidance team; and specialist teachers for children with physical or visual disabilities or hearing impairments.

'School Action' and 'School Action Plus' are the responsibility of the school. Class teachers should know which children have been identified for additional or special support at 'School Action' and 'School Action Plus', contribute information about children's progress at each stage and be aware of the content of children's Individual Education Plans (IEPs). They are also expected to take a leading role in monitoring and recording children's progress and to work with the school's SENCO and with professionals from outside the school.

After the stage of School Action Plus a request for a statutory assessment might be made. If so, the process is handled by the school and the LA, and may result in a Statement of Special Educational Needs that outlines special educational provision determined by the LA.

Code of Practice in England

In England schools, further education colleges and other settings have clear duties under the *Special Educational Needs and Disability Code of Practice: 0 to 25 Years* (DfE, 2014) and must 'have regard' to its contents. They should either follow its guidance or else be able to explain why they have not done so and the alternative provision that has been made.

Changes from the previous Code, which was published in England in 2001, reflect the new (2014) law and include:

- guidance on provision for disabled children and young people aged 0–25 years, as well as those with SEN, to improve outcomes;
- a stronger focus on the participation of students and their families in decision-making;
- guidance on joint commissioning of services to ensure co-operation between education, health services and social care, and a new co-ordinated assessment process with Education, Health and Care plans to replace statements;
- guidance on what must be included in the Local Offer;
- advice for schools and colleges to adopt a graduated approach to identifying and providing for students with SEN with four stages of action: assess, plan, do, review, to replace the previous 'School Action' and 'School Action Plus' categories The first step to supporting individual children's needs is high quality teaching by classroom teachers, differentiated for individual students;
- guidance on access to impartial advice that LAs must provide for families and students with SEN;
- guidance about record-keeping, with evidence of pupil progress, a focus on outcomes, and a rigorous approach for monitoring and evaluation of support that has been provided;
- guidance about funding. The notional SEN budget is not ring-fenced. The school should provide high quality support from the whole budget. The school should provide additional support up to a nationally prescribed threshold with the LA providing top-up funding where the cost of the SEN provision exceeds the threshold.

Individual plans for children and young people

The Code (§ 6.17) in England advises class and subject teachers, supported by the senior leadership team. to identify pupils who make less than expected progress by making regular assessments of the progress of all pupils. Gathering of information about pupils should include discussion early on with both the pupil and their parents so that all can be clear about the pupil's areas of strength and difficulty, any concerns the parent(s) might have, the outcomes agreed for the child and the next steps. If a pupil is identified as having SEN, schools are exhorted to remove barriers to learning and put effective special provision, to be known as 'SEN provision', in place through a graduated approach in the form of a four-part cycle of assessment, planning, intervention and review (assess→plan→do→review) where previous decisions and actions are revisited, refined and revised as staff and parents understand more about what supports the pupil in making good progress. This approach should utilise more frequent review and more specialist expertise in successive cycles as required to match interventions to the educational needs of children and young people.

Where, despite appropriate interventions, a pupil continues to make less than expected progress, the school should consider involving specialists, including from outside agencies. Together, the SENCO, class teacher, specialists, and parents/family, should consider a range of approaches to support the child's progress and agree the outcomes and a date by which progress will be reviewed.

If the child or young person still does not make the progress that is expected, the school or parents should consider requesting an Education, Health and Care needs assessment and provide evidence of the action taken by the school as part of its SEN support.

Guidance given in the 2014 Code about EHC plans is discussed in the section on statutory assessment below.

Code of Practice in Scotland

In Scotland, a revised *Supporting Children's Learning Code of Practice* was published in 2010 (Scottish Government, 2010) to reflect changes in the law in Scotland that had taken place in 2009. Within this document (p. 9) the purpose of this Code is defined as:

> It explains the duties on education authorities and other agencies to support children's and young people's learning. It provides guidance on the Act's provisions as well as on the supporting framework of secondary legislation. ... It also sets out arrangements for avoiding and resolving differences between families and education authorities.

The Code (§ 81) sets out a phased approach to addressing individual needs. A process of 'personal learning planning' (PLP) is considered appropriate to address many needs:

> All children with additional support needs should be engaged in personal learning planning and for many this process will be sufficient to address their additional support needs.

Personal learning planning (PLP) sets out aims and goals that relate to the young person's own circumstances. These must be manageable, realistic and reflect strengths as well as needs. Monitoring progress in achieving will determine the effectiveness of the additional support offered at that point. The child should be given the opportunity regularly to discuss his/her progress with a member of staff. If a particular type of support is not effective, an alternative approach should be explored. The parent(s), child and school should be fully involved in the PLP process.

The Code (§ 82) goes on to note how, if required, a PLP can be supported by an individualised educational programme. In Scotland, if children or young people require more detailed planning for their learning than can be made through PLP, they may have an individualised educational programme (IEP). This details the nature of a child's or young person's additional support needs, the ways these are to be met, the learning outcomes to be achieved and specifies what additional support is needed. At this point support from other agencies such as health, social work, or voluntary agencies may be required. If so, the relevant agencies should be involved in developing the child's IEP so that the work is properly co-ordinated. Again, the parent(s) and the child should be fully involved in the process.

STATUTORY ASSESSMENT OF SPECIAL EDUCATIONAL NEEDS AND DISABILITY

According to Ofsted (2010), about 1.7 million school-age children in England, that is, just over one in five pupils, were identified as experiencing special educational needs of various kinds. As discussed above, current legislation and guidance across the UK refers to individual plans for recording the nature of a student's difficulties and how they are going to be addressed. It is expected that both parents and students will be actively involved in creating and assessing the effectiveness of the individual. The plan might include adaptations to normal classroom activities, or a special programme of individual work for the child, or both. It should also include criteria for judging success, a section for recording outcomes and a date for reviewing the plan. The student's progress can then be reviewed regularly to see if the aims of the plan are being achieved.

A number of criticisms have been levelled at this kind of individual planning. It can be too bureaucratic. It may include targets for the child which can be de-motivating if focused only on weaknesses that the student should attempt to overcome. Sometimes targets are written by teachers or TAs without any consultation with the individual learner and may not be appropriate or intelligible to the student. They may focus only on the student and not take account of factors in the learning environment that may be contributing to his or her difficulties. However, the process of assessment and planning can also be used very effectively in analysing needs and planning the next steps in a learning programme. This process should be negotiated between all of those working with a student as well as the student him/herself so that it will be meaningful and have a direct impact on ways of thinking and working.

If however a child fails to make 'adequate progress' then additional or different action should be taken. What constitutes 'adequate progress' might be defined in a number of ways. It might, for instance, as in the Code in Wales, be progress which:

- closes the attainment gap between the child and the child's peers;
- prevents the attainment gap growing wider;
- is similar to that of peers starting from the same attainment base-line, but less than that of the majority of peers;
- matches or betters the child's previous rate of progress;
- ensures access to the full curriculum;
- demonstrates an improvement in self-help, social or personal skills;
- demonstrates improvements in the pupil's behaviour.

(NAW, 2004, § 4.14)

Of the children that schools identify as having SEN, those who have longer term or more severe disabilities or difficulties may the subject of statutory assessment.

Statementing in Wales and Northern Ireland

In Wales and Northern Ireland such assessment may result in the issuing of a Statement. Provisions specified on it are mandatory. Statements of Special Educational Needs are usually drawn up for one of two reasons. Either the child needs guaranteed access to special resources and expertise, a special curriculum, or an environment with higher than normal staff support; or their parents, or the professionals responsible for them, want them to attend a special school, or some other form of special provision such as a resource base in a mainstream school.

By law a Statement has to describe the child's special educational needs, and the special educational provision required to meet those needs. This must include the objectives of the requisite provision, the resourcing, how progress will be monitored, the name of the school, and any 'non-educational' needs and provision that have been identified. These might include services to meet medical needs.

The special provision listed must be provided by law, and the school named must admit the child. Chapter Seven, the 'Statutory Assessment of Special Educational Needs in the 2004', Code of Practice in Wales, for example, outlines the assessment and identification process that is required. The LA has to involve parents at many points, and parents have a number of legal rights. The LA must also collect evidence and advice from several professionals, including the child's head teacher, a doctor and an educational psychologist.

Education, Health and Care Plans in England

In England, schools and colleges should identify and support young people with SEN and/or a disability either from within their own resources under what is now to be called 'SEN Support' or, where the degree of need is such that it requires a higher level of resourcing than is available from these resources, through an Education, Health and Care (EHC) Plan. LAs, not schools, colleges or parents, have the legal duty to carry out an EHC needs assessment, issue an EHC plan and ensure the special educational provision that has been specified in an EHC plan. An LA has a clear duty to assess a child or young person's education, health and care needs where s/he may have SEN and may need special educational provision to be made at a level or of a kind which requires an EHC plan. An EHC needs assessment can only be requested if the young person has or may have educational needs, *not* where there are only health and/or care needs, no matter how severe.

The test which local authorities must apply in coming to a decision about an EHC plan is set out in the Children and Families Act 2014 (§37 (1)). Based on the evidence gathered:

1   Where, in the light of an EHC needs assessment, it is necessary for special educational provision to be made for a child or young person in accordance with an EHC plan -
    a   the local authority must secure that an EHC plan is prepared for the child or young person, and
    b   once an EHC plan has been prepared, it must maintain the plan.

There are specific requirements for the contents of an EHC Plan. An EHC plan specifies:

- the child's or young person's special educational needs;
- the outcomes sought for him or her;
- the special educational provision required by him or her;
- any health care provision reasonably required by the learning difficulties and disabilities which result in him or her having special educational needs;
- social care provision which is being made for the child/young person under the Chronically Sick and Disabled Persons Act 1970 and any social care provision reasonably required by the learning difficulties and disabilities which result in the child or young person having special educational needs, to the extent that the provision is not already specified in the plan.

If an EHC plan does not contain all of the sections which are needed, it will not be legally compliant.

Co-ordinated support plans (Scotland)

In Scotland, provision for children and young people with additional support needs associated with complex or multiple factors which require a high degree of support from education authorities and other agencies is organised through the provision of a statutory document called a 'co-ordinated support plan'. The Code in Scotland (§ 2, p. 74) lists the criteria required for a plan:

a   an education authority is responsible for the school education of the child or young person,
b   the child or young person has additional support needs arising from-
    i   one or more complex factors,[7] or
    ii   multiple factors,
c   those needs are likely to continue for more than a year, and
d   those needs require significant additional support to be provided-
    i   by the education authority in the exercise of any of their other functions as well as in the exercise of their functions relating to education, or
    ii   by one or more appropriate agencies (within the meaning of section 23(2)) as well as by the education authority themselves.

During the preparation of the plan the views of the following should be sought and recorded: the parents, the young person, representatives of relevant agencies and any others who provide support. If the decision of the local authority is to issue a plan, there are statutory requirements[8] related to its contents:

- the education authority's conclusions about:
    - the factor(s) from which the additional support needs arise;
    - the intended educational objectives;
    - the additional support required to achieve the objectives
- details of who should provide this support.
- the name of the school the young person is to attend
- the details of the person who will co-ordinate the additional support;
- the details of a contact person within the local authority who can offer advice and further information.

The Code (§ 50) also states that:

The plan should be clear and succinct, and refer to needs that will, or are likely to, continue for more than a year. Short-term objectives would continue to be contained within personal learning planning or an individualised educational programme or other plan.

It should include a focus on positive aspects of the young person's life, and include a review timetable.

Parents and young people have the right to refer particular matters, for example, statutory parts of the plan and prescribed decisions, to the Additional Support Needs Tribunals for Scotland.

THE SPECIAL EDUCATIONAL NEEDS CO-ORDINATOR (SENCO)

In England, Wales and Northern Ireland the role of the special educational needs co-ordinator (SENCO) developed in response to the introduction of legislation related to the identification of children with SEN and a statutory requirement to meet their needs in schools. In the Code of Practice that retains the status of statutory guidance in Wales, for example, the responsibilities in primary and secondary schools (NAW, 2004, 5.32, 6.35) are defined as:

- overseeing the day-to-day operation of the school's SEN policy
- co-ordinating provision for children with special educational needs
- liaising with and advising fellow teachers
- managing learning support assistants
- overseeing the records of all children with special educational needs
- liaising with parents of children with special educational needs
- contributing to the in-service training of staff
- liaising with external agencies including the LEAs support and educational psychology services, health and social service and voluntary bodies.

Cole (2005) notes how the ethos of the school and the values of individual head teachers have a direct impact on the role, status and, therefore, power of the SENCO to work towards an inclusive culture in the school. Without the support of the senior management team SENCOs can face a very heavy workload with vulnerable children who are not particularly popular in schools in competition with each other for position in league tables of pupil outcomes.

In many places the role of the SENCO has developed considerably since the publication of the (2001) Code. It may be allocated to members of the school senior management team or class teachers. SENCOs may have responsibilities both at the level of the individual children and the whole school. They may take charge of budgeting, resource allocation, timetabling and other managerial and administrative roles. They may also work with individual students, as well as advising, appraising and training staff, and liaising with outside agencies, professionals and parents. The new (2014) *SEN and Disability Code of Practice* that operates in England highlights the strategic nature of the role at the level of the senior management team in a school or college:

> The SENCO has an important role to play with the headteacher and governing body, in determining the strategic development of SEN policy and provision in the school. They will be most effective in that role if they are part of the school leadership team.
>
> (DfE, 2014, § 6.87)

The day-to-day responsibility of the SENCO is outlined as:

> the operation of SEN policy and co-ordination of specific provision made to support individual pupils with SEN, including those who have an EHC plan.
>
> (DfE, 2014, § 6.88)

One of the issues for many SENCOs is how to cope with the time demands of the role and, in particular, of the bureaucratic demands of assessment and planning for individual young people, evaluation of progress and the requirement for record-keeping that accompanies this. These days some SENCOs have dispensed with individual plans for some children and use group plans instead. Some may rely on 'provision maps' which can be either documents that identify provision for individual children, or whole-school provision with analyses of student outcomes and value for money, or both.

In England, in order to ensure that the SENCO is in a position to carry out this role schools and colleges are advised to ensure that the SENCO has sufficient time and resources to carry out these functions. This should include providing the SENCO with sufficient administrative support and time away from teaching to enable them to fulfil their responsibilities in a similar way to other important strategic roles within a school.

(DfE, 2014, § 6.90)

LOCAL AND REGIONAL DIFFERENCES

Around the UK the different practices and policies of Local Authorities (Library Boards, in Northern Ireland) as well as issues of ethnicity and socio-economic factors associated with the family, age and gender have resulted in very different levels and kinds of provision for students. The Ofsted (2010) review of special educational needs reported that, for some young people, the current system works well and supports clear educational progress. Schools and outside agencies collaborated effectively to serve the child's best interests rather than their own priorities. What seemed to make the difference was rigorous monitoring of children's progress, speedy intervention and thorough evaluation of the impact, together with high expectations for the child and a determination to support young people's self-direction. However, this does not seem to be the norm. Consistency in the identification of special educational needs varied widely, between and within different local areas. Between the three children's services, education, health and social care, there were widely different thresholds for qualifying for additional support. Access to a range of appropriate provision for children with the most severe needs was relatively quick, however, and started at an early age. Identification of need and entitlement to additional provision for young people between 16 and 19 also varied across education providers.

Ofsted (2010) reported that the young people interviewed during their review of special educational needs identified that what they wanted for their future was the same as other young people might wish for: successful friendships and relationships, personal choice about who to live with and what to do in their leisure time, and the opportunity of employment. Parents and families often felt that current provision for their children was not supporting them to attain their goals. Identification of their children's needs and fair access to high-quality services to meet those needs was inconsistent. Some felt that the system forced them to 'fight for the rights' of their children, and that the only way to guarantee additional support was through a Statement.

In 2010 the outlook for pupils identified as having special educational needs overall was not particularly positive. Ofsted reported that, as a group, they were disproportionately from disadvantaged backgrounds, were more likely to be absent from school or to experience periods of exclusion, and their academic achievement and progress at any specific age is comparatively poorer than their peers. These outcomes had not changed very much over previous years. Once they had passed the age of compulsory education, young people who experience difficulties in learning or disabilities comprised one of the groups most likely to be unemployed and/or not to be in education.

DISABILITY EQUALITY LEGISLATION ACROSS THE UK

Other legislation affects learning and teaching in schools. Since 2000 a number of pieces of legislation relating to disability equality have been passed across the UK,[9] in 2001, 2005 and, most recently, in the Equality Act 2010, the intention of which was to consolidate previous legislation relating to discrimination, including discrimination related to disability. The Equality Act passed into law on 6 April 2010. It stresses planned approaches to eliminating discrimination and improving access and is nationwide (including private education), imposing duties on schools and local authorities. In other words organisations such as schools and colleges are expected to be proactive in anticipating and responding to the needs of their disabled students.

A child or young person is disabled under the Equality Act 2010 (section 6) if s/he has a physical or mental impairment which has a substantial and long-term adverse effect on his/her ability to carry out normal day-to-day activities. 'Substantial' means more than minor or trivial and 'long-term' means lasting more than one year or likely to last more than one year. Not all children or young people with special educational needs will be disabled and not all disabled children or young people will have special educational needs. The vast majority, however, will fall under both legal definitions. Similar points may be made about children and young people with additional support needs in Scotland. However, given the broad definition of the term 'additional support needs' there will be many children with additional support needs who are not disabled. See Appendix A in the document 'Planning Improvements for Disabled Pupils' Access to Education' (Scottish Government, 2014) for a description of the overlap between the Equality Act, 2010, and the Education (Additional Support for Learning) (Scotland) Act (as amended).

In Scotland the Education (Disability Strategies and Pupils' Educational Records) (Scotland) Act 2002 requires education authorities and the proprietors and managers of independent and grant-aided schools, respectively, to prepare accessibility strategies which

- increase disabled pupils' participation in the curriculum;
- improve the physical environment of the school, or schools, to enable better access to education and associated services provided; and
- improve communication with disabled pupils. In particular, relating to the provision of information in appropriate alternative formats and taking account of any preferences expressed by them or their parents, that would be provided in writing to pupils who do not have a disability.

Detailed guidance on preparing accessibility strategies is provided in the Scottish Government publication 'Planning Improvements for Disabled Pupils' Access to Education', as above.

Early years settings, schools, colleges and local authorities have clear legal duties to act to prevent unlawful discrimination, whether directly or indirectly. For example, Paragraph 85 of the Equality Act 2010 states that there must be no discrimination by a school, for example

2 a in the way it provides education for the pupil;
   b in the way it affords the pupil access to a benefit, facility or service;
   c by not providing education for the pupil;
   d by not affording the pupil access to a benefit, facility or service;

Educational institutions must therefore ensure that they do not treat children and young people with disabilities less favourably than others. Although in the original 1981 Act in England and Wales there was a legal duty to include children in mainstream schools, there were three conditions that had to be met. Firstly the child must receive the special provision that he or she required. Next, the child's placement must be compatible with the 'efficient education' of other children in the same school. Finally, the child's placement must be compatible with efficient use of available resources. These three conditions meant that some LAs could argue that some children should go to special schools, even against their parents' wishes. Over time this law has now been changed to increase children's rights to be educated in mainstream. Stronger rights to a place in a mainstream school have made it unlawful for schools and LAs to discriminate against disabled students, particularly in relation to admission arrangements and the educational provision in school. Paragraph 85 of the 2010 Equality Act, for example, also states that there must be no discrimination by a school against a young person:

1 a in the arrangements it makes for deciding who is offered admission as a pupil;
  b as to the terms on which it offers to admit the person as a pupil;
  c by not admitting the person as a pupil.

A child who has special educational needs and a statement of special educational needs must now be educated in mainstream school subject to two conditions: the wishes of the child's parents and the provision of efficient education of other children.

The 2010 Equality Act gives parents (and/or young people of a responsible age in Scotland) the right of appeal to a Tribunal, if they feel their child has suffered discrimination. The Tribunal in England is the First-tier Tribunal, in Wales the Special Educational Needs Tribunal for Wales, and in Scotland an Additional Support Needs Tribunal for Scotland.

Educational institutions also have a duty to make reasonable adjustments – to change what they do or were proposing to do – to ensure a child or young person is not disadvantaged. This includes the provision of aids and services to support a child or young person. Schedule 13, of the Equality Act 2010 reads:

4 In relation to each requirement, the relevant matters are –
   a deciding who is offered admission as a pupil;
   b provision of education or access to a benefit, facility or service.

In Northern Ireland the relevant disability equality legislation is the Disability Discrimination (Northern Ireland) Order 2006. This Order extends previous legislation, the Disability Discrimination Act, 1995, to bring the functions of public authorities within the scope of disability legislation and imposes a new duty to promote positive attitudes towards disabled people and encourage participation in public life (§49A).

CREATING A POSITIVE LEARNING ENVIRONMENT FOR ALL

The various Codes of Practice make the assumption that teachers will offer differentiated learning opportunities for all students, including those with special educational needs and disabilities. For example, the 2014 Code in England (§ 6.12) reads:

> All pupils should have access to a broad and balanced curriculum. The National Curriculum Inclusion Statement states that teachers should set high expectations for every pupil, whatever their prior attainment. Teachers should use appropriate assessment to set targets which are deliberately ambitious. Potential areas of difficulty should be identified and addressed at the outset. Lessons should be planned to address potential areas of difficulty and to remove barriers to pupil achievement. In many cases, such planning will mean that pupils with SEN and disabilities will be able to study the full national curriculum.

Recent research confirms that strategies recommended for particular special educational needs are useful for most other students (Lewis and Norwich, 2000). It might therefore be sensible for newly qualified teachers to concentrate at first on strategies which improve the learning environment and increase the range of teaching strategies rather than assuming that something different has to be organised for every individual.

SUMMARY

Over the years, the conceptualisations of differences between people, the development of notions of entitlements and human rights, and the change in focus of, and on, education itself, have all contributed to the complexity and changing nature of the field of special educational needs.

The term 'special educational needs', used since Warnock (DES, 1978), is part of the discourse which, according to Salmon (1995) and Corbett (1996), for example, suggests a deficit model. At the same time we must recognise, along with the Disability Movement, that failing to acknowledge difference can be counterproductive to the learning needs of a student and be interpreted as disrespectful to that person's life experiences. Whatever an individual's view, parents, teachers and other professionals in education have to conform to aspects of the official definitions when engaged in formal processes under the Act, such as assessment and statementing.

In England, the aspect of law currently relating to special educational needs and disabilities is the 2014 Children and Families Act, Part 3, in Wales (at the time of writing) it is the 1996 Education Act, Part 1V, in Northern Ireland it is Part 11 of the Education Order (Northern Ireland) 1996 with revisions and additions made in the Special Educational Needs and Disability (Northern Ireland) Order 2005, together with their associated Regulations and statutory guidance documents. In Scotland it is the Education (Additional Support for Learning) (Scotland) Act 2004, subsequently amended by the Education (Additional Support for Learning) (Scotland) Act 2009. In addition, aspects of legislation related to disability equality also apply to education provision. The Equality Act 2010 consolidates previous discrimination legislation and is nationwide, operating across all the UK, but not in Northern Ireland.

NOTES

1   It is interesting to note that teachers in special schools for children with visual and auditory impairments still require specialist qualifications but those in some other kinds of special educational institutions do not.
2   Child or young person in England.
3   Or disability in England.

4   See below for an explanation of statutory assessment of special educational needs that previously might have resulted in a statement of SEN, but now may result in an EHC plan.

5   I.e., most recent at the time of writing (February, 2015).

6   The 2001 Code has now been superseded as a result of the change in legislation in England in 2014.

7   Factors are interpreted as 'complex' if they have, or are likely to have, 'a significant adverse effect on the school education of the child or young person' (Code, p. 77, § 13). Examples given in the Code as the source of such factors are the learning environment, family circumstances, disability of health and social and emotional factors.

8   See the Additional Support for Learning (Co-ordinated Support Plan) (Scotland) Amendment Regulations 2005 (SSI 2005/518).

9   This does not apply in Northern Ireland, where policy related to disability is devolved to the Northern Ireland Assembly.

UNDERSTANDING AND ADDRESSING DIFFICULTIES IN COMMUNICATION AND INTERACTION

INTRODUCTION

The chapter will focus on communication and interaction, the first of the four broad areas of need outlined in the *Special Educational Needs Code of Practice for Wales* (NAW, 2004, § 7.52), and the *SEN and Disability Code of Practice 0 to 25 Years* (DfE, 2014, § 5.32) in England. In the Code (DENI, 1998) in Northern Ireland there is an appendix in which 'speech and language difficulties' are defined in a way that is broadly similar. Young people's experience of 'language and communication difficulties' is also acknowledged in the Code in Scotland as potentially requiring the 'use of specialist learning and teaching approaches' (Scottish Government, 2010, § 77, p. 53).

There is an obvious overlap between descriptions of difficulties in communication and interaction, and cognition and learning. In the current chapter, particular attention will be given to speech and language delay, autistic spectrum disorders, moderate to severe learning difficulties exemplified by Down's syndrome, and profound and multiple learning disabilities, to illustrate:

- what is known about these delays and disorders from rigorous, high quality research studies,

- the relationship between such delay, impairment and/or disorder and learning,
- ways that the difficulties experienced by young people can be addressed through attention to the learning environment, curriculum and teaching approaches.

Issues related to permanent sensory impairment will be discussed in Chapter 6.

COMMUNICATION, LANGUAGE AND COGNITION

Communication is vital in everyday life. It allows us to build and sustain relationships, to share experiences, to express our thoughts and feelings and understand those of others, and to learn. As the National Deaf Children's Society states (2010, p. 8), there is a close link between language and communication. However, they are not synonymous. Language is 'the words (vocabulary), phrases, grammar and expressions we use and how we organise them to communicate'. Language ability can be seen as both receptive (that is, comprehending what is said and/or written) or expressive (that is, putting thoughts coherently into words, verbal or written). During their first year of life babies usually acquire a lot of receptive language. By the age of one, children can often understand quite a lot of what is said. However, they are less able to express themselves verbally. 'Communication is really more the means by which we convey language, both to get our meaning across and to understand the meaning of others' (2010). Communication is crucial for social and emotional development. It involves not only language, but also 'other things like eye contact, gesture, tone of voice, facial expressions and body language'.

STUDENTS WITH LANGUAGE IMPAIRMENT

Difficulties in language acquisition may involve receptive or expressive language impairments. The first of these is less obvious than the second and can create barriers to learning if overlooked. It is really important for teachers to get to know their students very well and to check carefully that what has been said is properly understood.

PRAGMATIC LANGUAGE IMPAIRMENT (FORMERLY 'SEMANTIC PRAGMATIC DISORDER')

Pragmatic language impairment (PLI), previously called 'semantic pragmatic disorder', is an impairment often associated with autism (Adams & Lloyd, 2007). Young people experiencing PLI have special challenges with the pragmatics of language, that is, using language appropriately in social situations, and/or semantic aspects of language, that is, the meaning of what is said. Children identified as having such an impairment can provide great challenges in the classroom, given that so much of the teaching in schools and colleges depends on spoken and written forms of language (Adams & Lloyd, 2007; Smedley, 1990). Many children experience significant difficulties in understanding language and developing vocabulary (Bishop & Adams, 1989; Botting & Conti-Ramsden, 1999). Children who have PLI have difficulties developing conversational skills, such as turn taking and adhering to the topic of the conversation (Bishop, 2000). Some are insensitive to their listeners and talk endlessly about their own preoccupations and interests. Some experience problems understanding discourse and telling stories in a logical order (Norbury & Bishop, 2003); and have problems with over-literal use of language, and making and understanding inferences (Leinonen & Letts, 1997). Some children are competent in using the formal structure of language whilst experiencing difficulties in semantic understanding (Rapin & Allen, 1983). There are no accurate figures for children who experience these difficulties (Law *et al.* 2002). Teachers and speech and language therapists report that there are increasing numbers of these children, although Rutter (2005) suggests that the increased numbers may relate to better identification rather than a real increase in prevalence.

Adams and Lloyd's (2007, pp. 229–230) description of a successful classroom intervention illustrates how both immediate and hidden meanings of language and communication, as well as the pragmatics of grammatical structure, have to be made explicit to some children. Their intervention had three principal aspects. Firstly good practice 'in interacting at an appropriate social and language level with the child' was established. The language demands in the classroom were modified, typically by 'having an assistant translate language into short meaningful utterances' accompanied by a visual demonstration.

Then the children were taught 'the vocabulary of social situations and insight' into others' emotions. Changes to routines were added in small steps, and these were discussed before they were implemented. Children were supported to understand 'social and verbal inferences, metaphors and hidden meaning in language'. Finally, work on the pragmatics of language focused on 'explicit exercises and classroom support in exchange structure, turn-taking, topic management, conversational skills, building sequences, cohesion and coherence in narrative and discourse'. The teaching methods that were used included 'modelling and individual practice; role-play; practising specific pragmatic skills in conversations; ... promoting self-monitoring and coping strategies'.

THE EXAMPLE OF 'AUTISM'

In 1934, Leo Kanner (Kanner, 1943) identified a difficulty in a small group of young children that seemed to centre on excessive focus on the self. He called it 'early infantile autism' from the Greek αυτος (autos) meaning 'self'. This difficulty was marked by inability to relate to people and social situations from early life marked by profound 'aloneness', failure to use language fluently to communicate and anxious and obsessive desire to maintain sameness. It was also characterised by fascination for objects which are handled with skill in fine motor movements, a good rote memory, over-sensitivity to stimuli, and apparently good cognitive potential.

A number of publications have been written by writers reflecting on their own experiences of being autistic. Higashida (2013, p. 47), for example, has explained what it feels like to spend so much time on his own:

'Ah, don't worry about him – he'd rather been on his own.'

How many times have we heard this? I can't believe that anyone born as a human being really wants to be left all on their own, not really. No, for people with autism, what we're anxious about is that we're causing trouble for the rest of you, or even getting on your nerves. This is why it's hard for us to stay around other people.

Around the same time as Kanner, Hans Asperger in 1944 used the term 'autistic' to denote a range of traits in some ways similar to that commented on by Kanner. As Wing (1996) notes, this range included extreme egocentricity and an inability to relate to others, speech and language peculiarities, repetitive routines, motor clumsiness, narrow interests, and non-verbal communication problems. Asperger identified features additional to those already seen by Kanner. These were, firstly, sensory sensitivities and unusual responses to some sensory experiences: auditory, visual, olfactory (smell), taste and touch. In her recollections, Grandin (1996) described her hearing as like a microphone in a hearing aid, permanently at the full volume position. She saw herself as having two choices, either to turn the microphone off altogether, or turn it on and be swamped with sound. Another account of autism (Barron, 1992) includes a description of a boy's supersensitivity to the texture of food and needing to touch and feel it before it went into his mouth. Food had to be of one kind, for example, bread could not be made into sandwiches with fillings otherwise it provoked vomiting.

Asperger also noticed an uneven developmental profile, a good rote memory and circumscribed special interests, and motor co-ordination difficulties. He noted, too, that one in ten people with autism spectrum disorder (ASD) have what appear to be extremely well developed skills in one specific area. These skills are often found in areas such as music, art, mathematical calculations, and calendrical calculation.

Wing and Gould (1979) identified a 'triad of impairments' in a broader group of 'autistic' children, about 15 in 10,000. This triad covers difficulty in social interaction (difficulty with social relationships, for example, appearing aloof and indifferent to other people), social communication, both verbal and non-verbal, and imagination. In addition to this triad, repetitive behaviour patterns are a notable feature, as well as a resistance to change in routine.

While the groups share the same triad, there is some difference in emphasis. People with Asperger syndrome tend not to experience the levels of learning difficulties that are associated with autism, and delay in speech and language development is not likely. They often have measured levels of intelligence that are average or above (National Autistic Society, 2015b, http://www.autism.org.uk/about-autism.aspx, accessed 08.05.15). In autism, however, three quarters of the population have difficulties in learning, some at a severe level.

Each area within the triad implies particular barriers to learning. Impaired social understanding and relating clearly affect interactions with other children and adults. A child who lacks social understanding is unlikely to understand unwritten social rules, recognise other's feelings, or seek comfort from others. Grandin (1996) recalls pulling away when others tried to give her a hug because being touched over-stimulated her senses and overwhelmed her. Autistic children may appear to behave 'strangely' or inappropriately, and may often prefer to be alone. Grandin remembers always wanting to participate in activities with other children but not knowing how and never fitting in. She tried to work out how to behave from observing other people and learning through trial and error. Difficulties in social communication mean that people on the autistic spectrum often find it hard to understand the meaning of gestures, facial expressions or tone of voice. Difficulties with social imagination mean people with ASDs are unable to think and behave flexibly. This may result in restricted, obsessional or repetitive activities and difficulties in developing the skills of playing with others. Children often find it hard to understand and interpret other people's thoughts, feelings and actions, predict what will or could happen next and understand the concept of danger. They may also find it hard to engage in imaginative play, prepare for change and plan for the future, and cope in new or unfamiliar situations.

All is not insurmountable, however. Dumortier (2004) comments from his experience that many of his problems could be avoided by prior planning. Schedules were very important to him and he needed to know well in advance what was going to happen, how it would happen, who would be involved and so on. Any change of plan, including either being late or being early, could lead to feelings of frustration, powerlessness, anger and anxiety.

Specialist approaches to addressing autism

Typically, autism in young people is identified through agreed diagnostic criteria consisting of a profile of symptoms and characteristics of autistic behaviour. According to the National Autistic Society in the UK (2015a, http://www.autism.org.uk/News-and-events/Media-Centre/Position-statements/Causes-of-autism.aspx, accessed 08.03.15), the exact causes of autism are still not known, although there is evidence that genetic factors are implicated. Research also indicates that a variety of conditions affecting brain development which occur before, at, or soon after birth are associated with autism. What is needed in educational terms to support the learning of students with severe forms of autism is a specialist approach and structured support. Indeed, among the core principles of 'good practice in autism education' in a report by the Autism Education Trust/CRAE (2011, p. 44) are to:

> Embed specialist, evidence-informed approaches in quality-first teaching practice to remove barriers for pupils on the autism spectrum
> [...]
> Build and consolidate autism expertise at a consistently high level by maintaining an on-going programme of training and CPD on autism for all staff.

so that staff can:

> Use innovative and individualised methods of adapting the curriculum, utilising pupils' strengths and interests, to make it accessible and rewarding for pupils with autism.

Nind (1999) makes the point that much of the literature on autism emphasises an innate inability to learn from natural interactive processes (Jordan & Powell, 1995; Trevarthen *et al.*, 1998). Many of the approaches for children with autism, for example, TEACHH and Lovaas (Jordan, Jones & Murray, 1998) rely on training or teacher direction, and less on intuitive responding. In the current climate, the prevalent position is that individuals with autism need direct training and behavioural intervention (Nind, 1999).

The Treatment and Education of Autistic and related Communication Handicapped Children (TEACHH, 1998) is what might be described as a 'cultural' approach to addressing difficulties related to autism. Cultivating individual strengths and interests is combined with structured teaching. TEACHH's approach is that it does not look 'simply for environmental stimuli that might trigger particular behaviours'. Instead it considers the way the child 'reads' their environment. The principles guiding the TEACCH approach include improving skills through education and modifying the environment to accommodate individual autistic students, structured teaching rather than more informal approaches, and parents collaborating with professionals as co-therapists so that techniques can be continued at home.

> TEACHH considers the environment in terms of how the child will be able to interact and learn from it ... a TEACHH-influenced classroom places a large emphasis on physically structuring the room to facilitate learning interactions.
>
> (Sheehy, 2004, p. 347)

The Lovaas approach, on the other hand, is a form of applied behaviour analysis (ABA) which is built on behavioural methods such as reducing identified tasks into small discrete 'teachable' steps reinforcing appropriate behaviours associated with each step, and using highly structured intensive teaching strategies. (See Chapter 5 for discussion of ABA.) ABA is used to reduce stereotypical autistic behaviours such as repetitive body movement through 'extinction' and the learning of socially acceptable alternatives to such behaviours.

General approaches to addressing autism in the classroom and at home

In classrooms teachers can address the learning and behavioural needs of children on the autistic spectrum in a number of ways. For example, a teacher can pay close attention to clarity and order, reduce extraneous and unnecessary material in order that children know where their attention needs to be directed, and maintain a predictable physical environment with very predictable and regular routines, ensuring that everything is kept in the same place. Children might be taught agreed signals to be quiet or to call for attention. Teachers might provide specific low-arousal work areas free from visual distractions. Headphones might be made available to reduce sound. They might also provide a visual timetable with clear symbols to represent the various activities for the day, and a simple visual timer with, for example, an arrow that is moved across a simple timeline to show how much time has passed and how much is left.

The use of Alternative and Augmentative Communication (AAC) is quite common where young people experience particular difficulties in verbal communication. AAC may be any kind of communication that replaces standard means of communication such as speech. Augmentative communication systems are designed to complement and/or enhance standard means of communication (http://www.autism.org.uk/living-with-autism/strategies-and-approaches/alternative-and-augmentative-communication/picture-exchange-communication-system.aspx, accessed 18.05.15). One form of AAC is the Picture Exchange Communication System (PECS), in which a child is taught to communicate with an adult by being given a card with a picture on it. In PECS, the adult teaches the child to exchange a picture of something for an item s/he wants, for example, to exchange a picture of a drink for a drink. Pictures can be used progressively to make whole sentences or express preferences, but it may take a long time to reach this stage of development in communication. The use of PECS is a key to a number of approaches such as the TEACCH programme. A development on the use of single pictures is that of visual scheduling, that is a visual timetable of events that are to take place during the day. Establishing daily routines in autistic children's lives may well be important in providing predictability and so reducing anxiety about what is happening around them. Providing visual schedules enables them to see clearly what is happening and when. One mother of an autistic 7-year-old boy commented (Smith, personal communication, 20.02.15):

> We regularly use scheduling with picture cards at home. The cards have pictures of what we do during the day, places we visit, and tasks to be completed. At the beginning of the day, we choose pictures that represent what will happen that day. We stick the cards on a velcro strip, and as we complete activities through the day we unstick each card and 'post' it in a 'completed' box. The benefit is that my son can see the whole day's happenings and can predict what will happen next. I have found that using schedules has reduced my son's stress, and built his confidence and, over time, has increased his flexibility. If the schedule needs to change, it can be discussed and my son can see that the rest of the schedule remains unaltered, which can be reassuring to him.

The future quality of life for young people with ASD may well depend on how far they can learn to understand and interact with others rather than solely on the academic skills and qualifications they may have gained (Jordan & Powell, 1995). In order to develop greater understanding of personal emotions children might be taught in a very deliberate, overt and structured way to name their feelings and relate these to their own experiences, predict how they are likely to feel at particular times and in particular circumstances, and recognise the signs of extreme emotions such as anger. A visual gauge showing graduated degrees of anger in different shades of colour can often be helpful here.

Pupils might also be taught, again very deliberately and in small steps, to identify and name others' feelings and link these to possible causes, and identify appropriate responses to others' emotions. They might, for example, keep a feelings diary in which they record times when they feel happy, sad or frightened, and what they can do about this. Teachers might use art, drama and social stories to identify the different kinds of emotions and/or explore their physical aspects and/or talk through situations that need to be resolved. Above all it is really important to get to know the pupil really well and to understand his/her individuality, strengths, weakness, likes and dislikes, and so on.

CONDITIONS ASSOCIATED WITH MODERATE TO SEVERE LEARNING DIFFICULTIES: THE EXAMPLE OF DOWN'S SYNDROME

There are a number of conditions often associated with some impairment of cognitive, including language, ability. One of these is Down's syndrome. Children with Down's syndrome tend to have a lower-than-average cognitive ability, often ranging from mild to moderate difficulties in learning. A small number have severe to profound mental disability. The average IQ of children with Down's syndrome is around 50 (Dykens & Kasari, 1997), compared to the average IQ of 100.

Language skills show a difference between understanding speech and expressing speech, and commonly individuals with Down's syndrome have a speech delay (Bird & Thomas, 2002). Fine motor skills are delayed and often lag behind gross motor skills and can interfere with cognitive development. Effects of the disorder on the development of gross motor skills are quite variable. Some children will begin walking at around 2 years of age, while others will not walk until age 4. Physiotherapy and/or participation in other specially adapted programmes of physical education may promote enhanced development of gross motor skills.

A 'syndrome' is a group of recognisable characteristics occurring together. Down's syndrome (Down syndrome in the United States and some other countries) was first described in detail by an English doctor, John Langdon Down, in 1866. It is a congenital condition which randomly affects about 1 in 1,000 babies born throughout the world, male and female alike. A 'congenital' syndrome is one present at birth.

Down's can occur in any family of any race, culture, religion or socio-economic class. It occurs because each of the body's cells contain an extra copy of chromosome 21. It can be identified in a foetus with amniocentesis during pregnancy, or in a baby at birth. It is chromosomal, not caused by anything the parents may have done before or during pregnancy.

In the United Kingdom, around one baby in every thousand, around 775 per year (http://www.nhs.uk/conditions/downs-syndrome/pages/introduction.aspx, accessed 18.05.15), is born with Down's syndrome, although it is statistically much more common with older mothers. At maternal age 20, the probability is one in 1450; at age 30 the probability is one in 940, at age 40 the probability is one in 85, and at age 45 it is one in 35 (Morris *et al.*, 2003). There is also data to suggest that paternal age, especially beyond 42 also increases the risk of a child with Down's syndrome (Fisch *et al.*, 2003).

PHYSICAL CHARACTERISTICS

Down's syndrome is recognisable at birth because of the typical physical characteristics (Selikowitz, 2008). Common physical features include a small chin, round face, protruding or oversized tongue, almond shape to the eyes, shorter limbs, a single instead of a double crease across one or both palms, poor muscle tone, and a larger than normal space between the big and second toes. The medical consequences of the extra genetic material are highly variable and may affect the function of any organ system or bodily process. Health concerns for individuals with Down's include a higher risk of congenital heart defects, recurrent ear infections, obstructive sleep apnea, and thyroid dysfunctions (Selikowitz, 2008). The incidence of congenital heart disease in children with Down's syndrome is up to 50 per cent (Freeman *et al.*, 1998). Eye disorders are relatively common. For example, almost half have strabismus, in which the two eyes do not move in tandem (Yurdakul *et al.*, 2006). In the past, prior to current treatment, there was also a high incidence of hearing loss in children with Down's syndrome. These days, however, with more systematic diagnosis and treatment of ear disease, for example, 'glue-ear' (see Chapter 6) almost all children have normal hearing levels.

When some of the cells in the body are normal and other cells have trisomy 21, it is called mosaic. There is considerable variability in the fraction of trisomy 21, both as a whole and among tissues.

COGNITIVE DEVELOPMENT

Overall cognitive development in children with Down's syndrome is quite variable. It is not currently possible at birth to predict the capabilities of any individual reliably, nor are the number or appearance of physical features predictive of future ability. Children with Down's syndrome have a wide range of abilities, and success at school can vary greatly, which underlines the importance of evaluating children individually (Selikowitz, 2008).

Individuals with Down's syndrome differ considerably in their language and communication skills. It is common for receptive language skills to exceed expressive skills. Augmentative and alternative communication (AAC) methods (see pp. 95–96), such as pointing, body language, objects or graphics are often used to aid communication.

ISSUES OF HUMAN RIGHTS

Some of the ways in which children with Down's syndrome were portrayed in the past and the treatment that some received illustrate a number of the issues related to human rights and values discussed already in this book. For example, owing to his perception that children with Down's syndrome shared physical facial similarities such as folds in the upper eyelids (epicanthal folds) with those of the Mongolian race as identified by the German physiologist and anthropologist, Johann Friedrich Blumenbach, John Langdon Down used the term *mongoloid*. He wrote in 1866: 'A very large number of congenital idiots are typical Mongols. So marked is this, that when placed side by side, it is difficult to believe that the specimens compared are not children of the same parents. The number of idiots who arrange themselves around the Mongolian type is so great, and they present such a close resemblance to one another in mental power, that I shall describe an idiot member of this racial division, selected from the large number that have fallen under my observation' (Down, 1866, p. 259). With the rise of the eugenics movement in the first half of the twentieth century, a number of countries, including certain states in the USA, began programmes of forced sterilisation of individuals with Down's syndrome. 'Action T4' was a programme of the systematic murder of individuals with Down's syndrome and other comparable disabilities in Nazi Germany, for example (Lifton, 2000). Since the Second World War, however, laws relating to such sterilisation programmes have been repealed.

In 1961, a number of geneticists wrote to the editor of *The Lancet*, suggesting that Mongolian idiocy had 'misleading connotations', had become 'an embarrassing term', and should be changed (Gordon, 1961). *The Lancet* advocated using the term Down's syndrome. The World Health Organisation (WHO) officially dropped references to mongolism in 1965 after a request by the Mongolian delegate (Howard-Jones, 1979).

Down's syndrome cannot be cured, but the learning and other difficulties associated with it can be addressed if people with the syndrome are offered appropriate help and if other people accept and include them. Above all it is important to stress that children with Down's syndrome are individuals and vary in their abilities and achievements. Although they have features in common, they also closely resemble their parents and family. Any one child will only have some of the characteristics associated with Down's syndrome. Each child has a unique appearance, personality and set of abilities. The extent to which a child shows the physical characteristics of the syndrome is no indication of his or her intellectual capacity.

PUPILS WITH PROFOUND AND MULTIPLE LEARNING DISABILITIES

Children with profound and multiple learning disabilities are individual human beings. Some may have autism or Down's syndrome. Others may have Rett syndrome, Tuberous Sclerosis, Batten's Disease or another disorder. One common factor for everyone is that they experience great difficulty communicating. Mencap (undated, p. 4) notes how many people with profound and multiple learning disabilities 'rely on facial expressions, vocal sounds, body language and behaviour to communicate'. Some people may only 'use a small range of formal communication, such as speech, symbols or signs'. Another factor is that learning is likely to be very slow. 'Short-term memory may well be very limited and children may need frequent repetition of the same concepts in the same situations' (Mencap, undated). Some may not reach the stage where they can communicate intentionally. Many may find it hard to understand what others are trying to communicate to them. It is very important, therefore, that those people who support people with profound and multiple learning disabilities 'spend time getting to know their means of communication and finding effective ways to interact with them' (Mencap, undated). Many people will also have additional sensory, physical and/or motor disabilities, or complex health needs.

For very many years there was a general assumption that children with multiple and profound difficulties were ineducable. However, as we saw in Chapter 2, more recently there has been a realisation that they can learn throughout their lives if appropriate support is made available. In England and Wales, for example, the 1970 Education Act acknowledged the right of all children to an appropriate education, irrespective of the degree of difficulty in learning.

Encouraging communication skills in pupils with profound and multiple learning difficulties is really important. There are a number of ways in which pupils' can be encouraged and supported to communicate with adults and peers, including electronically.

INTENSIVE INTERACTION

'Intensive Interaction' is aimed at facilitating the development of fundamental social and communication skills for children and young people with the most severe learning difficulties. As Nind (1999) comments, Intensive Interaction is based on the model of 'natural' interactions between caregivers and infants. It is designed to support practitioners to adopt a holistic, nurturing and problem-solving frame-work for interaction (Yoder, 1990). The teacher (or other practitioner) begins by trying to 'connect' with the learner and developing into 'a familiar repertoire of mutually enjoyable interactive games and playful ritualised routines based on the learner's own preferences'. The teacher or caregiver modifies his/her facial expressions, body language, vocal and gaze behaviours and so on to fit the rhythms of the learner's behaviour. The teacher's/caregiver's behaviour deliberately responds to the learner as if his/her behaviour has 'intentional and communicative significance' (Nind, 1999, p. 97). The repertoire of playful routines provides a safe context for learning the conversational rules of turn-taking and mutual interactions (Field, 1979).

The group for whom Intensive Interaction is appropriate may include some children with autism. As Nind (1999) comments, approaches to autism based on applied behaviour analysis assume that learning to communicate can be broken down into sub-tasks that can be taught separately. However, non-directive interactive routes to developing communication skills adopt a different approach. One premise underlying Intensive Interaction is that communication is complex and holistic. Hence Intensive Interaction favours the holistic model of caregiver–infant interaction for encouraging communication skills.

OBJECTS OF REFERENCE AND SYMBOL SYSTEMS

Objects of reference, and electronic banks of pictograms forms of alternative and augmentative communication (AAC) (see pp. 95–96) are also often used to assist children with varying degrees of cognitive difficulties to communicate.

'Objects of reference' refer to physical objects used to represent those things about which humans communicate: activities, events, people, ideas, and so on. These objects can be used as a 'bridge' to more abstract forms of communication such as sign, symbol or word. Objects of reference are often chosen because of their multi-sensory properties to give the individual a clue about what is about to happen, for example, a piece of soap to signify that washing is about to take place, or a seat buckle to signify a car journey. It is essential that the same item is always used to signify the same event (http://www.communicationmatters.org.uk/, accessed 18.05.15). The contexts in which various objects gain significance and meaning are different for different people. Park (2003) gives the example of Dawn, who has learned to use a bottle of bubble bath as her object of reference for 'bath'. He also describes Janet, who likes to lie on a trampoline and uses a piece of the cushion material to ask someone to help her climb onto the trampoline in the garden.

An example of the use of pictograms for communication

Symbol-based language programs have been developed over many years, for example, by Widgit Software. Widgit has produced an array of software that uses pictorial symbols to support the development of communication skills. In some ways we might see these as similar to 'icons' in Brunerian terms (see Chapter 4). However, whereas icons relate to a single item of information, Widgit symbols have a consistent visual structure with a wide vocabulary that can be used in a combined sequence to convey a broader meaning and build more precise information.

Widgit describes its Symbol Set as 'comprehensive collections of images' designed to 'support text, making the meaning clearer and easier to understand' by providing a 'visual representation of a concept'. The Symbol Set often 'follows a schematic structure, or set of design "rules"', that enables the reader to develop his/her own receptive and expressive language skills as exemplified below.

(Widgit Symbols © Widgit Software 2002–2014 www.widgit.com, accessed 18.05.15)

THE USE OF ICT TO SUPPORT COMMUNICATION

As a number of researchers have noted, Computer-Assisted Learning has the potential to be used as a tool for reducing barriers to learning (Singleton, 1994; Moseley, 1992; Florian & Hegarty, 2004). Two of these barriers are difficulties in cognition and communication (Wearmouth, 2009).

Many assistive devices are available to enable students to communicate: electronic language boards, voice synthesisers and voice recognition software. For example, screen magnifiers, or screen magnifiers with a speech facility, are intended to support students who experience visual difficulties to access on-screen text, graphics, tool bars, icons through magnification, colour-changing options, speech, Braille output, and so on (http://www.inclusive. co.uk/product-list?Text=screen%20magnifier, accessed 18.05.15).

The standard computer keyboard is designed to be used with two hands, and it favours right-handed people with the numeric keypad on the right. It is also very sensitive so that a string of letters may appear on the screen if a key is held down for slightly too long. The way the keyboard behaves can be changed, however, by using some of the accessibility in, for example, Windows (http://www. microsoft.com/resources/documentation/windows/xp/all/ proddocs/en-us/access, accessed 08.03.15). The use of 'StickyKeys' enables one finger to be used to operate shift, control and alt keys. 'FilterKeys' allow adjustment to the length of time a key needs to be held down before it appears on the screen. 'MouseKeys' enable the mouse pointer to be moved around using the numeric keypad keys. Keyguards with holes positioned over each key can make it impossible to press two keys at once whilst it is possible to rest hands and arms on the guard without pressing keys (http://www.bltt.org/ quicktips/foakeyguards.htm, accessed 08.03.15). They can be removed and fitted for use only when required. Instead of this, 'IntelliKeys' can be used as a programmable alternative keyboard that plugs into the keyboard or USB port to enable users who have difficulty using a standard keyboard as a result of physical, visual or cognitive disabilities to type, enter numbers, navigate on-screen displays and carry out menu commands. IntelliKeys has no keys. Instead, overlays with large, well-spaced keys in high contrast colours to help students find letters, numbers, words, and directional arrows slide over its programmable surface to create keyboards for different students and curriculum areas (http://www.inclusive.co.uk/intellikeys-usb-keyboard-p2392#, accessed 08.03.15).

Different sizes and shapes of keyboards can also replace the standard keyboard, and the position of the keyboard can be changed to accommodate individual needs. Small keyboards that suit single-handed users can fit between the arms of a standard wheelchair, for example. Separate numeric keypads are also available, if appropriate to the young person's need. Keyboards with larger or brightly coloured keys are also available. Retractable lap trays bolted under the desk can hold the keyboard to enable a lower typing position if needed. Keyboards can be tilted, and switches and pointers can be fixed in specific positions where they can be handled more easily. Alternatively, on-screen keyboards enabling letters to be selected by a mouse or trackball can be used to make the selection. Some on screen keyboards also have a facility for word prediction to make typing quicker (http://windows.microsoft.com/en-us/windows/type-without-keyboard#type-without-keyboard=windows-7, accessed 08.03.15).

It is also possible to adjust the way the mouse operates, for example, the speed, and the amount of time needed for double clicking. The buttons can also be swapped over for left-handed use. Mice also come in different sizes and shapes; and require varying amounts of pressure on buttons. A trackball is like an upturned mouse but it is a static device with the ball on the top which is moved with fingers, thumbs and palms (http://www.trackballmouse.org/, accessed 08.03.15). Larger trackballs can be moved with feet.

Voice recognition is an alternative to typing on a keyboard. Talking to the computer results in words appearing on the screen. This software is useful for those who find typing difficult, painful or impossible. Voice recognition software can also help those with spelling difficulties, including dyslexic users, because recognised words are always correctly spelled.

There can be a difficulty in the use of voice recognition software to support the writing of text, however, where students' speech is unclear and their words are not sufficiently differentiated, clear or consistent to be encoded into text. With screen-based devices such as a touch screens and a light pen, which is a light-sensitive stylus wired to a video terminal that is used to draw pictures or choose an option from a menu, selections and movements can be made by pointing at the screen surface. However, where a user is physically or cognitively unable to use any keyboard or pointing device, then a starting point can be to use a switch, a button which sends a signal to the computer to drive the software. Switches come in a variety of shapes and sizes and can be operated by any controlled movement of the body.

Many of the symbol communication systems used by students who experience multiple and profound difficulties in communication are supported by software programs to facilitate writing, as exemplified in Chapter 4.

Using ICT to support young people with multiple and profound difficulties and/or disabilities

Lilley (2004, pp. 82–4) offers a number of examples of individual programmes developed to incorporate the use of ICT for students with multiple and profound difficulties in learning and/or disabilities. For example, 13-year-old Samantha with cerebral palsy and poor fine and gross motor control was provided with 'an ultra-compact keyboard with guard and a gated joystick' that enabled her to move the cursor on the screen. A large 'jelly-bean' switch replaced the left-click function on a normal mouse. A 'Mouser 3' linked the mouse and the computer to allow switches to be used instead of the mouse buttons. 11-year-old Ann was confined to a wheelchair after a road accident when she lost expressive language. A jelly-bean switch was fixed to a specially adapted tray on her wheelchair, and Ann was encouraged to use a range of software programs designed to help learners understand the principle of cause and effect – a press of the switch causes a reaction on the computer screen. When she had mastered simple switch use she was encouraged to work on 'simple scanning software (Clicker 4 – a widely-used piece of software that allows children to click on pictures and phrases which the computer can speak if desired) that can easily be customized'.

(Lilley, 2004, p. 84)

Use of the Internet appears, at face value, to be a very useful medium for supporting the learning of some students who experience difficulty. Recent developments have come a long way in making access a reality for many students with special learning needs. However, this needs careful consideration of students' special learning needs (Paveley, 2002). Findings from the 1998 NCET project (Wearmouth, 2000, pp. 203–204) indicated that 'real' time access to raw information from the Worldwide Web is unrealistic for many students. Interesting or useful web materials often need to be saved to disk for future use. Further, where students are isolated from peers for whatever reason, for example, the location of their home, or difficulties with mobility, it may be especially important for students to make contact through e-mail or video-conferencing with peers elsewhere. Use of e-mail provides purpose for reading and writing skills and is highly motivating to students. An e-mail system which integrates the use of a concept keyboard, symbols, a talking word processor and text, and which automatically deletes headers when messages are received would be useful. However, the way in which students are given choice of e-mail and video-conferencing partners has to be negotiated very carefully.

SUMMARY

Communication is a vital part of building relationships, sharing experiences and learning. A number of conditions are associated with difficulties in this area, for example, pragmatic language impairment, autism and profound and multiple learning difficulties. Whilst it is clearly important to understand the condition in order to respond effectively to children's learning needs, this is only part of the story. Also important is getting to know the individual child, his/her strengths and interests and the wishes of the family.

In the next chapter we consider issues related to difficulties in cognition and learning, and some of the ways in which these might be addressed.

UNDERSTANDING AND ADDRESSING DIFFICULTIES IN COGNITION AND LEARNING

INTRODUCTION

The chapter will focus on the second of the four broad areas of need outlined in the Code of Practice in both England (DfE, 2014) and Wales (NAW, 2004): cognition and learning. We have already discussed the issue of profound difficulties in learning in Chapter 3. Here we look at difficulties more generally and particularly to the kinds of challenges faced by young people identified as experiencing 'moderate' learning difficulties. We go on to look at what is often called a 'specific learning difficulty', a term that is also used in the appendix of the Code in Northern Ireland (DENI, 1998) and that relates to a particular area of learning and not to overall attainment and cognitive ability terminology. We discuss one example of a specific learning difficulty: dyslexia.

UNDERSTANDING COGNITION AND DIFFICULTIES IN COGNITION

The Latin root of the word 'cognition' is 'cognoscere', which means 'to get to know', or 'to recognise'. In general terms, the frame of reference within which 'cognition' is used in the (2001) Code of Practice relates largely to information-processing associated with problem-solving, language, perception and memory and the development of concepts. The cognitive difficulties experienced by some students clearly extend to the area of communication and interaction discussed in Chapter 3. It is obvious, for example, that language acquisition and use are integral to thinking, problem-solving and communication (Wearmouth, 2009).

UNDERSTANDING CHILDREN'S MODES OF LEARNING

One very useful frame of reference within which to think about the level of learning at which a child is operating and the difficulty s/he might be experiencing is Bruner's (1966) model of the different modes of representation of reality used by humans as they develop their conceptual understanding of the world. As discussed previously (see p. 27), Bruner outlines three modes: 'enactive', where we 'do' and then we understand and know; 'iconic', where we understand reality through visual representations of the real thing; and 'symbolic', where we understand and can use abstract representations of reality. As Grauberg (2002) notes, one common feature that can be readily identified in children who experience cognitive difficulties is weakness in understanding and remembering that a symbol can represent something else, for example, something concrete or an action.

Whilst these three modes appear to imply that learning occurs in discrete stages, it is, of course continuous. Children may experience difficulty at any point in their development. Those who experience difficulties in cognition are very likely to need much more time to absorb and understand new concepts with representation more through concrete objects if necessary, using an enactive mode to learn by doing.

MODERATE LEARNING DIFFICULTIES

Although movement through the three modes above can be seen as developmental, it must be said that they are not necessarily age-dependent or invariant. As adults, we habitually use all three modes (Bruner, 1966).

ADDRESSING MODERATE DIFFICULTIES IN RECEPTIVE LANGUAGE

In Chapter 3 we differentiated between receptive and expressive language skills. Children who experience difficulty in understanding spoken language might learn effectively from teachers who understand that children learn by doing first. The Primary National Strategy (2005, ref 1235/2005) suggests that, whenever possible, pupils should have direct experience of a concept before it is used. Some pupils need time to formulate a reply to a question, so it might be appropriate to forewarn some pupils that they will be asked a question. Some pupils also benefit from being prepared for transitions between different activities and different parts of the classroom and school by, for example, having visual timetables and schedules and being told when and where they are going to move during the school day. Children often get the gist of what is meant from nonverbal clues, so it is important not always to speak in terms that are immediately understood by students otherwise their language will never develop. It is important to ensure that students realise they are being spoken to, and when they are being asked a question. They may need to be taught the skills of whole-class listening.

To ensure that all students understand what is said, including those with difficulties in receptive language, as Wearmouth (2009) notes, teachers should check that they speak calmly and evenly, and their faces are clearly visible. They might use visual aids related to the topics being discussed, and explain something several different ways if they have not been understood the first time. They might also make a point of repeating what students say in discussion or question and answer sessions.

STRATEGIES TO DEVELOP ORAL SKILLS

Children will only want to read a text if they can understand what it is that they are reading. To do this they need prior knowledge and experience. Low performance on tests of reading comprehension can also reflect students' limited vocabulary, and/or limited experience in talking about characters and events within stories or concepts of various kinds, and relating these to their own knowledge and experience. Talking is an essential intellectual and social skill that is shaped by how we think and forms part of how we communicate with others and make sense of the world. The young child's thought development begins through interpersonal negotiation with others, caregivers, teachers and peers at school and this is internalised into personal understanding (Vygotsky, 1962). It is clearly very important, therefore, to build up students' oral language skills, by supporting them to talk about what they have been reading and about how what they have been reading connects with what they already know. The potential of a meaningful 'talk to expand literacy' approach that goes beyond studying letters and words is supported by a number of research studies.

From the time a child first begins to understand the world s/he appears to do so by means of story. 'Any understanding we have of reality is in terms of our stories and our story-creating possibilities' (Mair, 1988, p. 128). Sarbin (1986) notes that it is through story that children learn to become functioning members of the society into which they are born. 'It is through hearing stories ... that children learn or mislearn both what a child and what a parent is, what the cast of characters may be in the drama into which they have been born and what the ways of the world are'. There is no way to enable children to understand society 'except through the stock of stories which constitute its initial dramatic resources'. If children are deprived of stories 'you leave them unscripted, anxious stutterers in their actions as in their words' (Sarbin, 1986, p. 201).

There is an important question about how learners can take the step 'from speaking to understanding writing on a page or screen, to realise that knowledge of life and language can help them make sense of words and texts' (Gregory, 1996, p. 95). Orally told stories, rhymes, songs, prayers and routines for meeting and greeting people, all have an important role in literacy acquisition and are promoted within many cultures long before children begin any form of formal education. Gregory (1996, p. 112) advocates addressing the issue of building from the known into new literacy acquisition by explicit scaffolding of children's learning through 'recognising children's existing linguistic skills and cultural knowledge' and then deliberately 'building these into both teaching content and teaching strategies'. She describes a reading session that draws on children's oral language and makes use of puppets to mediate learning. This should draw on the child's emotions, for example, fear, love, sympathy, hate, and aim to tell an adventure or drama. Well-chosen stories told in the classroom by the teacher can scaffold children's learning about written texts in a way that conversation cannot. Chapters for reading should include 'memorable stories and texts from all times and places', perhaps containing 'universal truths, values and morals, fear and security' which relate to pupils of all levels and ages (Gregory, 1996, p. 122).Ways in which beginning readers might be introduced to story-reading sessions include: explicitly discussing the context for the story, one or more of the characters, and the plot; reading the story slowly, clearly, with 'lively intonation' and without interruption; discussing the story and the themes, and relating these to the children's lives. Gregory (1996, p. 120) gives an example of a text, 'The Clay Flute' by Mats Rehnman, that seems complex but is popular with children. It is set in the Arabian Desert and tells the story of a poor boy who suffers many misfortunes but finally 'makes good'. The language is difficult but rich in imagery and emotive vocabulary (witch, horrible, grab, scream, kiss, tear, sword, heart and so on). Gregory identifies the reasons for its popularity as its clear purpose in the way the plot develops, its portrayal of the universal values of courage and kindness, and the way good is seen to triumph over evil.

Understanding written text

Having the ability to handle written text with confidence is a key part of coping with the day-to-day expectations of life. Commonly, difficulties in receptive language may include barriers relating to reading comprehension.

Developing reading comprehension

First, it is important to be able to judge the level of difficulty of any text used in class, for example, sentence length and complexity, word length and familiarity and the degree of conciseness in the explanation of concepts. It is also important to consider carefully (Lunzer & Gardner, 1979) the interest level of the text and/or prior knowledge of the subject matter. If students are interested in what they are reading or are familiar with the subject material, they can cope with more difficult text. Further, more students can understand higher level concepts if ideas are expanded and explained step by step.

Strategies for developing reading comprehension can include adding pictures, subheadings and summaries to the text and teaching students to take notes, underline key passages or write summaries. Students can be taught to scan the text before reading in depth, including focusing on pictures, diagrams, captions, subheadings and highlighted words (Wearmouth, 2009, pp. 42–43). They can be taught to think consciously about the text as they read: whether it fits in with what they already know, whether they have understood it, or what questions they might ask themselves about the meaning of a text as they read it through. The amount read before questions are raised can be shortened. This may mean a page by page reading, or even a paragraph by paragraph reading. Close consideration must be given to the constitution of student groups in this case. As students pay more attention to the messages conveyed by text the amount of text read before questions are asked can be lengthened. Groups of students can be encouraged to share the reading of a book and then discuss topics such as: how did the main character feel?; has anything like this ever happened to you?; what happens next? Cloze can be used to make sure that students are reading for meaning. Here every fifth word or so is deleted from the text, and the student is asked to fill in the gaps with a suitable, meaningful word.

Often students need to gain more experience in reading in order to increase word identification, knowledge of letter/sound combinations and use of contextual information and inference (Duke & Pearson, 2002). Excellent ways in which to develop these skills and also the related writing skills of language structure, organisation of thought and creative writing are following the text with the eyes while listening to a recording (which has to be word-perfect), 'paired reading' (Topping, 2001) or 'reading buddies'.

ICT support for reading

The use of symbols on some computer programmes acts as scaffolding for reading. Symbols can be used with one student and gradually withdrawn until s/he can read without them. The left–right directionality of reading can be reinforced through the *Clicker* programme (http://www.cricksoft.com/uk/products/clicker/home/writer.aspx, accessed 08.03.15). Sound to support reading and writing can be used in many different ways. Word processors with speech synthesis can be very powerful. Learners can hear what they have written, either as they are writing, or the whole text after they have finished.

Sound can be introduced to text by dropping it into a standard text to speech utility or talking word processor. The text may also be dropped into a programme such as *Writing with Symbols* (Widgit computing) which gives a symbolic version that can be printed out and spoken aloud. Talking word processors may be particularly useful tools to enable students to decode text downloaded from the Internet.

An example of a program to develop switch-accessible stories and slide shows is 'SwitchIt! Maker 2' (http://www.switchitmaker2.com/, accessed 08.03.15). Each activity has a sequence of on-screen pages which can have a picture, video or text-based material, music or recorded speech. Pages can be turned by a simple switch, the computer's spacebar, the mouse buttons or IntelliKeys (see p. 104 for a description of this hardware).

EXPRESSIVE LANGUAGE

Students who experience difficulty in expressing themselves need frequent opportunities for exploratory talk in every area of the curriculum in order to put new information and ideas into their own words and link subject matter to what they already know. Strategies that facilitate oral language development might include exploratory talk in small groups, problem-solving aloud, explanations of how something is made, or how and why things happen, dramatisation and role-play, interviews (live or taped) and group discussion.

Writing

Learners who experience problems in expressing themselves in writing may often benefit from structured support to help them develop skills for different types of writing. Allowing a student to dictate text onto an audio recorder and then transcribing it for him/her will help him/her to get thoughts and ideas down on paper. Alternatively the student can be allowed to dictate text while the teacher/older student/parent scribes.

Using ICT can also facilitate writing for some pupils. Word-processing can offer 'a means of drafting and re-drafting that is easy, efficient and accessible and so is a great equaliser in presentation. ... Pupils can work more quickly and demonstrate different types of writing exercise and have the opportunity to experiment ... and thus demonstrate their true ability' (Lilley, 2004, p. 89).

An example of a writing support and multimedia tool for children of all abilities is 'Clicker Writer' (http://www.cricksoft. com/uk/products/clicker/home/writer.aspx, accessed 08.03.15). At the top of the screen is a word processor. At the bottom of the screen is the 'Clicker Grid'. This has 'cells' containing letters, words or phrases that teachers can click on, to send them into Clicker Writer so that students can write sentences without actually writing or using the keyboard.

ENGLISH AS AN ADDITIONAL LANGUAGE AND SPECIAL EDUCATIONAL NEEDS

The various Codes of Practice across the UK note that the identification and assessment of the special educational needs of young people whose first language is not English requires particular care. The 2014 Code in England (§ 5.30), for example, advises that

> practitioners should look carefully at all aspects of a child's learning and development to establish whether any delay is related to learning English as an additional language or if it arises from SEN or disability. Difficulties related solely to learning English as an additional language are not SEN.

The *Special Educational Needs Code of Practice for Wales* (NAW, 2004, § 7.56) acknowledges that some students require 'support to compensate for the impact of a communication difficulty on learning in English or Welsh as an additional language'. The 2010 Code in Scotland (p. 13) recognises that 'children or young people may require additional support for a variety of reasons and may include those who ... have English as an additional language'. However, it cautions that it should not 'be assumed that inclusion in the list inevitably implies that additional support will be necessary'. These Codes clearly recognise that lack of competence in English (or Welsh) cannot be equated with general difficulties in learning, or particular difficulties in language acquisition, as understood in this Code. Students learning English (or Welsh) may say little or nothing for some time, but are learning nevertheless.

There is no possibility of making sense of what bears no relation to one's own ways of making sense of things. Unfamiliarity with local culture, customs and language on entering school can result in complete bewilderment and an inability to understand the expectations and norms of the literacy curriculum. Gregory (1996, p. 33) notes, for example, how 'Tony' arrived at school, aged four years and ten months, with an 'eye for detail' and a 'disciplined and structured approach to reading from his Chinese school'. In his Chinese school he had been 'given an exercise book where he had to divide the page into columns and practise ideographs over and over again until they are perfect' (p. 32). The carefully and clearly delineated and constrained tasks set by the previous teacher contrasted sharply with the range of personal choice given to 'Tony' and his classmates in the mainstream classroom in Northampton, England. His aimless wandering around the classroom while peers chose activities for themselves indicated that he appeared unable to cope with the non-realisation of his expectations about what school should be about. Having said this, we cannot assume that their language status or unfamiliar or conflicting expectations are the only reason for students who learn English as an additional language to make slow progress. They may also experience general cognitive difficulties. This may be a very sensitive area that requires specialist help. If by providing contextual support cognitively demanding tasks can be accomplished the needs are linguistic; if not, they may be educational. It is important always to try to obtain a first language assessment. Standardised tests are often culturally or linguistically biased so it is also important to check whether norm-referencing was on a bilingual population.

MEMORY PROBLEMS

Within the area of moderate learning difficulties, very poor memory is a problem for a number of students. There are a number of common reasons for this. For example, students may not have grasped the information clearly in the first place. They may not have linked the new information to previous knowledge sufficiently. Or they may not have distinguished new knowledge from what is already known, so that the new information interferes with the old. It may therefore not be a good idea to introduce concepts with clear similarities together. For example, if we were to introduce a donkey and a pony at the same time and tell the child that the donkey is the one with the big ears, it may be that the child is forever afterwards confused about which is which.

There are a number of frames of reference against which to conceptualise what happens in the human memory system. In one, memory is seen as having two distinctive parts: long-term memory and short-term or 'working' memory. Long-term memory itself is also often seen as consisting of two parts: knowing *that* (declarative or semantic memory), and knowing *how* (procedural memory). There is clearly a big difference between knowing a fact, for example, a date, and knowing how to do something. Memory can be accessed through recall or through recognition. Of these, recognition is usually easier than recall, although if the context in which the initial learning occurred is very similar to the context in which recall is needed and there are strong memory cues, then recall can be easier.

Many students with short term memory difficulties have problems absorbing and recalling information or responding to and carrying out instructions within a busy classroom situation. They may find it difficult to copy from the blackboard as they are unable to memorise what they have seen and transpose it to the paper on the desk. As well as this they are required to rotate this visual image through 90 degrees from the vertical to the horizontal and also to change the size of the letters involved. Young children have to learn sequences of certain items relating to particular areas that are important for everyday living: letters of the alphabet, months of the year, days of the week and numbers, for example. There are many students who, even in secondary schools, cannot recite either the alphabet or the months of the year in the correct order.

Difficulties in this area, however, can be improved with training. Teachers and/or families might try increasing the span of items that are to be remembered and the length of time between presenting the sequence and asking for recall. As memory span increases, an intervening task can be given between presentation and recall. They might also try gradually increasing sequences of instructions, beginning with one or two only: 'Please go to the cupboard and get some pencils', and subsequently, perhaps: 'Please go to the cupboard, get some pencils, give one to Jane and one to Aaron.' They could ask the student to give a verbal message to deliver to another teacher, secretary or administrator, and increasing the length of the message as the student is successful. It is important to encourage the student to repeat the instruction before carrying it out and use his/her own voice to aid his/her memory. After reading a short story, they could make a point of asking the student to identify the main characters, sequence of events and outcome. They might also encourage students to think up their own mnemonic and visualisation techniques and, if possible, both together, or to repeat aloud and rehearse items to be remembered, and use a multi-sensory mode of learning through oral, visual, auditory and kinaesthetic modes. The learner should be able to see, hear, say and, if possible, touch the materials to be learned. This reinforces the input stimuli and helps to consolidate the information for use, meaning and transfer to other areas. Teachers can keep verbal instructions clear and concise and ensure students are attending before teachers start to speak. It can help to preface instructions with a warning (for example, Peter, in a moment I am going to ask you) to ensure that the student is ready to listen. They might also encourage students to repeat back key points as well as to talk through tasks in their own voice to help to direct their motor movements, and try supplementing auditory verbal material with visual cues and practical demonstrations. In some cases, written checklists or pictorial reminders may be beneficial (Wearmouth, 2009, p. 48).

DIFFICULTIES EXPERIENCED IN THE LEARNING OF MATHEMATICS

Much teaching and assessment in the area of mathematics takes place in the context of a symbolic representation of mathematics, that is, through written text and pictures (Rogers, 2007, p. 2). Many children appear to adopt mathematical symbols and algorithms without having grasped the concepts that underpin them (Borthwick & Harcourt-Heath, 2007). While activities involving reading and writing numbers may tell us something about children's ability to read and write numbers, they do not necessarily tell us anything about children's conceptual understanding of 'number-ness'. Learners' ability to understand symbolic representation depends on understanding of the first-hand experience to which the symbolic representation refers. In the case of younger learners this may involve, for example, the handling and counting of everyday items. Learning to use number symbols is likely to occur simultaneously with acquiring the alphabetic principle and sound–symbol correspondence in literacy acquisition and, as Grauberg (2002) comments, 'Where is the "f" in 5?' It is possible to use other number systems, for example, tally charts, first, where one bundle represents five and clearly made up of five. Rogers (2007, p. 13) notes that there is a weak conceptual framework for understanding number in the early years on which to begin formal mathematics teaching:

> make it both difficult to engage children (Department of Education and Science, 1989) and to correct later (Nunes *et al.*, 1997), It is also well documented that such difficulties soon become compounded, resulting in distress and further delay (Adult Literacy and Basic Skills Unit, 1992). Attention needs to be paid to the negative effects of incomprehension of a prominent part of the mathematics curriculum in which young children are involved on a daily basis. It may be that such incomprehension prompts the early lack of confidence in mathematics that characterises further failure and poor problem-solving during the later school years. They can often learn to count up and down 'in ones' and can take part in counting games and activities. However, understanding that a number, for example five, is not just the last number in the series 1–5 (the ordinal principle), but also means the whole set of five (the principle of cardinality) is another matter.

Pictorial symbols or icons are clearly different from abstract symbols used at the symbolic stage of reasoning in Bruner's framework. If we take the example of mathematics learning in schools, lack of symbolic understanding can lead to difficulties in the written recording of number work, relational signs: 'plus', 'minus', 'equal(s)', place value and 'zero', money and time, as Grauberg (2002, p. 5) notes.

Relational signs: 'plus', 'minus', 'equal(s)'

Adding and subtracting both imply actions. Without an understanding of what the action is there is little point in trying to encourage the use of the symbol. '=' is often interpreted to children as 'makes', but, as we are all aware, a child's notion of 'makes' is clearly not what the symbol '=' means, mathematically.

Very great care must be taken in working out ways to support children's understanding by making clear links from one small step to the next. Primary schools in particular have a lot of equipment that can be used to play games in adding, subtracting and balancing. Bearing in mind Bruner's three modes of representation, for some children it might be important to use concrete aids to establish number learning, for example, Cuisenaire rods and/or an abacus, for much longer than for other children. A major question is how to move from the act of adding, taking away or balancing to competent use of the abstract symbols. One way to do this might be to spend time thinking about ways in which children will move into and through the iconic mode of representation and to encourage children to devise their own symbols for the actions first so that the icon visibly represents their own understandings.

Common problems: the examples of place value and 'zero'

Difficulties with the concept of place value and 'zero' can be experienced by students to the end of their secondary education.

Common conceptual difficulties in mathematics

As the head of learning support in an upper (13–18) school I observed numbers of students in mainstream lessons struggling with mathematical concepts that regular mainstream teachers assumed they had grasped a long time before. In their mathematics lessons I was still trying to support them to develop a basic understanding of place value. In other areas of the curriculum they were expected to cope with the concept of hundreds, thousands and millions which they found so frustratingly complex and difficult that their behaviour became disruptive. An example is geography or social studies lessons where population density was expressed in thousands per square mile. Some students could not handle the concepts of thousands and millions competently and confidently, either in an ordinal or cardinal sense, and became very frustrated.

Zero is another problematic concept, mathematically. I was once asked by 14-year-old students in a mixed comprehensive school how nought multiplied by a number could possibly equal nought. How could a number suddenly equal nothing? I replied by taking a handful of nothing and putting it down on the desk 44 times to prove the point.

(Wearmouth, 2009, p. 138)

Without understanding the whole concept of place value the use of zero as a place holder in a multi-digit line is difficult to comprehend for some students. One way to start to address problems with place value might be to continue to use concrete equipment such as Dienes materials – unit cubes, 'longs' of 10 cm cubes, and 'flats' of 100 cm cubes – for much longer than the teacher might have anticipated, providing that this can be done without embarrassing the child(ren). For example, 54 might be written down at first as 50 with the 4 superimposed over the 0. 504 would be written down as 500 with the 4 superimposed over the last 0. Alternatively, as Grauberg (2002) notes, the numbers may be written on transparencies and then superimposed.

UNDERSTANDING NUMBER-NESS

Teaching number in the early years through the use of number sequences seems to be common in the UK and the USA (Grauberg, 2002). In some other countries in Europe and the Far East, for example, Japan, the preference is for emphasising recognition of small quantities without counting. Recognising a small number, for example, four, as a quantity involves one operation of matching a sound symbol or visual symbol to an amount. This seems, logically, easier than recognising four from a number sequence. This latter involves remembering that four comes after three and before five, and simultaneously counting up to the total amount. It will take a lot of concrete activities in a variety of different contexts before a child with cognitive difficulties understands the concept of 'numberness':

which means the concept of 'twoness', 'threeness', 'nness'. Through his [*sic*] experience with many different materials we want him to see what is common to all (the fact that there are, for instance, 'two' of each) and we want him to learn to ignore what is irrelevant (e.g. size, colour, feel).

(Grauberg, 2002, p. 12)

Time

'Time' is a complex concept for children to develop. As Piaget (1969) notes, it includes points in time, duration and sequence of events, frequency of events, and intervals between them.

Concepts of time vary, as Grauberg (2002) points out. Supporting a student to acquire a concept of time is a very different proposition from teaching him/her to tell the time. There is no constant point of reference in relation to many indicators of time. 'Late' can refer to a time in the morning, if a student should have arrived earlier, or to a point at night when, for example, that student could be early or on time. Our sense of the passage of time is not constant either. It often seems to distort depending on the activity and our engagement with, or enjoyment of, it. For example, the few days before a birthday often seem to young children to pass much more slowly than most other days.

Bruner's three modes of representation – enactive, iconic and symbolic – again offer a framework for thinking about activities and approaches for students who experience difficulties in the acquisition of time-related concepts. Using a timer or some sort might help in the initial stages to enact the representation of time passing. Concentrating on the sounds emitted on striking a percussion instrument themselves might encourage a sense of the frequency of events. To encourage the concept of sequence, a teacher might first organise an activity for children to act out a regular sequence of events in their own lives and then represent sequence pictorially (Bruner's iconic mode of representation). These days the concept of a visual timetable for use in schools with young children and older children who experience cognitive difficulties is quite common (Selikowitz, 2008).

To tell the time, use of a digital timer is a simpler option than a traditional clock face. However, there are other considerations. The hands of the traditional clock face can be seen to move in the context of the twelve hour cycle, but the numbers on a digital timepiece simply change (Wearmouth, 2009).

SPECIFIC LEARNING DIFFICULTIES

Some young people experience difficulties in learning in specific areas that appear to be unrelated to their overall ability. One of these areas of difficulty is often linked to the concept of dyslexia.

THE EXAMPLE OF DYSLEXIA

'Dyslexia' is a concept about which there is much controversy. Some of this relates to whether or not there is an identifiable entity that we might term 'dyslexia' and, if so, what its precise nature, causes and explanations might be (Stanovitch, 2000). Some concerns best practice in identification, assessment and teaching. There are also issues of equity in resourcing individual learning needs by privileging certain groups of students. One of the 'major' tensions in dyslexia research results from the potential conflict between the different agendas of individual and interest groups: researchers and practitioners, parents and teachers, teachers and educational psychologists, schools and local authorities, and local authorities and governments (Fawcett, 2002). The issue of funding provision for individual dyslexic students can force the various interest groups into opposition, for example.

'Dyslexia' is a psychological explanation of difficulties in learning. The information-processing system of 'dyslexic' individuals is seen as different from that of non-dyslexics in ways which have an impact on a number of areas of performance. Pumfrey (1996) describes dyslexia as a 'variable syndrome', implying that definitions of dyslexia may vary and be interpreted in different ways. Some definitions relate only to difficulty in acquiring literacy, as reflected by its derivation from Classical Greek: δυσ (dys), meaning 'bad' or 'difficult', and λεξίς (lexis), meaning 'word', or 'speech'. Other definitions are wider and include reference to difficulties in co-ordination, personal organisation, balance, patterning, directionality (right/left confusion), sequencing, rhythm, orientation, memory and so on.

In terms of literacy acquisition, the difficulties experienced by dyslexic students are usually related to difficulties in processing either visual or/and auditory information and making the connections between the visual symbols and the sounds they represent, commonly called 'decoding'. In relation to visual factors, learners may experience difficulty in any of the following areas (Wearmouth, 2009): recognition of the visual cues of letters and words, familiarity with left–right orientation, recognition of word patterns and recognition of letter and word shapes. Or they may encounter problems with any of the following auditory factors: recognition of letter sounds, recognition of sounds and letter groups or patterns, sequencing of sounds, corresponding sounds to visual stimuli, discriminating sounds from other sounds and/or discriminating sounds within words. The British Psychological Society (BPS) working party adopted this narrower view of dyslexia related solely to literacy:

> Dyslexia is evident when accurate and fluent reading and or spelling develops very incompletely or with great difficulty. This focuses on literacy learning at the 'word level' and implies that the problem is severe and persistent despite appropriate learning opportunities. It provides the basis for a staged process of assessment through teaching.
> (British Psychological Society, 1999, p. 18)

A wider definition espoused by the British Dyslexia Association (BDA) includes difficulty in the development of literacy and language related skills, particularly in phonological processing, and also in working memory, the speed of processing information and the automatic development of skills that may not reflect the level of other cognitive abilities. 'Conventional' teaching methods may not suffice in addressing such difficulties but information technology and individual counselling may lessen the effects (http://www.bdadyslexia. org.uk/dyslexic, accessed 18.05.15).

The Rose Review on identifying and teaching dyslexic children concurs with this wider view (Rose, 2009, p. 30). This Review identifies dyslexia as a learning difficulty associated with 'difficulties in phonological awareness, verbal memory and verbal processing speed' that 'affects the skills involved in accurate and fluent word reading and spelling', but also acknowledges a wider range of information-processing difficulties in various 'aspects of language, motor co-ordination, mental calculation, concentration and personal organisation'. However, these aspects alone are not markers of dyslexia. A 'good indication' is the extent to which 'the individual responds or has responded to well-founded intervention'. In other words, as the BPS (1999) implies also, if a child experiences difficulties but has not received good teaching, then it cannot be assumed that s/he is dyslexic.

ASSOCIATION BETWEEN DYSLEXIA AND INTELLIGENCE

One debate around dyslexia relates to whether a child is dyslexic if his/her difficulties in literacy can be attributed to general low ability. Two methods used to identify dyslexia, both of which utilise IQ, can be compared to highlight the implications for practice: the 'cut-off method' and the 'regression' method. Both have resource implications for the type of teaching programmes and provision allocated. The regression method essentially looks at the discrepancy between IQ and the reading level which would be predicted based on a child's IQ score. This means that a child with a high IQ score who may be around or only slightly below his age level in reading can still be identified as dyslexic because the reading level may still be below that expected for the IQ level. On the other hand the cut-off method means that any child with an average or above IQ but who is lagging in their reading level by at least 18 months can be described as dyslexic. As the British Psychological Society (1999, p. 67) notes, both these methods can be problematic for two reasons. Both rely on the validity of the IQ measure as a robust indicator of a child's abilities. Also, measures of IQ and reading ages can change over time and a child who qualifies for additional help on account of any of these measures may make an improvement in reading which would exclude them, using the discrepancy criteria, from continuing to use the label dyslexia or qualify for extra help. In practice, therefore, a child receiving additional help may lose this support if s/he makes gains which narrow the discrepancy gap between reading and IQ.

EFFECTS ON PERFORMANCE

Riddick, Wolfe and Lumsdon (2002, pp. 12–13) describe how dyslexia affects young children's performance in various areas. At pre-school level there may be a delay in spoken language, including difficulty in learning nursery rhymes and verbal sequencing, for example, days of the week and letters of the alphabet. There may also be poor gross motor co-ordination, for example, in learning to ride a bicycle or swim, poor fine motor skills, for example, in copying shapes and letters, and poor short term memory, for example, remembering a sequence of instructions and/or names. At primary age a child is likely to experience difficulties in reading, writing, spelling and number work. The child may be unable to identify rhythm and alliteration, or read single words accurately. S/he may reverse some words, for example, 'pot' and 'top', miss out whole lines and read some sections of text twice without realising it, and have better understanding of text than word accuracy. Reading age for fluency and accuracy is likely to be below chronological age. Children who begin school with poor letter knowledge and poor rhythmic ability may be at risk of developing difficulties in reading. Snowling (2000, p. 213–214), for example, says that difficulties in encoding the phonological features of words (that is, the sound system of a language) is core to dyslexic children's difficulties. 'Dyslexia is a specific form of language impairment that affects the way in which the brain encodes the phonological features of spoken words. The core deficit is in phonological processing ... Dyslexia specifically affects the development of reading and spelling skills'. A child may spell the same word different ways in the same text, spell incorrectly words learnt for spelling tests, make several attempts to spell words with frequent crossings out, spell phonetically but incorrectly, use what look like bizarre spellings for example, 'bidar' for 'because', leave out syllables, for example, 'onge' for 'orange', or part of a letter blend especially when there is a blend of three letters, for example, 'sred' for 'shred', reverse letters, especially 'b' and 'd', 'p' and 'q'. S/he may experience difficulty copying from the board, produce work that is chaotic or very untidy, begin writing anywhere on the page, confuse upper and lower case letters, produce very little output and what there is may be unintelligible even to the child.

Dyslexic children experience a number of difficulties in mathematics, including the learning of number bonds and multiplication tables and the understanding of concepts involving directionality (Weavers, 2003). Time and spatial concepts can prove difficult. Children may find sequencing activities and orientation or both numbers and processes hard. Confusion can arise through having to process different operations in different directions, for example, the conventional right to left calculation of addition and subtraction, and left to right of division. There may be limited spatial awareness and visual discrimination, resulting in confusion of signs and reversal of digits. Children may also have very poor mental arithmetic (mental manipulation of number/symbols in short term memory) (Wearmouth, 2009).

Addressing difficulties experienced by primary-aged dyslexic pupils in mathematics

Riddick, Wolfe and Lumsdon (2002, p. 50) offer a number of suggestions about teaching such students:

- make sure they understand basic symbols = + −, etc;
- make sure they understand basic number language e.g. subtract, multiply, etc.;
- repeat learning and revision of number facts;
- teach child to estimate a sensible answer;
- teach child to check their answer against the set question;
- be alert for reversals which lead to child making a wrong calculation;
- practise counting forwards and backwards in sequences, e.g. in ones, then two, etc.;
- use pattern methods to teach number bonds;
- teach multiplication using table squares;
- use squared paper to aid correct setting out of calculations;
- give a sample strip with digits in correct orientation for checking reversals;
- use multi-sensory teaching; rehearse what has just been learnt with oral revision at the end of the lesson;
- teach using logic rather than just rules so conceptual ability can be utilised.

At secondary level, students may become withdrawn, subdued, anxious about reading out loud or taking written tests, socially isolated and may experience psychosomatic difficulties, for example, sickness and headaches (Riddick *et al.*, 2002). S/he is likely also to feel very tired because of the exertion involved in trying to cope with increasing literacy demands (Wearmouth, 2004a).

THEORIES EXPLAINING DYSLEXIA

There are a number of theories that attempt to explain the difficulties experienced by dyslexic learners.

Visual-based theories

As Everatt (2002) explains, there are visual-based theories which propose that dyslexia may be the consequence of an abnormality in the neural pathways of the visual system. There are others suggesting a lower level of activity in the areas of the visual cortex thought to be responsible for identifying the direction of movement (Eden *et al.*, 1996). There is also a view that visual difficulties may be caused by over-sensitivity to certain wavelengths (or colours) of light. This is sometimes referred to as scotopic sensitivity syndrome (Irlen, 1991). The significance of this is that coloured filters, overlays or lenses which are said to alleviate reading problems for some learners (Wilkins *et al.*, 1994) have increasingly been incorporated into teachers' practice, with variable results.

Cerebellar deficit hypothesis

Nicolson and Fawcett (1994) developed the cerebellar deficit hypothesis in order to account for common patterns of difficulties among individuals identified as 'dyslexic: problems in balance, speed and phonological skill. The cerebellum is a densely packed and deeply folded subcortical brain structure, also known as the 'hind brain' (Fawcett & Nicolson, 2001). In humans it accounts for 10 per cent to 15 per cent of brain weight, 40 per cent of brain surface area, and 50 per cent of the brain's neurones. Damage to different parts of the cerebellum can lead to different symptoms in humans, ranging from disturbances in posture and balance to limb rigidity, loss of muscle tone, lack of co-ordination and impaired timing of rapid pre-planned automatic movements.

The results of a number of studies investigating the role of the cerebellum and its implications for dyslexia (Fawcett *et al.*, 1996; Nicolson & Fawcett, 1999; Finch *et al.*, 2002) indicate that dyslexic children showed, firstly, clinical symptoms of cerebellar abnormality. Also, there were abnormalities in cerebellar activation in automatic processing and in new learning. Greater frontal lobe activation suggested they were by-passing the cerebellum to some extent. Overall this indicates that dyslexic children may use different methods in sequential learning and automatic performance. Fawcett and Nicolson hypothesise that the causal chain between cerebellar problems, phonological difficulties, and eventual reading problems accounts for three criterial difficulties of dyslexia: writing, reading and spelling.

The 'Balance Model' of reading and dyslexia

The 'Balance Model' of reading and dyslexia is another example of a biological model (Bakker & Robertson, 2002). The balance model hypothesises that early and advanced reading, that is, reading through decoding and attention to perceptual features of text, and reading for meaning, are mediated by the right and left hemispheres of the brain respectively. This model predicts that some children, P (perceptual)-type dyslexics, rely too much on the perceptual features of text and may not be able to shift from right to left in the hemispheric mediation of reading. Some other children, L (linguistic)-type dyslexics, rely on linguistic features of text to read fast and construct meaning, but pay too little attention to perceptual features of text.

The results of these investigations indicate that P- and L-dyslexics differ with regard to the speed of processing of reading-related information. P-types are faster than L-types in deciding whether all letters in an array are the same or different but P-types are slower than L-types when it comes to the question of whether a word is real or not (Licht, 1994; Bakker, 1990; Fabbro *et al.*, 2001).

The allocation to sub-types is based largely on observation of pupil performance in the particular aspects of the reading process which are causing concern (Bakker & Robertson, 2002).

Intervention therefore can aim to directly adapt learning behaviour in line with the identified weaknesses in reading behaviour.

Phonological deficit hypothesis

Since the 1980s the dominant theory used to explain dyslexia has been the phonological deficit hypothesis (Bradley & Bryant, 1983; Snowling, 2000; Stanovich, 2000). Phonological representations can be interpreted as the knowledge about sounds which a reader brings to the task of reading. Phonological processing is strongly related to the development of reading. Difficulties experienced at the level of phonological representation and the relationships between symbols and the sounds they represent constrain reading development. Hatcher and Snowling (2002) comment that one of the effects of this is that learners who experience difficulties at the phonological level are less able to generalise knowledge about the phonological properties of sounds and words they are taught. Activities such as non-word reading are problematic because of the difficulties associated with sound–symbol relationships. Hatcher and Snowling feel that this can be viewed as one of the most robust signs of dyslexia.

Hatcher and Snowling suggest that the most crucial factor in the individual profiles of dyslexic children is the severity of the lack of development in phonological representations. This can account for the differences between dyslexic children's profiles and the different presenting characteristics of the dyslexic group. Additionally dyslexic children with poorer phonological representations will have fewer compensatory word attack strategies to draw on and this will further undermine their reading performance.

Hatcher and Snowling conclude that assessment of phonological skills is therefore necessary, by, for example, providing examples of tasks: rhyme recognition, rhyme production, phonological manipulation such as phoneme deletion and letter knowledge, which can be found in some of the established tests available for this purpose. This view has considerable implications for intervention programmes in the early years.

ADDRESSING DIFFICULTIES ASSOCIATED WITH DYSLEXIA

In their review of dyslexia, Rice and Brooks (2004) conclude that research appears not to indicate that 'dyslexics' and 'ordinary poor readers' should be taught by different methods. The same kind of approaches to addressing reading, writing and mathematical difficulties that are appropriate for dyslexic learners can also be useful for other students.

Teaching approaches for dyslexic students can be grouped into those that are designed to enable the child to overcome the difficulties that are experienced as far as possible – almost to train the personal information-processing system to become more organised in a deliberately systematic and focused way (personal reflections) – and those that enable to child to cope.

Phonological awareness training

When children are very young it may be difficult for them to realise that speech can be broken down into individual words or that words can also be broken down into sounds. Phonemic awareness develops only when there is good experience of speaking and listening. It can be encouraged by playing rhyming games, making up nonsense rhymes, repeating rhyming strings, and playing other games which require the manipulation of sounds. Hatcher and Snowling (2002) outline examples of phonological awareness training such as rhyme activities, identifying words as units within sentences, syllable awareness and blending tasks.

As Hatcher and Snowling comment, whilst it is important to train phonological awareness it is also important to establish the relationship between sounds and written forms of words. Interventions that rely exclusively on training in phonological awareness are less effective than those that combine phonological training with print and meaning in the context of sentences in text. Interventions that address difficulties in co-ordination, personal organisation, directionality, balance and patterning may also be needed for some students.

Acquisition of fluency in reading and writing

At almost any age, paired reading arrangements can enable dyslexic individuals to gain more experience in reading ('reading mileage', Clay, 1993, 1998) to enable greater experience in reading and in visual tracking of the text in order to increase word identification, knowledge of letter/sound combinations and use of contextual information and inference. Students might be encouraged to choose reading material of high interest to themselves, irrespective of its readability level, and both children might read out loud together, with the reading partner modulating his/her speed to match that of the dyslexic pupil. Or children might be encouraged to use recordings of books that they really want to read, tracking through the text with their eyes while listening to the CD.

In terms of writing, allowing students to dictate their thoughts onto a digital recorder and then transcribing them for him/her, or allowing him/her to dictate thoughts to the teacher/an older child/ the parent, in the first instance is a coping strategy. Encouraging the child to listen to the recording of his/her own thoughts and then write the text from this is one way to separate out the conceptual thinking around content and the mechanical aspects of writing with which the child is likely to experience difficulty.

Pupils might also be provided with writing frames to support extended writing and encourage logical sequencing (Wray, 2002).

Multi-sensory approaches to learning

As we also saw in Chapter 3, multi-sensory approaches are a very important way to harness all the senses to support students' learning. Introducing visual, tactile, auditory and kinaesthetic modes to teaching and learning enables students who need extra reinforcement in their learning to see, touch, hear and move, sometimes simultaneously, in their learning activities. The principles of multi-sensory teaching which apply to language work also apply to the mathematics field, for example, introducing new mathematical concepts and processes using concrete materials, diagrams, pictures and verbal explanation. Progress should be carefully monitored at each stage, checking that a particular concept has been thoroughly mastered and understood before moving on to the next step.

'Metacognitive' strategies

'Metacognitive' strategies can also help dyslexic and other students to think about their own thinking processes so that those who experience difficulty in particular areas of learning can develop alternative routes to accessing these areas. 'Mind-mapping' (Buzan, 2000) that encourages learners first to produce a visual representation of all those areas to be covered in the text before beginning on the written task is an example of one way to develop a structure for producing extended text.

COPING STRATEGIES

Research (Florian & Hegarty, 2004) stresses the motivational value of computer-assisted learning, for example, word-processing, which can increase the time that students are willing to practise writing. Spell-checkers can remove much of a pupil's inhibition about writing that comes from poor spelling. Drafting and correcting becomes less laborious and the printed copy can be corrected away from the machine by the student or the teacher and improved versions created without difficulty. Everything can be saved and re-used easily, allowing work to be done in small amounts. Presentation is improved; when the final version is printed it is legible and well presented. Optical comfort is also important. A choice of screen colours can be helpful to students.

Visual discrimination/spatial analysis

Strategies to enable pupils to cope with particular difficulties in the area of spatial analysis and visual discrimination in the classroom might include keeping all visually presented materials simple in format and uncluttered by excessive stimuli and assisting the student in planning and organising assigned tasks written on paper by providing visual cues and providing step-by-step instructions (Wearmouth, 2009). When giving directions it is often helpful for teachers and others to be specific and use concrete cues. New concepts might be introduced where appropriate by beginning with the identification of individual parts and moving to integrated wholes.

'Reasonable adjustments': examination concessions

Where a young person has a formal assessment of severe dyslexia it may be the case that this is interpreted as a disability under the terms of the 2010 Equality Act. If this is the case then, as discussed above (see p. 84), s/he is entitled to 'reasonable adjustments' to enable access to the school or college curriculum, including internal and external examinations. The school might give internal examination concessions (extra time, answers in note form, oral test to support written examination, use of word processor in coursework, examinations etc.) and 25 per cent additional time. Examination papers might be duplicated so that the pupil can see both sides of a page at the same time, enlarged or printed on coloured paper, along with the use of highlighting pens to help with the analysis of questions. Guidelines for access arrangement during external examinations have been issued by some qualifications bodies to ensure compliance with the 2010 Equality Act, for example, the Qualifications and Curriculum Authority (QCA) (2014) in relation to secondary students.

MARKING STUDENTS' WORK

In school there may be considerable differences of opinion about the extent to which corrections should be made to a script which contains very many mistakes. Before deciding how to mark individual students' written work teachers new to a school would be well advised to find out about the school's marking policy. On the one hand it can be argued that, for some students, repeatedly receiving back scripts covered with marks indicating errors is very demoralising. On the other, there has to be a rational, structured approach to ensuring that students make progress in recognising mistakes and learning how to correct them. Teachers may feel it is appropriate to encourage students to proof read their own, or peers', work before handing it in, and/or, perhaps, to correct only words or sentence structure with which they feel students should already be familiar.

SUMMARY

As practitioners, teachers need to bear in mind factors related to the individual child, to the condition (if one has been identified) associated with that child, the wider cultural and social factors, the curriculum and also the school context. The view that failure to learn can result from social arrangements that fail to support students' engagement with their learning as much as from attributes of individuals (Lave, 1993, p. 10) can lead to a very positive approach to overcoming the difficulties that are experienced. It has the advantage of giving teachers and students more control over learning in that appropriate attention to these areas can lead to improved student learning. Also teachers can have confidence that students will learn and make progress if appropriate strategies are devised to address their difficulties and facilitate children's increasing participation in school.

5

UNDERSTANDING AND ADDRESSING DIFFICULTIES IN SOCIAL, EMOTIONAL AND MENTAL HEALTH

INTRODUCTION

This chapter focuses on difficulties experienced by children and young people who demonstrate features of social, emotional and mental health difficulties and the kinds of behaviour commonly associated with such difficulties. The Code in England, for example, advises:

> Children and young people may experience a wide range of social and emotional difficulties which manifest themselves in many ways. These may include becoming withdrawn or isolated, as well as displaying challenging, disruptive or disturbing behaviour. These behaviours may reflect underlying mental health difficulties such as anxiety or depression, self-harming, substance misuse, eating disorders or physical symptoms that are medically unexplained. Other children and young people may have disorders such as attention deficit disorder, attention deficit hyperactive disorder or attachment disorder.
>
> (DfE, 2014, § 6.32)

Similar kinds of behaviours are outlined in the Code in Wales in the description of young people with difficulties in behaviour, social and emotional development:

Children and young people who demonstrate features of emotional and behavioural difficulties, who are withdrawn or isolated, disruptive and disturbing, hyperactive and lack concentration; those with immature social skills; and those presenting challenging behaviours arising from other complex special needs.

(NAW, 2004, § 7.60)

Special attention will be given to young people's behaviour experienced by teachers and others as extremely challenging, including attention deficit/hyperactivity disorder (AD/HD), physical violence and bullying, and withdrawn behaviour associated with trauma such as bereavement and emotional deprivation. The aim will be to illustrate

- what research tells us about these difficulties: causal factors and common indicators;
- the relationship between the experience of social and emotional difficulties and learning;
- ways that the barriers to learning experienced by young people with these difficulties can be addressed in school and elsewhere.

Interpretations of, and responses to, behaviour perceived as challenging at home and/or in schools often generate a great deal of heated debate. Schools play a critical part in shaping a child's identity as a learner (Bruner, 1996). This chapter takes as its main frame of reference for understanding pupil behaviour that the human mind actively constructs its own reality and makes its own sense of every situation and context. Young people's behaviour must therefore relate to the way that they make sense of their worlds. Rejecting schooling is nearly always a strongly emotional experience (Furlong, 1985). For this reason careful account needs to be taken of students' own sense-making, even if this may be experienced as uncomfortable at times. The chapter also takes the view that:

- belonging is a fundamental human need, as Maslow's hierarchy (1943), for example, clearly indicates;
- teachers and families can put themselves into a much stronger position to deal with problematic behaviour by recognising that the way students behave may be explained by factors within

classrooms and within schools as well as factors associated with those students (Wearmouth *et al.*, 2005);

- student behaviour occurs in interaction between the learning environment and the individual.

Effectively addressing difficult student behaviour associated with social, emotional and mental health difficulties must relate to the way that students make sense of their own worlds as well to consideration of the learning environment in which that behaviour occurs (Wearmouth *et al.*, 2005).

FRAMES OF REFERENCE IN THE AREA OF BEHAVIOUR DIFFICULTIES

Schooling is an integral part of society, not simply a way of preparing for entry to that society (Bruner, 1996). 'Difficult' neighbourhoods tend to produce more 'difficult' students than neighbourhoods in more affluent circumstances (Watkins & Wagner, 2000). However, economic impoverishment in the neighbourhood does not necessarily lead to disruptive behaviour in schools (Rutter *et al.*, 1979; Ofsted, 2001). Even in areas of disadvantage, good classroom management, as well as interventions with individual students, can make a difference to student behaviour, learning and future life chances.

The frames of reference for understanding problematic behaviour really matter. In schools this can have a strong effect on the way teachers deal with students and their parents or carers. We might take the example of 'Maladjusted Jack' and consider how different interpretations of his behaviour might lead to different kinds of intervention.

The example of 'Maladjusted Jack'

'Maladjusted Jack' was a participant in a series of interviews with adult male inmates in one of HM prisons (Wearmouth, 1999). He gives an account of how he was born into an unsettled family and was taken into care at an early age as a result of his parents' divorce and his sister's inability to provide for him adequately:

My parents split up when I was 3 and I went to live with my sister. She already had two children of her own, and she couldn't cope with me as well. She put me into care.

Social Services were involved in his life from an early stage. When he started infant school he was deemed to be out of control because he used to run around, disrupt classrooms, upset the dustbins in the school yard and climb on to the roof. He was quickly referred to an educational psychologist for an assessment of his behaviour.

NURTURING YOUNG CHILDREN IN SCHOOLS

One psychological theory of human development that has had considerable influence over educational provision for young children such as Jack whose behaviour is of concern to teachers is that of attachment theory (Bowlby, 1952). As Holmes (1993, p. 39) notes, implicit in this theory is the view that:

> children deprived of maternal care ... may be seriously affected in their physical, intellectual, emotional and social development ... prolonged separation of a child from his mother (or mother substitute) during the first five years of life stands foremost among the causes of delinquent character development.
>
> (Bowlby, 1944; Bowlby, 1952)

Babies quickly attach themselves emotionally to their adult carers and progress through well-recognised stages of development towards maturity. Successful development depends on needs being adequately met at an earlier stage. Where this is not the case, then children will persist in inappropriate attachment behaviour, being over-anxious, avoidant or aggressive, or becoming incapable of warm attachment and positive human relationships (Harris-Hendriks & Figueroa, 1995; Bennathan, 2000).

Attachment theory has influenced education in the early years through the development of 'nurture groups' in some infant schools, originally in the Inner London Education Authority in 1970–1 by

Marjorie Boxall, an educational psychologist, and re-established more recently by some local authorities. The Boxall Profile is an observational tool that was developed as a way of assessing the level of skills children possessed to access learning and of identifying their developmental needs to support the work being done in nurture groups. It was originally standardised for children aged 3–8 years but has recently been developed for use in secondary schools. Boxall (2002) argues that learning, personality and behaviour difficulties, which are more likely in the young children of families experiencing disadvantage and deprivation, can be the result of inadequate early care and support from parents who struggle with poverty, damaged relationships and harsh and stressful living conditions. The underlying assumption of the nurture group is that children such as Jack who have fared badly though the learning processes of early childhood need extra support and appropriate experiences. This means recreating in school the total experience of a normally developing child from babyhood onwards and planning the routine of the nurture group day to provide a predictable, reliable structure in which children can go on to interact and learn in regular settings (Bennathan, 2000).

Features of nurture groups

The nurture group attempts to create the features of adequate parenting within school with opportunities to develop trust, security, positive mood and identity through attachment to a reliable, attentive and caring adult, as well as autonomy through the provision of controlled and graduated experiences in familiar surroundings. Some features of such groups include: easy physical contact between adult and child; warmth, intimacy and a family atmosphere; good-humoured acceptance of children and their behaviour; familiar regular routines; a focus on tidying up and putting away; the provision of food in structured contexts; opportunities to play and the appropriate participation of the adults; adults talking about, and encouraging reflection by children on, trouble-provoking situations and their own feelings; opportunities for children

> to develop increasing autonomy. These opportunities incor-
> porate visits outside the nurture group, participation in
> games, visits to regular classrooms and children's eventual
> full-time inclusion in a mainstream class.
>
> (Wearmouth, 2009, p. 167)

Bennathan (2000) comments that nurture groups accept and work with children with serious social behaviour developmental difficulties who present major challenges to regular class teachers and other students so that they can be included in mainstream schooling. If Jack had been included in a nurture group, the critical challenge would have been to ensure that the group role remained a short term developmental one and that Jack would be included in regular classrooms after a relatively short time.

Nurture groups had only been established in Inner London when Jack was young, however, not in his home area. The psychologist to whom he was referred assessed him as 'maladjusted' and Social Services and the local education authority decided to send him away to a boarding school for 'maladjusted' pupils at the age of 6. Thus began his career in special schools, firstly through his primary years and then through secondary.

Examination of the rise and demise of this category is an interesting example of the way in which the use of labels attaching problems to children can pervade the education system to suit the existing national context.

The case of 'maladjustment'

Until 1945 there was no formal category of 'maladjustment' enshrined in Ministry of Education regulations. It had its origins in the creation of a group of children identified as moral imbeciles or defectives under the terms of the 1913 Act. Children who displayed emotionally disturbed or disruptive behaviour came to be associated with both mental defect and moral defect (Galloway et al., 1994, p. 110). Board of Education

Reports in the 1920s, for example, identified 'unstable', 'nervous', 'difficult and maladjusted' children as in need of child guidance (Galloway *et al.*, 1994, p. 112).

After 1945 all LEAs had a responsibility to establish special educational treatment in special or ordinary schools for students defined as 'maladjusted'. The concept was still relatively new when the Underwood Committee was set up in 1950 to enquire into 'maladjusted' students' medical, educational and social problems. The (1955) Underwood Report (Chapter IV, para. 96) lists six symptoms of 'maladjustment' requiring professional help from psychologists, child guidance clinics or doctors: 'nervous disorders', e.g. fears, depression, apathy, excitability, 'habit disorders', e.g. speech defects, sleepwalking, twitching and incontinence, 'behaviour disorders', e.g. defiance, aggression, jealousy and stealing, 'organic disorders', e.g. cerebral tumours, psychotic behaviour, e.g. delusions, bizarre behaviour, and 'educational and vocational difficulties', e.g. inability to concentrate or keep jobs.

An overall definition proved difficult. There has never been a consensus on what defines 'problem behaviour', of the sort categorised by the term 'maladjusted'. As Galloway and Goodwin (1987, p. 32) comment: 'the common point to emerge from attempts to clarify behavioural disorders and types of maladjustment is that it is a ragbag term describing any kind of behaviour that teachers and parents find disturbing'.

'Maladjustment' was often used pragmatically to justify special educational provision for those students for whom segregation from peers has been seen as necessary. Invent the category, create the student. Between 1945 and 1960, the numbers of students classified as maladjusted rose from 0 to 1742. 'Psychiatrists have sometimes been prone to see pathology in all kinds of variations of personality and styles of life' (Rutter *et al.*, 1970, p. 178).

In 1970, Rutter *et al.* attempted to assess the prevalence of specific categories of difficulties in the school student population. Estimates of maladjustment in the child population varied across the country from 5 to 25 per cent (Brandon, 1961). Furlong (1985) notes that, by 1975, there were 13,000 students labelled as 'maladjusted'. Ravenette's (1984, p. 4) identification of three situations where the word 'maladjustment' was commonly used shows clearly how the maladjusted descriptor was used to explain Jack's behaviour:

1 There is a breakdown in the relationship between a child and others which is chronic rather than transitory.
2 The adults in the situation are worried by the behaviour which points to a breakdown and by their inability to do anything about it.
3 It is then a signal to others that the situation is intolerable, that the institution is entitled to some special help or relief and that perhaps the child should be placed in a more appropriate institution, or be rendered 'normal' by treatment.

(Adapted from Wearmouth, 2009, p. 21)

These days Jack would not be identified as maladjusted because the term no longer exists as a formal descriptor of student behaviour in schools. 'Maladjusted' has been replaced by descriptors such as 'emotional and behavioural difficulties' (EBD), or 'social, emotional and behavioural difficulties (SEBD) which still enable removal of students from mainstream on occasions.

EMOTIONAL AND BEHAVIOURAL DIFFICULTIES

The frame of reference relating to the terms 'emotional and behavioural difficulties' (EBD), first formally used by Warnock (DES, 1978), or 'social, emotional and behavioural difficulties' (SEBD), or, as now in England, 'social, emotional and mental health' difficulties is just as ill-defined as that relating to maladjustment.

Use of this term to explain why some students behave badly or inappropriately is not always helpful to parents and/or teachers. Poulou and Norwich (2002, p. 112), for example, found from a review of international studies that it can influence teachers' confidence in their abilities to respond to students' needs in classrooms and 'can generate feelings of helplessness and incompetence' (Lennox, 1991; Bennett, 1992; Leadbetter & Leadbetter, 1993; Chazan *et al.*, 1994; Gray *et al.*, 1996). The more teachers thought student behaviour stemmed from problems within the students themselves, such as the 'child wants to attract attention' or the 'child's innate personality', 'the more they experienced feelings of "stress", "offence" and even "helplessness", especially for conduct and mixed behaviour difficulties' (Poulou & Norwich, 2002, p. 125).

Young people's behaviour does not occur in a vacuum (Watkins and Wagner, 2000). Teachers see themselves as able to deal with a student's problematic behaviour if they consider that students' problems generally are caused by 'factors originating from teachers themselves, like their personality, manners towards the child with EBD, or teaching style' (2000). In other words, if they think they can control the cause of a difficulty they believe 'that they can also sufficiently treat it. In addition, they perceived themselves in such cases as even more responsible for finding an effective solution for the child's problem' (Poulou & Norwich, 2002, p. 112).

As already discussed in Chapter 2, most commonly, understandings and strategies in classroom management are based on principles from a behaviourist psychology frame of reference (Skinner, 1938; Baer *et al.*, 1968). Behavioural methodologies hold that all (mis)behaviour is learned and, therefore, that learning and (mis)behaviour can be modified through intervening in a systematic, consistent, predictable way in the environment. Classroom and school rules are examples of antecedent conditions (or setting events) that are intended to signify behaviour that is acceptable or appropriate. Such rules can also provide punishing consequences for behaviour that is unacceptable.

Ten principles for controlling and modifying behaviour

Ten principles for controlling and modifying students' behaviour in schools are summarised below from Berryman and Glynn (2001). The first four aim to manage behaviour through attending to the antecedent conditions, that is, aspects of the context, that precede or accompany it. The other six principles aim to modify unwanted behaviours through changing the contingencies of reinforcement, that is, the rewards or punishment, that follow it.

Changing behaviour by altering the antecedents of the behaviour

1 Careful planning ahead to foresee possible behaviour difficulties that are likely to arise, and preparing strategies and responses ahead of time, can help to avoid challenging or undesirable behaviours.

2 Altering aspects of the context in which undesirable behaviour occurs can influence that behaviour. For example, ensuring that classroom equipment is properly organised and available and re-arranging desks and chairs, can make a difference.

3 Give clear instructions that are polite, clear and concise as an antecedent condition for compliant behaviour. Before an instruction is given, gain the child's or student's full attention to avoid unnecessary repeating of instructions which can undermine their effectiveness.

4 Model the behaviour that is wanted, that is, specific ways of behaving in particular situations. Pupils then may imitate that behaviour in similar situations. Students may imitate negative as well as positive behaviour however, for example, abusive or sarcastic language. Modelling may have even stronger effects if the observer sees the modeller being rewarded (Bandura, 1969).

Changing behaviours by altering the contingencies of reinforcement

5 Provide positive predictable consequences. Behaviour learnt most readily is that which consistently has positive consequences. This can include social attention, praise, recognition, access to favourite activities, and so on.

6 Intervene at an early stage. The earlier the intervention to check undesirable behaviour, the easier it is to prevent behaviour from escalating into a major problem.

7 Accept gradual improvement. It is important to provide positive consequences for quite small changes in behaviour to begin with.

8 A little and often. The frequency of opportunities students have to experience the consequences of their behaviour is important.

9 Define and select another behaviour the student can perform that is incompatible with the undesirable or unacceptable behaviour, and reinforce this with positive consequences.

10 Clearly define sanctions, explain them to children, and very carefully implement them for a specified length of time. Implementing these sanctions should not either model or provoke further physical or verbal abuse and should never be accompanied by emotional or angry 'put down' and abusive comments. Sanctions should be removed when specific behaviour change criteria have been met.

The boarding primary school that Maladjusted Jack was sent to appears from his description to have been run along strict behaviourist lines. He appears to have thrived in a context where he could see purpose in what he was expected to do, and where discipline was strict but very fair. He recalled with respect a particular teacher who:

> wasn't too bad a bloke really. He was very fair – very strict, though. He played a game called Leggo because if you misbehaved you got a slap

across the legs with this metre ruler and you went: 'Oh, that hurt!' That's why we called it Leggo.

He remembered with affection a woman teacher who used social reinforcers of praise and extra attention to reinforce behaviour that she saw as acceptable and desirable:

Mrs F. She was probably my best teacher ever. She really did try and help me a lot. She took me under her wing. She saw the potential in me, and tried to bring out the best in me. She was very motherly to me – she stuck up for me when no one else would.

Lack of structure and disorganisation in the secondary special school for maladjusted pupils to which he was transferred, however, led very predictably to frustration, rage and very uncontrolled behaviour:

The school was total crap. It was rubbish. It was totally unorganised. There was no foresight in the school at all. There was no purpose. I wasn't studying towards exams, I was going over the same things again. The things they tried to teach me, I'd already done it. ... I was laughing in their face because I knew how far they could push, how far they can go. I've been in children's homes and in boarding schools, so I know exactly how far they can go with you. When they overstepped the mark I was the first one to step in there and say: 'You can't do that!'

Finally he was sent to a secure psychiatric unit:

I was in there for seven months. 'Beyond control', they actually said. I was locked up, wasn't I? It was just another institution where you had to learn to run the rules and bend them to your best advantage ... I was totally out of it. I thought: 'You've ruined my education, now you watch me, putting you through it, putting you through the grinding mill.' ... I was out to beat them any way I could do.

(Wearmouth, 1997, p. 32)

BEREAVEMENT IN CHILDHOOD

One of the events in childhood that is likely to affect children's behaviour very profoundly, and, indeed, may have resonances later on in life, is that of the death of the primary caregiver, most often the mother, or of close family members. According to Cruse Bereavement Care (2015), one in 29 children aged 5–16 in the UK has been bereaved of a parent or sibling, and one in sixteen has lost a close friend (http://www.cruse.org.uk/, accessed 18.05.15). The deep distress that results from a child's bereavement may create a special educational need of a short- or long-term nature.

Children need a secure, affectionate and continuous experience of care from a small number of caregivers in order to grow into emotionally secure and sociable adults. When children are born there follows a period of developing mutual attachment between child and caregiver. The pattern of attachment that is established between the child and primary caregiver is a source of security that remains important throughout life. Black (1998) notes that: 'Infant attachment is at its height at about 3 years of age and then becomes increasingly diffused by the development of other relationships, but it remains important throughout life, with later relationships qualitatively echoing the other ones' (Black, 1998, p. 931).

Infants' and toddlers' reactions to long-term or permanent separation from an attachment figure generally follow a predictable pattern. Crying, searching restlessly and high anxiety are followed by a period of despair and, eventually 'pathological states of detachment and indifference may ensue' (1998). Children who have lost one caregiver often become very anxious about the safety of others. They may also have feeding, sleeping and other kinds of difficulties.

Personal reflections on separation from a parent

My mother was taken into hospital for a long period of about three months when I was four years old. I couldn't eat or sleep and became very thin. I was sent to stay with an aunt, and I can remember being distraught when she went out anywhere without me. I didn't realise why, at the time. I had never been particularly close to her.

Five years later my mother died and I developed a stutter. I just couldn't get the words out. It wasn't a coincidence.

(Wearmouth, unpublished)

Some people may assume that a young person who loses a parent, caregiver, sibling or grandparent will not be affected too deeply as s/he is too young. However, emotional disturbances that are not immediately obvious may become apparent later and last for several years (Rutter, 1966). Weller *et al.* (1991), for example, found that over one third of their sample of bereaved children had serious depressive reactions a year after bereavement. Cruse Bereavement Care (2015) comments that it is common for 'some bereaved children and young people to delay their grief for months or sometimes years'. Subsequently, 'other life changing incidents such as moving home, acquiring a step parent or experiencing a further bereavement can serve to release the bereaved child or young person's delayed or unresolved grief'. There seems to be no way to divert grief. 'ultimately, regardless of how long the child or young person has managed to deny their grief, they will have to go through the grieving process eventually' (Cruse Bereavement Care, 2015, http://www.cruse.org.uk/for-schools/symptoms, accessed 09.03.15).

Commonly children and adolescents long to be reunited with the dead parent and may experience suicidal thoughts. When the death is of the mother, the quality of the care given to the child may also be reduced (Black, 1998). Where the death in the family is of a sibling, the child may feel guilty at having survived when the brother or sister has died. The child may also believe that s/he is to blame in some way for the death. This may lead to profound changes in the child's behaviour (Black, 1998).

SUPPORT FOR BEREAVED CHILDREN

Studies of grief among bereaved adults indicate that the process and period of mourning is assisted if children are told in advance that the parent is likely to die (Parkes, 1986). Children who know beforehand experience lower levels of anxiety than those who do not (Rosenheim and Reicher, 1985).

Long-term support for practical aspects of child care are clearly very important for the welfare of the bereaved child. Family therapy that focuses on sharing the experience of loss and grief in the family and supports talking about the dead parent or caregiver can help the grieving process (Black and Urbanowicz, 1987; Weller *et al.*, 1991).

Children need to grieve, too

Children need to be allowed to attend the funeral as part of the grieving process, but should be protected from the raw grief that may be expressed (Black, 1998).

I was 9 when my mother died. My dad didn't let my sister and I go to the funeral. I guess it was because he couldn't cope himself. I was 32 before I found out where my mum's grave was. When I first saw it, it was like she had died just yesterday. The grief was overwhelming.

(Wearmouth, unpublished)

As Cruse Bereavement Care (2015, *About Grief*, http://www.cruse. org.uk, accessed 18.05.15) notes, above all, young people need to be given the opportunity to grieve. Ignoring or averting the child's grief is not supportive, but can prove extremely damaging as the child becomes an adult. Young people need to be allowed to talk about their feelings. Everyone has their own way of grieving. Not all young people will experience the same emotions, behave the same way or respond similarly to other people who have lost close friends or relations.

MEDICAL AND BIOLOGICAL EXPLANATIONS OF BEHAVIOUR

In the context of school the differences in world views held by different professional groups and their different ways of working may have a very important influence over students' educational experiences in schools. Medical and biological explanations of behaviour theorise problems as inherent to an individual. From a medical or biological view, behaviour experienced by others as difficult or challenging is the result of an underlying condition, disease or dysfunction which an individual has and which requires treatment.

ATTENTION DEFICIT/HYPERACTIVITY DISORDER (AD/HD)

One of the conditions that is sometimes attributed to a biological cause is Attention Deficit/Hyperactivity Disorder (AD/HD). AD/HD is described by Norwich *et al.* (2002, p. 182) as '... a medical diagnosis of the American Psychiatric Association' that is 'characterised by chronic and pervasive (to home and school) problems of inattention, impulsiveness, and/or excessive motor activity which have seriously debilitating effects on individuals' social, emotional and educational development, and are sometimes disruptive to the home and/or school environment'. According to the British Psychological Society (1996), between 2 and 5 per cent of British school students are believed to experience this condition. There are interesting differences in the reported incidence of AD/HD internationally which are explained by some researchers as related to prevailing variations in cultural practices. There is a strict requirement for 'pervasiveness and persistence' across a range of contexts. This means that behaviour which is seen largely in one context only does not constitute grounds for a diagnosis.

Defining AD/HD as a mental disorder is problematic. 'We have evidence that children given the diagnosis AD/HD don't attend, don't wait and don't sit still. But just because they don't do all these things does not mean that they cannot do them' (BPS, 1996, p. 23).

As the AD/HD Association of New Zealand suggests, while no one really knows what causes AD/HD, the general consensus among the medical and scientific community is that AD/HD is biological in nature. Many believe that it results from a chemical imbalance in the brain.

In some cases, a medical diagnosis of the cause of challenging or inappropriate behaviour in schools result in a prescription for particular kinds of medication. The use of psychostimulants is based on a theory of biochemical imbalance. 'The medication stimulates areas of the brain regulating arousal and alertness and can result in immediate short-term improvements in concentration and impulse control. The precise mechanism is poorly understood and the specific locus of action within the central nervous system remains speculative' (BPS, 1996, p. 50–51). Some researchers suspect that stimulants work through the release of neurotransmitters, powerful chemical messengers. Neurons in the brain do not actually connect to each other. There is a gap between them. Neurons communicate through neurotransmitters that are passed between them. Many researchers have suspected that AD/HD may result from problems related to communication between neurons. Of the most commonly used stimulants, methylphenidate (Ritalin) is most widely prescribed. It is usually administered in the form of tablets to be taken regularly.

One major concern about the use of such psycho-stimulants relates to the effects and side effects of these drugs. There is also an ethical issue concerning the lack of adequate monitoring of the day-to-day classroom learning and behavioural outcomes of medication prescribed for many students.

> [E]ducational practitioners are concerned about the so-called 'zombie' effect (Sharron, 1995) which may be the result of inappropriate doses and poor monitoring. There is also evidence of 'behavioural rebound' in the afternoons when the medication wears off. These concerns illustrate the practical issues of managing medication at home and at school [as well as the ethical risks in relying on medication alone, without providing appropriate learning tasks and activities that attract positive reinforcement, to bring about behaviour change at school].
>
> (BPS, 1996, pp. 51–52)

Although the prescription of a chemical psychostimulant is fairly common, as noted by the British Psychological Society (1996), apart from all the ethical considerations, prescribing a drug provides an insufficient response. 'Medication must not become the first, and definitely not the only, line of treatment' (BPS, 1996, p. 2). Also needed are appropriate social support mechanisms in school and outside, including ways to address barriers to learning within the classroom or school context. Focusing on the medical and/or biological bases alone to explain behaviour is likely to provide an insufficient remedy because it ignores the holistic nature of well-being and, therefore, all those other elements which contribute to it. Students' core values associated with self-identity, self-esteem and a sense of purpose as a functioning member of a social and cultural group must also be considered in addressing overall well-being. There is a great deal of room for exploring ways in which more inclusive pedagogies within classrooms and schools might improve the learning and behaviour of students who are diagnosed as having AD/HD.

The use of psychostimulants is not the only common response to the issue of behaviour related to AD/HD. In a summary of 150 intervention studies of students with AD/HD (BPS, 1996, pp. 47–48) seven approaches are identified which are based on a cognitive-behavioural viewpoint. These approaches focus on the effects of consequences through positive reinforcement, response cost and training in the reduction of behaviour viewed as problematic. Positive reinforcement or token reinforcement can result in reduced activity, increased 'time on task' and improved academic performance. 'Several studies showed that behaviour management and medication were most effective when combined.' Mildly aversive procedures (reprimands or redirection) can be effective with primary age children, especially when combined with positive reinforcement. A combination of positive and negative reinforcement procedures and 'response cost', that is, mild punishment designed to make the undesirable behaviour more difficult and more of an effort to perform, has also been successful in some studies. Biofeedback involving providing the child with some form of visual or auditory feedback on levels of physiological states (e.g. heart rate) with a view to the child learning to control and monitor those states has also had some measure of success.

There is also some evidence that a few students experience intolerance to particular foods and there is the suggestion of a link between this and difficult behaviour. 'Common allergens included additives, chocolate, dairy products, wheat, oranges and other fruit. These particular substances are found in many commercially produced foods and medicines' (BPS, 1996, p. 52). The area of the influence of diet over behaviour is largely under-researched and controversial.

The issue of physical restraint

Whatever label might be given to difficult behaviour, dealing with severe behaviour incidents is far more challenging and stressful for a teacher or others than dealing with mildly disruptive incidents. However, an appropriate response is often the same. On occasions, students may be aggressive, out of control and a danger to themselves and others. It is very important to minimise the risk of physical confrontation in the first instance, rather than having to take action after the event. It seems sensible for teachers to avoid confrontations with students where these can be avoided. However, many of us have experienced situations when they cannot be, for instance, if asked by a colleague to help in some crisis, or where a student's provocative behaviour may have become intolerable. Dunckley (1999) refers to physical restraint as a last resort that should only be used to manage a dangerous situation. It should be employed carefully and in accordance with school policies, which should indicate when restraint can be used. It may be necessary to remove a student from a group of peers. This can be achieved 'by asking the other students to leave. It may be more appropriate, and safer, to bring other staff to the place where the student is, rather than the other way around' (Dunckley, 1999, p. 10). It is important for those associated with schools to check school, local area and/or national policies on physical restraint of students in schools.

There are a number of important ethical issues surrounding the restraint of students against their will (Bowers, 1996; Cooper, 1999; Cornwall, 2000). There is a difference between physical restraint, to hold a student still until aggression (hitting, kicking, punching others) subsides, and punitive incarcerations such as locking the student away for extended periods of time, as can occur when the principles of 'time out' are misunderstood, or misapplied, often in the heat of the moment (Cornwall, 2004). Dunckley (1999, p. 16) comments that students who are 'in an agitated state' need 'guidance and direction to increase their sense of security ... where possible and appropriate give a choice, time for the student to respond, then, after an appropriate time, follow through with consequences.'

In a non-statutory advisory document on the use of 'reasonable' force in schools in England, (DfE, 2013, p. 4) school staff are advised that reasonable in this context means 'using no more force than is needed' to control or restrain young people.

- 'Control' means either passive physical contact, such as standing between pupils or blocking a pupil's path, or active physical contact such as leading a pupil by the arm out of a classroom.
- 'Restraint' means to hold back physically or to bring a pupil under control. It is typically used in more extreme circumstances, for example, when two pupils are fighting and refuse to separate without physical intervention.

School staff are urged always to try not to cause injury, but it is acknowledged that in extreme cases it may not always be possible to avoid injuring the pupil. All members of a school staff have the power to use such 'reasonable' force, and this includes searching pupils for 'prohibited items' such as knives or illegal drugs.

TOURETTE SYNDROME

Tourette syndrome (TS) is a neurological disorder characterised by motor and vocal tics: repetitive, stereotyped, involuntary movements and vocalisations. As NINDS (2005) outlines, motor tics are, commonly, sudden, brief, repetitive movements that may include eye blinking and other vision irregularities, facial grimacing, shoulder shrugging, and head or shoulder jerking, or, more dramatically, touching objects, hopping, jumping, bending, twisting, or motor movements that result in self-harm such as punching oneself in the face. Vocalisations often include repetitive throat-clearing, sniffing, or grunting sounds – or, at the extreme, 'coprolalia' (uttering swear words) or 'echolalia' (repeating the words or phrases of others). People with Tourette syndrome often report that tics are preceded by an urge or sensation in the affected muscles, commonly called a 'premonitory urge' that builds up to the point where it is expressed. Excitement, anxiety or particular physical experiences can trigger or worsen tics.

Across the world the prevalence among school children 'range from 1 to 10 per 1000, with a rate of 6 per 1000 replicated in several countries' (Piacenti *et al.*, 2010, p. 1929). Evidence from twin and family studies suggests that Tourette syndrome may be genetic (NINDS, 2005). Tics tend to start in early childhood, peak before the mid-teen years, and improve subsequently. Approximately 10 per cent of young people have symptoms that last into adulthood. Medication can be prescribed for young people whose tics are severe enough to interfere with their functioning. The most effective appear to be antipsychotics. However, as Piacenti *et al.* (2010, p. 1930) comment, these 'rarely eliminate tics and are often associated with unacceptable sedation, weight gain, cognitive dulling, and motor adverse effects', such as tremors.

In recent years particular interventions based on a behaviourist approach have been developed that seem, from small controlled trials, to be effective in reducing tic severity (NINDS, 2005). For example,'habit reversal training'acknowledges that tics have a neurological basis and also, in its design, takes into account the context in which the individual lives and works as well as the internal experience of premonitory urges. Piacenti *et al.* (2010, p. 1930) describe the main components of habit reversal as tic-awareness and 'competing-response training'. Awareness training comprises self-monitoring of tics and the early signs that a tic is about to occur. Competing-response training involves deliberately engaging in a behaviour that is not physically compatible with the tic as soon as the premonitory urge is felt. In this way tics are not suppressed. Instead, the individual is taught to manage the urge and initiate an alternative socially acceptable behaviour that replaces the tic. The competing response can be initiated when the patient notices that a tic is about to occur, during the tic, or after the tic has occurred. For vocal tics, the most commonly competing response that is taught is slow rhythmic breathing from the diaphragm. With practice, patients are able to complete the competing response without disengaging from routine activities.

Young people with Tourette syndrome often cope well in mainstream classrooms. However, frequent tics can interfere with academic performance or disrupt social relationships with peers. My own experience is that, in a well-managed classroom, other young people can be very understanding and supportive. All young people with Tourette syndrome, as with any other kind of special educational need, benefit from a learning environment that is supportive and flexible enough to accommodate their individual learning needs.

This may mean making special arrangements if the tics disrupt the pupil's ability to write, or problem-solving with the pupil on ways to reduce stress in the classroom or during examinations.

BULLYING BEHAVIOUR

An example of student behaviour which is the focus of teachers' concerns in many schools and which can be explained from a variety of viewpoints is that of bullying. Rigby (2002) concludes that, from his analysis of work on what constitutes bullying behaviour (for example, Olweus, 1993, 1999; Randall, 1991; Smith & Sharp, 1994; Farrington, 1993), bullying is a combination of the wish to hurt somebody together with hurtful action, an imbalance and unjust use of power, enjoyment on the part of the bully, the victim's feeling of oppression and, often, repetition of the bullying behaviour.

THE INFLUENCE OF SITUATIONAL FACTORS ON BULLYING BEHAVIOUR

The Second World War and then, later, the war in Vietnam stimulated interest in a clear focus within social psychology research projects into the issues of obedience to malign authority, and the influence of group pressure to conform to a group norm where the actions of one person or a group acting under the orders of an authoritative other were clearly to the detriment of another. For example, Milgram's (1963, 1974) 'electric shock' experiments were designed to investigate the extent to which individuals were prepared to obey authoritative instructions from others to deliver electric shocks to adult learners.

Studies on conformity and obedience typically indicate a 'fundamental attribution error' (Nisbett et al., 1973); that is, that people generally overestimate the role of the characteristics of individual people and underestimate the role of contextual factors in regulating human behaviour (Atkinson et al., 1993). Zimbardo's (1970) 'prison experiment' where volunteers acting the part of prison guards were prepared to humiliate and victimise other volunteers acting as 'prisoners' is an example of the kind of experiment designed to test the hypothesis that, under certain conditions, members of a group can lose their personal identities and experience a sense of mob aggression and much greater impulsive behaviour against other individuals.

Contemporary studies of bullying in schools in various countries indicate that the incidence of bullying by peers appears to be more common in some countries than others (Rigby, 2002). Within countries Rigby (1997) has shown that differences between schools in the incidence of bullying can also be considerable. It is noteworthy that, in schools, there is a negative relationship between the presence of teachers at break times and lunchtimes and bullying (Olweus, 1993).

THE CYCLE OF BULLYING

Bullying is often associated with an imbalance of power between victim and perpetrator. Once the victim begins to react to the bullying by showing signs of stress, the bully or bullies may experience great pleasure and enjoyment from their feelings of power and dominance. The cycle of bullying may continue and/or grow more intense and continue for a long time. Sometimes the victim may fight back (literally), sometimes she or he may find ways to avoid the bullying by hovering around teachers or staying at home.

One of the crucial factors in accounting for the degree of severity of bullying in schools is the behaviour of bystanders. Research on bystander behaviour assumed popularity after the murder of the New Yorker, Kitty Genovese in 1964, which became notorious as a result of the non-intervention of thirty-eight neighbours who heard her screams for help for over thirty minutes but failed to assist her (Atkinson et al., 1993). Social psychologists researching what they termed 'bystander apathy' found that the presence of others seems to deter individuals from intervening in difficult or dangerous situations where they could be of assistance to the person in danger or trouble. However, a training programme focusing on raising awareness of bystander apathy can be shown to make a significant difference to the preparedness of bystanders to help others in trouble (Beaman et al., 1978). The abduction in England of a young boy, James Bulger, was also witnessed by many bystanders who did nothing to intervene with the 10-year-olds who marched him around Liverpool before murdering him. Another factor which appears to be of consequence in inhibiting intervention is the perceived relationship between these boys. They were assumed to be brothers (Levine, 1999).

Group pressure to conform to a majority view can also be shown to influence individuals to act against their own judgements. In a classic series of studies Asch (1952, 1955, 1958) showed that individuals confronted with the unanimous views of a group about an issue were unlikely to disagree openly with the group's judgement even where this was clearly wrong. In Asch's experiments individuals were asked to judge the length of a line that was clearly estimated incorrectly by the group. Many subjects preferred to accede to the group's view rather than risk challenging the group's apparent competence and thus the fear of 'What will they think of me?' (Atkinson *et al.*, 1993).

Rigby (2002) warns against any assumption that the descriptors 'bully' and 'victim' should suggest a stable personality trait. Many of those who bully in their younger years do not repeat this behaviour later on. Some of those who bully in one situation would never do so in another.

It is tempting to think of bullies as being socially inadequate (Field, 1999). However, this may be a gross oversimplification. To take advantage of, and manipulate, other less powerful individuals, bullies may need to be very skilful in the social situation (Sutton *et al.*, 1999). On measures of self-esteem school bullies are average (Rigby, 1997). However, bullies tend to be less able to imagine another's point of view (Rigby, 2002) and to experience stronger feelings of depression (Slee, 1995). They also appear to be more positively disposed towards violence (Olweus, 1993).

Despite the risk of supporting the use of stereotypes, there does seem to be some consensus among researchers about the correlates of victimisation. For example, victims of bullying may have low self-worth and self-esteem, be non-assertive and have poor social skills, be introverted, relatively unco-operative and physically less strong than others. They may also be physically shorter than others, be lonely and isolated, and prone to anxiety, depression and suicide (Rigby, 2002, pp. 139–40).

Responses to bullying behaviour in schools often fall into one of two categories. There are those that assume bullying is an anti-social act which needs to be reduced through the application of responses from a behaviourist approach, such as various types of punishment contingencies. From this view 'we can best proceed by identifying and punishing behaviour we wish to stop' (Rigby, 2002, p. 463).

Typically any violation of rules is treated similarly whether major or minor. Policies may rely completely on 'rules and sanctions and zero tolerance for rule infractions' (Rigby, 2002, p. 238). Other responses focus on establishing respectful behaviour between people so as to minimise bullying through the abuse of power in personal relationships (Rigby, 2002). From this view, 'positive improvement in behaviour between people can be brought about through instruction, persuasion and modelling of respectful behaviour' (2002, p. 238).

'CIRCLE TIME'

One initiative associated with the resolution of students' disputes at primary school level in schools in the UK that depends on listening to the views of the student community in classrooms is that of 'Circle Time' (Mosley, 1996). As Tew (1998, p. 20) comments, in many traditional communities the circle is a symbol of 'unity, healing and power' and can be found in the traditions of groups as diverse 'as the North American Indians and Anglo Saxon monks'. Wearmouth et al. (2005) note that, in schools, 'Circle Time' is a meeting that follows strict protocols of involving all participants in discussion where both teachers and students are bound by rules that stipulate no one may put anyone down, no one may use any name negatively (creating 'safety' for all individuals including teachers and parents), and when individuals speak, everyone must listen. Everyone has a turn and a chance to speak, all views are taken seriously, members of the class team suggest ways of solving problems and individuals can accept the help or politely refuse it (Wearmouth et al., 2005, p. 184).

The rules must be followed strictly. If a student breaks a rule a visual warning is given. If this persists, time away from the circle follows.

RESTORATIVE PRACTICE

In some schools and local areas, particular programmes have been designed to focus on traditional community values in order to harness the necessary resources to address problems that have resulted in, and as a result of, unacceptable, unsociable behaviours

(Schweigert, 1999). One such initiative is based in general terms on the principles of 'restorative justice'. The prime focus in a restorative justice approach is on 'putting things right' between all those involved or affected by wrongdoing. Restorative justice can employ traditional conflict resolution processes and culturally appropriate mechanisms drawn from the external community to address and resolve tension and make justice visible and more productive in communities inside the school. In New Zealand, for example, where restorative justice practices are influenced by traditional Maori cultural values and preferred ways of responding to wrongdoing, the emphasis is on the restoration of harmony between the individual, the victim and the collective (tribe or sub-tribe). In order for restoration to take place, all those involved in the offence 'need to be heard in the process of seeking redress' (Restorative Practices Development Team, 2003, p. 11).

An example of a restorative approach

Wearmouth *et al.* (2007) describe an example of restorative practice where the teachers, mother and wider family members of 15-year-old 'Wiremu' had become increasingly concerned about his negative, challenging behaviour in school and anti-social activities outside. Things came to a head when he took his mother's car out joyriding and crashed into the neighbour's garden, damaging the gnomes given to the elderly neighbour by his deceased wife. The behaviour support teacher to whom he had been referred organised a meeting at the local rugby club where Wiremu was a keen member, and invited everyone who knew him to attend. When the boy arrived, unaware of the true reason why he was being taken to the club, everyone was given a chance to speak about him, teachers, community elders, friends and relations. Mostly it was in very glowing terms – about his captaincy of a rugby team, his personal qualities, and so on. Then his mother talked about the loss of the car that meant so much to the family, and the neighbour talked about his dead wife and the broken gnomes.

> What happened next had surprised everybody. Wiremu stood up to speak. He was crying. He turned to the elderly neighbour whose garden he had wrecked and asked to be forgiven. He offered to help mend the fence, to sort out the plants in the garden and to repair the garden gnomes. The [behaviour support] teacher recalled him saying: 'As a child I remember your wife ... she used to give my sister flowers to take to mum. She was always smiling and she had a nice face.' Wiremu hugged his mother and apologised over and over again.
>
> (Wearmouth *et al.*, 2007, p. 43)

Belonging is a fundamental human need. Even the most hardened pupils will experience intense and often contradictory emotions when they are challenging school. As Furlong (1991, p. 296) comments: 'Feelings of anger, fear, frustration, elation and guilt may all be present. In the classroom the peer group may be shown the more positive side when feelings of bravado and elation may be to the fore, while in the privacy of the head teacher's office the same pupils may express guilt and remorse at their actions.''Wiremu' might have been identified as deviant, suffering from AD/HD, or labelled as something else, and charged with illegal driving of a vehicle and criminal damage to property. Instead, he kept his word, repaired the damage he had caused, and, with the support of family and community, harmony was restored. As the behaviour support teacher commented:

> There was not a dry eye in that whare [meeting-room] and I will not forget it in a hurry. The meeting ended with everyone walking away with their mana [personal standing] and wairua [sense of spiritual well-being] strengthened by what they had seen.
>
> (Wearmouth *et al.*, 2007, p. 43)

SUMMARY

Anti-social or challenging behaviour in classrooms and around the school is sometimes explained as a problem that stems from the student him/herself and his/her family or circumstances. This may be the case with some students. However, student behaviour in schools does not occur in a vacuum. All students' behaviours are situated in a social context and result from interactions between people and their environments or social events. Participation in school activities involves the whole person in its combination of doing, talking, feeling, thinking and belonging. It refers both to taking part in activity and also to the connections with others during this process. Personal identity in schools is constituted in the way in which learners participate in activities with others and, therefore, by definition, non-participation. The implication is that the most important concern should be first to establish effective whole class management and positive classroom learning environments in which individual disruptive behaviour is much less likely to happen. Often individual students are blamed for their own failure and/or disturbing behaviour in schools rather than looking to explanations in the way society is structured to favour some children, or at the level of school structure, organisation, curriculum and classroom management. This has meant that there has been no real pressure to change society's ills or to make schools more responsive to students' needs (Armstrong, 1994, pp. 141–142).

6

UNDERSTANDING AND ADDRESSING SENSORY AND/OR PHYSICAL DIFFICULTIES AND NEEDS

INTRODUCTION

This chapter focuses on sensory and physical difficulties and the educational needs that may result. Particular attention is given to hearing and/or visual impairments and physical and motor difficulties to illustrate:

- what research studies tell us about these difficulties, including common indicators,
- the relationship between sensory and/or physical difficulties and needs and young people's learning and future life chances,
- ways that the barriers to learning experienced by young people with these difficulties can be addressed in school and elsewhere.

The frame of reference applied to assessing difficulties is generally taken from the identification and assessment of the extent of the child's sensory or physical impairment. However, as Miller and Ockleford (2005) comment, young people are individuals with different interests, background experiences and so on. As in other areas of special educational needs and disabilities in schools, a whole range of information is needed to ensure that support for an individual is appropriate. This includes the views of the child or young person and the parents/family, medical and school records.

HEARING IMPAIRMENTS

THE EAR AND HOW IT WORKS

The ear has two main functions. It receives sound and converts it into signals that the brain can understand. It also helps us to balance.

The hearing system consists of three parts, the outer, middle and inner ear, all of which must work well to allow sound to be heard properly. The outside part of the ear, known as the the pinna, catches sound waves and directs them down the ear canal to the eardrum. The soundwaves cause the eardrum to vibrate and the vibrations are passed across the middle ear by three tiny bones, the hammer, anvil and stirrup. These bones increase the strength of the vibrations before they pass into an organ called the cochlea in the inner ear. The cochlea is filled with fluid and contains thousands of tiny hair-like sound-sensitive cells. The vibrations entering the cochlea cause the fluid and sound-sensitive cells to move. As these cells move, they create a small electrical charge. The auditory nerve carries these signals to the brain, where they are interpreted as sound. Impaired hearing occurs when one or more parts of the system is/are not working effectively.

Balance

The semicircular canals in the inner ear are three tubes, filled with liquid and movement-sensitive hair cells. As we move, the fluid moves and creates signals about balance that are sent to the brain.

DEGREES OF DEAFNESS

There are different degrees of deafness. Most often these are classified as mild, moderate, severe or profound (Spencer & Marschak, 2010). Few children are totally deaf. Most deaf children can hear some sounds at certain pitches and volume. The quietest sound that

- those with mild deafness can hear is between 21 to 40dB. This can include speech, particularly in noisy situations;
- those with moderate deafness can hear is between 41 to 70dB. This can include speech without using a hearing aid;
- those with severe deafness can hear is between 71 to 90dB. Those who are severely deaf usually need to lip-read or use sign language, even with the use of a hearing aid;
- those who are profoundly deaf can hear is more than 90dB. Forms of communication often include lip-reading and sign language.

(Adapted from http://www.nhs.uk/Conditions/Hearing-impairment/Pages/Diagnosis.aspx, accessed 18.05.15)

DIFFERENT TYPES AND CAUSES OF DEAFNESS

Deafness can be of different types. Conductive deafness is when sound cannot pass efficiently through the outer and middle ear to the cochlea and auditory nerve. The most common type of conductive deafness in children is caused by 'glue ear' (NDCS, 2010). Glue ear is a build-up of fluid in the middle ear which affects about one in five children at any time. For most children, the glue ear clears up by itself. A few need surgery to insert 'grommets' into the eardrums, tiny plastic tubes that allow air to circulate in the middle ear and help to prevent the build-up of fluid. Sensori-neural deafness is permanent and occurs when there is a fault in the inner ear or auditory (hearing) nerve.

There are many reasons why a child can be born deaf or become deaf early in life. Around half the deaf children born in the UK every year are deaf for a genetic reason. Deafness can also be caused by complications during pregnancy. Infections, for example, rubella and herpes, can cause a child to be born deaf. Premature babies are often more liable to infections that can cause deafness. Severe jaundice, a lack of oxygen at some point can also cause deafness. Infections such as meningitis, measles and mumps, a head injury or exposure to loud noises can damage the hearing system (World Health Organisation, 2010).

A major problem with late identification of deafness is the effect on language development (Goldberg & Richberg, 2004; Moeller *et al.*, 2007). A delay in identification can mean a delay in establishing effective communication with the child. This in turn can have a long-term impact on his/her social and educational development. The consequences on development of undetected hearing impairment may be long-lasting (Yoshinaga-Itano, 2003). Children who do not hear clearly or whose hearing varies may be late to start talking, have difficulties with speech sounds, or fail to develop good listening skills. They may also have poor memory and language-processing skills, poor basic vocabularies as a result, reading and spelling problems, difficulty with sentence structure and comprehension, and achieve lower attainments in reading and mathematics. Pupils with a conductive hearing loss have a higher tendency to behaviour problems, poor motivation and attention, shyness and withdrawal (Spencer & Marschak, 2010). The most vulnerable are those whose conductive deafness started in early infancy and persisted undiagnosed for long periods.

INCLUDING CHILDREN WITH HEARING IMPAIRMENTS IN MAINSTREAM SCHOOLS

In 1908 regulations by the Board of Education in England and Wales laid down that teachers in schools for the blind and deaf must obtain, within two years of their appointment, an approved qualification. The 1908 regulations have broadly continued to the present day. These days many children with sensory impairments are in mainstream schools. It is essential, therefore, that non-specialist as well as specialist teachers understand how to include them most sensitively and effectively.

Key to successful inclusion is the ethos of the school in which the hearing impaired students are placed. The RNID (2004) strongly promotes the message that effective pedagogy for students who experience hearing difficulties is effective pedagogy for a whole range of other students also. They state that 'Reviewing and adapting teaching styles, presentation methods, listening conditions and differentiation of the curriculum to address the needs of deaf pupils will also improve the learning conditions for many other pupils in the school' (RNID, 2004, p. 8)

There are three major 'types' of approach: Auditory-Oral (or 'Oral/Aural'), Sign-Bilingual, or Total Communication. Whilst professionals may well be committed to one particular approach 'generally the evidence for any one method working better than another for deaf children as a whole is unclear, and all the approaches can point to some evidence which shows successful outcomes for children' (NDCS, 2010, p. 45). As the National Deaf Children's Society goes on to comment, 'The 'best' communication approach for any child and family is the one which works for them, both fitting in with the family's culture and values and most importantly, allowing the child to develop good self-esteem, a positive self-image, successful relationships, and to achieve her potential in all aspects of her life (NDCS, 2010, p. 50).

Auditory-Oral approaches emphasise the use of amplification such as hearing aids, cochlear implants and radio aids to maximise the use of the child's 'residual' hearing (Spencer & Marschak, 2006). The philosophy behind auditory-oral approaches is that oral language better supports the development of reading and writing, because written language is built on an understanding of the sounds and structure of the spoken language (Beattie, 2006). The aim of this approach therefore is that deaf children should learn to use whatever residual hearing they may have to develop good listening and speaking skills which will enable them to communicate and mix with hearing people as part of the wider hearing community. The most widely used of these approaches is the Natural Aural Approach promoted by the Deaf Education through the Speaking and Listening (DELTA) organisation. Here no sign language is used and children are not encouraged to rely on lip-reading (Lewis, 1996).

Sign Bilingualism uses sign language as the child's first language and the spoken language of the family is learned as a second language (Moores, 2008). In Sign Bilingualism in the UK, the languages are British Sign Language (or Irish Sign Language in Ireland) and whatever is the spoken language of the home. A sign bilingual approach to developing communication is rooted in the belief that a visual language is essential for deaf children to have full access to language learning, education, information and the world around them, together with a strong positive deaf identity.

British Sign Language is a complete language in its own right with its own grammar and linguistic rules. There is no written form. Its grammar is very different from English, so it is not used simultaneously with spoken language. BSL has developed over hundreds of years as a visual language which uses body language, head position, facial expressions and gesture as well as the hands. It also uses fingerspelling for some words which have no signs, such as names. British Sign Language (BSL) is the language of the UK Deaf community and it is estimated that about 70,000 people use it as their first or preferred language. Use of British Sign Language can therefore bring with it a connection with Deaf culture and the opportunity and expectation of taking part in the Deaf community as well as the hearing world (Burman *et al.*, 2006). Where a child uses BSL it is useful if the rest of the family learn to sign, as well as classmates and teachers in school.

Total Communication is based on the principle that deaf children can learn to communicate effectively by using any and all means that they can in whatever combination works best: sign, speech and hearing, finger-spelling, gesture, facial expression, lip-reading and cued speech. Signed/Signs Supported English (SSE) is a sign support system which uses signs taken from BSL, together with fingerspelling (Moores, 2001). It is used in the word order of English to supplement what is being spoken. Signed English, similarly, uses signs taken from BSL together with some specially developed 'markers' made with the hands, and finger-spelling, to give an exact representation of the word order and the grammar of English through sign. It is mainly used to support the teaching of reading and writing. In fingerspelling, each letter of the alphabet is indicated by using the fingers and palm of the hand (Padden & Gunsals, 2003). It is used to support Sign Language to spell names and places and for words that don't have an established BSL sign. Lip-reading is the process of reading words from the lip patterns of the person speaking (Spencer & Marschak, 2010). For a number of reasons lip-reading is never enough on its own. Many speech sounds are not visible on the lips. Lip patterns also vary from person to person. Further, lack of clarity around the face, for example, poor lighting conditions, beards or moustaches that obscure the mouth, or eating whilst talking can make lip-reading difficult. Lip-reading therefore is used to support other communication approaches. Cued Speech is a sound-based system that accompanies natural speech and uses eight hand shapes in four different positions (cues) to represent the sounds of English visually (Hage & Leybaert, 2006). Some spoken sounds cannot be fully lip-read: 'p', 'm' and 'b' all look the same on the lips; sounds like 'd', 'k' and 'g' cannot be seen on the lips. Hand shapes are 'cued' near to the mouth to make clear the sounds of English which look the same when lip-read. It is intended to make every sound and word clear to deaf children and therefore enable them to have full access to spoken language. The association between the sounds and letters of spoken English is intended to help develop literacy skills as well as spoken language.

ASSISTIVE DEVICES

As the NDCS (2008, p. 31) comments, deaf children often use assistive listening devices to assist them to hear what a speaker is saying, particularly in noisy listening conditions. Personal FM systems (often known as radio aids) are very useful, especially at school, college or at home. 'They can help reduce effects of background noise in, for example, a school classroom, and help a child to concentrate on one person's voice, often their teacher'. Radio aids have a transmitter with a microphone and a receiver. The person talking wears the transmitter and the sounds are transmitted by radio waves to the receiver. The deaf child wears the receiver which picks up the signal from the transmitter and converts it back to sound. The child's hearing aids or implants amplify the sound so that the child can hear what is said.

Classroom soundfield systems are designed for similar reasons as radio aids, but are not the same. A soundfield system includes a microphone worn by the speaker that is linked to an amplifier by either an FM radio transmitter or an infra-red transmitter so that the speaker can walk around a room with no need for wires. Loudspeakers are fitted around the room. The soundfield system amplifies the speaker's voice to produce a clear, consistent level of sound above the background noise (NDCS, 2008). Most children with hearing aids or cochlear implants will still need to use a radio aid in a classroom with a soundfield system.

Sound waves reverberate and increase the amount of background noise in rooms with hard surfaces (Moeller *et al.*, 2007). Soundfield systems and the acoustic treatment of teaching spaces can improve the listening environment for all students. It is important for class teachers to think carefully about the clarity of their spoken language (Wilkins & Ertmer, 2002). Teachers should use natural speech patterns and not exaggerate lip movements or shout, highlight key terms and key concepts and place themselves in a position appropriate for students to lip-read or benefit from a hearing aid, where the maximum range is often two metres. Deaf students may also need to be encouraged to see the faces of peers who are speaking. To acquire spoken and written English, students may also need the support of visual and written forms of language, as well as lip-reading or multi-sensory clues (Harris & Moreno, 2006). For example, with video materials, deaf students might benefit from advanced access to a summary of the programme and having new vocabulary and concepts explained, as well as sub-titles. In addition, auditory-oral approaches require 'consistent, efficient use of individual hearing aids, radio aids and/or cochlear implant devices' (RNID, 2004, p. 15).

As the RNID (2004, p. 15) notes, in 2000 the vast majority of all deaf children in English schools were reported to be using 'auditory-oral' approaches that do 'not use sign language or manually coded elements to support the understanding of spoken language'. These approaches assume that students have enough residual hearing to acquire and use spoken language without needing to use sign language or finger spelling, provided there is sufficient amplification of sound. Although some children make progress that is commensurate with their age, as Spencer & Marschak (2006) comment, many do not keep pace with hearing peers.

The listening environment is a crucial consideration (Spencer & Marschak, 2010), as is implied above. Intensity or loudness is measured in decibels (dB). Frequency (pitch) is measured in Hertz (Hz). All sounds are made up of different frequencies. Speech comprises vowels and consonants. Vowel sounds are low frequency and consonants are generally higher in frequency. Speech is usually a mix of high and low frequency sounds. The main issue for schools is that everyday building materials absorb the higher frequency sounds more easily than lower frequency sounds. This means that the consonants, which are required for speech clarity, are more likely to be absorbed than the vowels. Therefore additional special materials may need to be added to a room to absorb more of the lower frequency sounds (Moeller *et al.*, 2007). Noise in classrooms is mostly speech, mainly low frequency. If enough is reflected it masks important high frequency consonants, making it difficult to understand what the teacher is saying. As much low frequency reflection as possible therefore needs to be prevented.

Communicating with deaf children

The National Deaf Children's Society (NDCS) (2010, pp. 10–12) offers useful advice to teachers and families of children with hearing impairments. For example, it advises avoiding competing noise in the background that makes hearing difficult, bringing everyday sounds to the child's conscious attention and helping the child make the connection between the object and the sound it is making by looking at it. In the home it might be a vacuum cleaner. At school it might be the bell. Carpets, curtains and soft furnishings that do not reflect sound are more 'acoustically friendly' than wooden or ceramic flooring and blinds. The NDCS also suggests staying within the child's vision as much as possible to enable the child to use visual clues from body language, including facial expressions and lip-reading, and not placing the child facing the window so that s/he is looking into bright light. Wearing plain rather than patterned clothes means that the child can see the signed communication more easily. Visual supports, such as objects, books, toys or pictures, can help children to understand unfamiliar concepts. Deaf children's attention should be drawn to the variety of interactions and forms of communication going on around them. If everyone around deaf children uses signing with each other as well as with the children they can interpret verbal interactions between everyone around. People speaking to deaf children should face them, repeat and re-phrase if they do not understand. Most importantly, adults and peers should respond to their attempts to communicate and not speak for them.

VISUAL IMPAIRMENT

As discussed in Chapter 7 on assessment, visual impairment (VI) is a general term that indicates a continuum of sight loss (Mason *et al.*, 1997). VI is estimated to affect around 25,000 between the ages of 0 and 16 years in the UK (Tate *et al.*, 2005), and 15,000 between the ages of 17 and 25 years. At least four in every 10,000 children born in the UK are diagnosed as severely visually impaired or blind by their first birthday (Miller & Ockleford, 2005). VI might be the result of the following: genetic or hereditary illness, including congenital optic nerve and retinal disorders, damage to the eye before, during or sometime after birth, or damage to the visual cortex or to other areas of the brain concerned with information processing. Fifty per cent of blind and partially sighted children also have additional disabilities and this includes 30 per cent with severe or profound and multiple learning difficulties.

It has been estimated that around 3 per cent of blind and partially sighted pupils, aged 5 to 16, use Braille as their sole or main format for reading and writing (Morris & Smith, 2008).

INCLUDING PUPILS WITH A VISUAL IMPAIRMENT IN THE CLASSROOM

As a result of their visual difficulties, before going to school children may well have had less opportunity to explore their environment and learn through observing and copying the actions of others (Douglas & McLinden, 2005). Both academic progress and children's social skills may be influenced by this. Children may therefore need teaching of literacy development through specialist codes such as Braille or Moon or through print/modified print Braille, and/or specialist teaching of mobility, tactile and keyboard skills, as well as social and life skills generally. It is important to consider whether and when to withdraw the child from the mainstream classroom for specialist or additional teaching so that the pupil does not become socially isolated and the mainstream teacher maintains full responsibility for the pupil.

Davis (2003) notes that visually impaired children may become very tired as a result of the amount of concentration required to complete tasks, and/or need more time to complete tasks. Special consideration of the learning environment, in particular the classroom, may well be necessary, for example, where to site quiet or loud areas, Braille and/or tactile/large print signs, bulky equipment such as CCTV, a Brailler and computers, as well as classroom lighting (Mason, 2001).

Braille is the alphabet and numbers, designed to be read by fingers rather than eyes through a series of raised dots on a page. The RNIB

(2015) notes that a blind French schoolboy, Louis Braille, devised the code more than two hundred years ago. This code is based on six dots arranged in two columns of three. Different types of Braille codes use combinations of these dots, 63 in all, to represent letters of the alphabet, numbers, punctuation marks and common letter groups (see Figure 6.1).

There are two grades of Braille: uncontracted (previously Grade 1) and contracted (previously Grade 2). Uncontracted includes a letter for letter and number for number translation from print. Contracted has special signs for common words and letter combinations. This usually increases the speed of reading. Particular subject areas, for example, music, mathematics, science and foreign languages, have their own specialist codes.

The RNIB (2015) gives examples of reading schemes where printed books:

> have been adapted to include either uncontracted Braille (grade 1) or contracted Braille (grade 2) on interleaved clear plastic sheets, so that the pictures and print story can be seen underneath. This enables shared reading between sighted and blind readers as it is clearly useful for parent and child, teacher and child, and/or friends to share books.

Figure 6.1 Braille alphabet (136)

There are a number of common misconceptions about visual impairment, for example, as Mason (2001, p. 20) points out, holding a book close will not harm vision. Dim light will not harm eyes. Some conditions, for example, albinism, mean that a child may require a low level of lighting. Having a VI does not mean that other senses, for example, hearing or touch, are highly developed.

As Mason also comments, in order to plan appropriate support for pupils with VI, teachers and support staff need to consider whether the child has a preferred or dominant eye or a defect in field or colour vision. This is important for both seating and using appropriate teaching strategies. There may well be restrictions on physical activities which may constrain the child's participation with peers. Low-vision aids may have been prescribed, so it is important to know when they should be used and whether the child has been trained to use them. Also, a consideration of lighting levels as well as size and contrast of print is important to maximise the child's vision.

MULTI-SENSORY IMPAIRMENT

Multi-sensory impairment means difficulty with both vision and hearing. Children with multi-sensory impairment may be born with it or acquire it later as a result of illness or injury. Very few children are totally blind and deaf. In the past Rubella (German measles) during pregnancy was a main cause of deaf-blindness. However, as a result of vaccination against Rubella usually before girls reach the age of puberty it is now uncommon. Premature birth and/or severe infections during early childhood may also cause deaf-blindness.

The reduced and possibly distorted visual and auditory information that pupils with multi-sensory impairment receive means that they have limited and possibly confused experience of the world (Aitken, 2000). Some children become skilled at using touch as a means of learning about the world and a means of communicating. Others may become skilled in using the sense of smell. Others may sense movement around them from differences in air pressure. Taylor (2007, p. 205) notes the difficulties experienced by many of these children in communicating:

> These include: a reduced and confused experience of the world, becoming passive and isolated, and the tendency to be echolalic or

repeating the last word said to them, all of which limit their ability to make choices. Aitken and Millar (2002) also highlight the effects of hearing impairment on individuals' communication, including isolation from information and from other people. A physical impairment in association with communication difficulties will also present additional challenges. The child with MSI has all these difficulties compounded.

Bill

Taylor (2007, p. 206) describes a young man, Bill, aged 14, who had quadriplegic cerebral palsy, which caused weakness in all limbs, and epilepsy. His left arm and hand had some useful function for picking up objects, signing and gesturing. He had bilateral optic atrophy and was registered blind, with some peripheral vision in his left eye. He also had a conductive hearing loss. Other people communicated with him mainly through speech, objects and signing on the body, and expressively through sign, gesture, and vocalisation. He used a voice output communication aid (VOCA) to relay messages from home to school and to make some choices.

For those young people whose visual and vocal ability is severely affected, many assistive devices are available to enable students to communicate: electronic language boards, voice synthesisers and voice recognition software.

MULTI-SENSORY TEACHING

Multi-sensory teaching is simultaneous use of visual, auditory, and kinesthetic-tactile senses to enhance memory and learning. Links are consistently made between the visual (what we see), auditory (what we hear), and kinesthetic-tactile (what we feel) pathways in learning to read and spell.

The use of such an approach for children whose senses are compromised or greatly reduced could be effective if careful planning takes account of their individual sensory needs. Using a multi-sensory teaching approach means helping a child to learn through more than one of the senses. One possible approach is to involve the use of more of the child's senses, especially the use of touch and movement (kinetic). This will give the child's brain tactile and kinetic memories to hang on to, as well as the visual and auditory ones.

Helen Keller

Helen Keller is, perhaps, the best known deaf-blind child in history. A childhood illness had left her both blind and deaf. During the following few years, Helen became a very difficult child, with her violent outbursts, screaming and temper tantrums, born of frustration. When she was six her family found a teacher who herself was partially sighted and had been educated in an institution for visually impaired children. When she arrived, she immediately started teaching Helen to finger spell. At first Helen could not understand what Anne was trying to communicate to her. The breakthrough came when Anne pumped water over one of Helen's hands and spelled out the word 'water' in the other. Something about this made the connection between the word and its meaning. Helen made rapid progress after that. Anne taught her to read, firstly with raised letters and later with Braille, and to write with both ordinary and Braille typewriters.

MUSCULAR DYSTROPHY

An estimated 8,000 to 10,000 people in the UK have a form of muscular dystrophy (Pohlschmidt & Meadowcroft, 2010). The term is used to refer to a group of genetic muscle diseases associated with progressive weakness and wasting of muscles owing to the degeneration of muscle cells. This can include the heart.

There are over thirty different conditions that can be categorised into seven groups, including Duchenne, Becker, limb girdle, congenital, facioscapulohumeral, oculopharyngeal and Emery-

Dreifuss. The severity of muscular dystrophy is very variable. Symptoms can be obvious at birth or shortly thereafter. Sometimes the symptoms are very mild and are seen much later, between the ages of 40 and 50. Most of these involve a defect in a protein that plays a vital role in muscle cell function or repair.

To take one example, Duchenne muscular dystrophy affects only boys, with very rare exceptions. Around one boy in 35,000 is born with this condition – that is, about 100 boys born in the UK each year. In just over 50 per cent of all cases the mother carries the gene but is usually not herself affected by it. Each son of a carrier has a 50 per cent chance of being affected and each daughter has a 50 per cent chance of being a carrier. A problem in the genes results in a defect in dystrophin, which is an important protein in muscle fibres. Most boys with this condition develop the first signs of difficulty in walking at the age of 1 to 3 years and are usually unable to run or jump like their peers. By about 8 to 11 years boys become unable to walk. By their late teens or early twenties the muscle-wasting is severe enough to shorten life expectancy (Pohlschmidt & Meadowcroft, 2010).

Regular supervision from a clinic is very important to manage the condition as effectively as possible. Many children who experience difficulties in gross motor movement may use a wheelchair. Others may be unable to control or vary their posture efficiently.

> These children will need specialised equipment to aid their mobility, to support their posture and to protect and restore their body shape, muscle tone and quality of life. It is vital that children with physical needs have access to appropriate forms of therapy, for example physiotherapy and hydrotherapy, and that their carers receive training to enable them to manage their physical needs confidently on a day-to-day basis.
>
> (Mencap, undated, p. 5)

The kinds of physical access supported by ICT can considerably reduce physical barriers to the learning of some students. For example, a student who cannot use his/her hands can control the computer by pressing a switch with his/her head. 'A youngster who has problems with fine motor control can use a trackerball to move a pointer across the screen. He can select the options in a drawing package to draw a series of geometric shapes, with a confidence that the quality of the results will do justice to his intentions' (NCET, 1995, p. 4).

The example of Michael

Michael was a young 9-year-old boy with Duchenne muscular dystrophy who featured in an Open University video programme (Open University, 2000). He was a pupil in a mainstream primary school and participated in lessons in the same way as peers. A full-time learning support assistant was appointed to take care of his personal hygiene needs in school and to help him move around generally. For example, at his request she held up his hand in the classroom when he wanted to answer a question. There was a very close collaborative working relationship between her and Michael's family. Various members of outside agencies were involved in his health, well-being and academic progress. For example, he was monitored very carefully by a physiotherapist for signs of increasing problems with his mobility, and had regular physiotherapy in school time to alleviate as far as possible the development of contractures, that is the shortening of his muscles. A member of the local authority learning support team visited the school regularly to check whether he had appropriate equipment to meet his needs, for example, a laptop with peripherals that enabled him to connect to the computer easily as well as appropriate software to access the primary curriculum.

RESPONDING TO THE NEEDS OF PUPILS WITH SEVERE DIFFICULTIES IN MOTOR MOVEMENT

Individual children with severe motor difficulties:

> may have difficulties affecting some or all of their limbs, limited hand function, fine and gross motor difficulties and sometimes difficulties with speech and language. Most, though not all pupils will have a

medical diagnosis. A diagnosis may have been given at birth, at about the age of two or a later date, though deteriorating conditions such as muscular dystrophy may not be diagnosed until the child attends school. Some children may have physical difficulties as a result of an accident or illness, which can happen at any age. It must be remembered that, in the same way as other children, they may also have learning difficulties, dyslexia, dyspraxia, asthma, epilepsy, vision and hearing difficulties or hidden handicaps affecting their visual/auditory perception or eye/hand co-ordination etc.

(Pickles, 2001, p. 290)

A long-term plan for these pupils would take into account

dignity and emotional needs ... especially in positioning, toileting and transfers ... to enable pupils to be as independent as possible ... recognising that teaching methods may need to vary as needs change is all part of inclusion.

(Pickles, 2001, p. 292).

It would also need to include views of the student as a person, with hopes, expectations and rights, considerations of physical access to the school environment, ways in which the needs of the family and the student's place within it can be taken into account by the school, the role of the support assistant(s) and the kind of relationship that might be established with the student and the family, and any issues this raises and the role and function of information and communications technology and of any other appropriate techno-logical aids. How therapy might fit into the child's curriculum might also be very important. Staff in the school, and peers if appropriate, would need to be made aware of the child's strengths and needs.

LIAISING WITH SUPPORT STAFF

In general terms, one of the ways of approaching how to support students who experience visual, auditory or physical difficulties is to consider how best to liaise with support staff who may be employed to help address these students' learning needs. The Education (Specified Work) (England) Regulations 2012 (http://www. legislation.gov.uk/uksi/2012/762/made, accessed 18.05.15) specify circumstances in which certain kinds of school staff – such as support staff – may carry out 'specified work' relating to teaching and learning. The role of support staff in the classroom is to help the teacher make sure that each student engages positively in class activities and makes progress. Support staff can help to support the development of differentiated curricular approaches to meet the diversity of students' learning needs.

SUMMARY

The greatest challenge for a child with a sensory impairment is communication (Spencer & Marschak, 2010). A child who can see and hear will reach out and explore its surroundings naturally. A child with a sensory impairment will not necessarily do this and may need encouragement to explore and interact with others. For a deaf child, normal progress in language may be hard. Intensive education and support may be needed throughout the child's life. Early intervention in the child's life is clearly very important. A unique communication method may be developed for the child but whatever the means of communication it should enable that child to develop cognitive and other skills, whether it is symbols, objects of reference, sign language, Braille, or something else.

However much is known about a child's sensory of physical difficulties though, as Miller and Ockleford (2005) aptly comment, that child is still an individual with his/her own personal strengths and needs, interests, experiences, background, and so on that, together with his/her own views, must all be taken into account when drawing up any intervention plan.

7

ASSESSMENT AND PLANNING FOR CHILDREN WITH SPECIAL EDUCATIONAL NEEDS

INTRODUCTION

This chapter will open by explaining how some children can be supported to make huge learning gains and, consequently, will feel much more positively about themselves as learners if teachers, parents and others clearly understand the power of some forms of assessment, monitoring and focused feedback. It will continue by discussing the following topics:

- principles of different kinds of assessment of difficulties in learning
  - summative and standardised;
  - on-going formative assessment and constructive feedback to students;
  - criterion referenced assessment.
- ways of assessing behaviour experienced as problematic or challenging, including assessments from a biological and/or medical perspective
- assessment of sensory impairments
- the significance of understanding the barriers to learning from the student's and family's perspective
- framework for planning

- developing, implementing, monitoring and evaluating an individual plan to address different experiences of difficulties at different ages and stages.

THE PLACE OF ASSESSMENT IN SUPPORTING LEARNING AND BEHAVIOUR NEEDS

In education generally, and certainly in the area of special educational needs and disability, there are a number of different frames of reference for conceptualising how a child's learning and behaviour and the difficulties that are experienced should be assessed and, therefore, what the starting point might be for developing appropriate ways to meet that child's learning or behavioural needs. For example, deciding whether a child's need is 'special' by definition means using a form of assessment, often very formal, summative by nature and standardised against national norms, that enables comparison with the learning achievement and behaviour patterns of peers, or norms for sight, hearing, movement and so on. After all, by law, a child[1] has special educational needs if he or she has a learning difficulty[2] which calls for special educational provision to be made for him or her (Education Act, 1996, Part 1V, § 312(1), Education Order (Northern Ireland) 1996, Part 11, § 3(1); (Children and Families Act, 2014, Part 3, § 20 (1)) and the educational provision that is required to meet the needs is 'special'. There are some obvious questions raised by this definition, for example, how to measure 'significantly greater difficulty in learning', how to compare one student to the majority, how to gauge the contexts in which what is already provided is insufficient so that appropriate provision is therefore 'special', and how to ensure that a child whose attainment levels are demonstrated to be very poor in comparison with peers does not feel so demoralised that s/he will not try any more. There is plenty of evidence to indicate that assessment itself can serve to reinforce or undermine the motivation to strive for future achievement in schools (Murphy, 2002).

We do not always wish to compare one child with others, however. It is always important to have a sense of children's on-going progress in learning through on-going continuous formative assessment that can provide teachers and others with opportunities to notice what is happening during learning activities, recognise the level and direction of the learning of individuals and see how they can help to take that learning further.

Sometimes also we need to know whether a child has reached a particular threshold or level in his/her learning. So-called criterion referencing means comparing a child's achievements with clearly stated criteria for learning outcomes and clear descriptors of particular levels of performance within them. Setting out criteria for an assessment not only clarifies what is required of learners but also assists teachers or others in deciding what they need to teach. Criterion referencing can also improve the quality of feedback offered to learners as the descriptors of levels of performance and the overall criteria should be clear enough to serve as indicators of what learners have to do to succeed (Wearmouth, 2009).

Anyone considering assessing a child needs to be fully conversant with test procedures, their aims and rationale as well as wider cultural and social factors, the school, the area of the curriculum concerned, and also attributes of the individual child and above all, of course, what useful information the assessment can give.

FORMAL, NORM-REFERENCED (STANDARDISED) TESTS

Identification of the students who are 'different' and, therefore, who is eligible for special educational provision may depend on the results of norm-referenced assessment that is designed to indicate a learner's achievement in comparison with others. Whatever is assessed here has to be measurable, otherwise it is not possible to compare one child's score with another. For example, it is very common to use norm-referenced tests in the area of reading. One example is the Neale Analysis of Reading Ability (Neale, 1999) which provides normative scores in both reading accuracy and comprehension.

To understand the use and, potentially, misuse, of standardised testing it is important to understand the test standardisation process, as well as a number of important concepts related to standardised tests and test procedures: 'measure of spread' of scores, validity and reliability, the usefulness of standardised scores and interpretations of percentile ranks, confidence bands and reading ages.

THE STANDARDISATION PROCESS

One way to make test scores such as 21 out of 36 more readily understandable and comparable to another test score such as 11 out of 30 would be to convert them to percentages (58 per cent and 37 per cent, to the nearest whole number). However, these percentages on their own do not tell us either the average score of all children taking the same tests and therefore how well or badly children are doing in comparison with peers, or how spread out the scores are. Standardisng a test score involves assessing a large, nationally representative sample using that particular test and then adjusting the mean (average) to a score of 100. It is easy to compare a child's result with this score of 100.

An important concept associated with standardised tests is that of the 'measure of the spread' of scores, the so-called 'standard deviation'. This is usually set to 15 for educational attainment and ability tests. Irrespective of the difficulty of the test, about 68 per cent of students in a national sample will have a standardised score within one standard deviation (15 points) of the average (that is, between 85 and 115) and about 95 per cent will have a standardised score within two standard deviations (30 points) of the average (between 70 and 130). These examples come from a frequency distribution, known as the 'normal distribution', which is shown in Figure 7.1.

VALIDITY AND RELIABILITY

The terms 'validity' and 'reliability' are often used in relation to both formal and informal tests. In general, the 'validity' of a test is the degree to which that test assesses what it is intended to test. We might ask, for example, whether a test of cognitive ability or reading that has been developed and standardised in Britain would be valid for young people from a completely different culture and new to the UK, or how valid is the concept of 'reading age' and whether and/ or how this might relate to adults. We might also ask whether the test tests what we expect it to test in the context in which it is being used, in other words whether a test has 'context validity'.

'Reliability', on the other hand, generally means whether we would obtain the same result on the same test with the same cohort of individuals if we did the test procedure again.

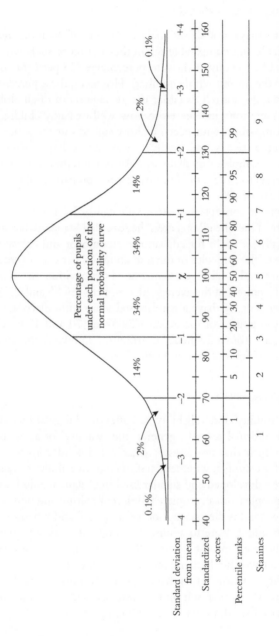

Figure 7.1 The relationship between standardised scores, percentile ranks and stanines under a normal distribution curve (145)

USEFULNESS OF STANDARDISED SCORES

The use of standardised scores is often thought to be useful for a number of reasons. Firstly, it produces a scale that enables a comparison of results so that we can see whether a child is above or below the national average. The date when the test was standardised is important here, however. An old test might well be out of date in terms of comparisons of individuals with national norms. Re-standardisation of an old test might well give different national norms in relation to the current generation of children. Secondly, scores are standardised so that the ages of the children are taken into account. When looking at a child's score on a standardised assessment against national norms, we will be able to tell whether that child is above or below other children of the same age. Thirdly, using standardised scores allows us to compare a child's performance on a test in one area of the curriculum, for example, reading, with another, for example, mathematics. Or we might compare a child's performance in two different aspects of the same area, for example, reading comprehension and reading accuracy, which might be important in assessing whether a child is dyslexic.

PERCENTILE RANKS

There is a constant relationship between percentile ranks and standardised scores when the same average score and standard deviation are used. The percentile rank is the percentage of students in the sample of the same age who gained a score at the same level or below that of the child's score. So performance at the 50th percentile indicates that the child performed as well as, or better than 50 per cent of the sample when age is taken into account.

CONFIDENCE BANDS

'Confidence bands' indicate the range of scores within which the accurate assessment of attainment is likely to fall. It is not possible to obtain the 'true score', that is the hypothetically perfect measurement of the individual's ability. Tests of the sort discussed here measure attainment, that is, the outcome of the student's work at any particular time, not 'ability'. In addition, however carefully educational tests are put together and administered, errors can result from factors such as the child's state of health, tiredness, lack of familiarity with formal assessments, and so on.

THE CONCEPT OF 'READING AGE'

'Reading age' is a very commonly used concept in relation to norm-referenced assessments of literacy learning, for example, in standardised assessments such as the Neale Analysis of Reading Ability (Neale, 1999). Reading age indicates the age at which a given raw score was the average. It is obtained by working out for each age group the average raw score of all of the children in the sample of that age and then smoothing out any irregularities in the resulting graph. Increases in performance with age are smaller for older age groups. This raises issues for using this measurement with older students, because accuracy and rate of reading would show no improvement beyond a certain point.

Reading ages represent snapshots of a progression in literacy development. They are not fixed and exact measures of reading attainment. Reading is a learned behaviour that is closely aligned with development and age. Thus a low reading score does not necessarily suggest general low ability, slow developmental growth, and so on. However, if we use these normative scores while taking into account the confidence bands attributed to the known score we can then view reading ages as estimates of reading ability at the time of testing.

ISSUES ASSOCIATED WITH NORM-REFERENCING

Standardised tests alone are not designed to diagnose the root of difficulties in learning experienced by a learner. Anyone considering assessing a child needs to be fully conversant with test procedures, their aims and rationale as well as wider cultural and social factors, the school, the area of the curriculum concerned, and also attributes of the individual child and above all, of course, what useful information the assessment can give. Additionally there are a number of issues associated with normative assessment, including equity and the link between achievement norms and teacher expectations of particular learners.

Firstly, in relation to the question of equity, some students may be allocated additional resources after achieving only very low scores on norm-referenced tests. However, there is a very grey area around the cut-off point above which other students will receive no additional provision.

Then there is the issue that when an individual student's test score lies within the bottom 'tail' of a normal distribution curve there is often an assumption that the student's innate ability is very low. Using standardised forms of tests means that we can pinpoint those students whose scores fall into the lowest 2 per cent or so. However, poor scores on normative tests can also mean that students' failure to achieve in school is automatically 'blamed' on poor ability, or the family, or the ethnic group. Sometimes this is known as the 'deficit' view of children who experience difficulties. This view can limit teachers' expectations of what to expect of certain students and, therefore, lead to continued poor achievement (Rosenthal & Jacobson, 1968). It also absolves schools from responsibility for that learner's progress in school rather than opening up discussion of how classroom teaching practices and the school curriculum generally can be adapted to suit students' learning and behaviour better. 'Success' and 'failure' on norm-referenced tests are not just the result of children's natural ability, however (Tomlinson, 1988). Some families cannot support their own children adequately as a result of the circumstances in which they find themselves and the way that schools are structured, as much as of a lack of innate ability in the child.

FORMATIVE ASSESSMENT

'There is no evidence that increasing the amount of testing will enhance learning' on its own (Assessment Reform Group, 1999, p. 2). Results from externally imposed summative tests, especially where there are very high stakes attached to these results in countries such as England, can have very negative effects on students (Wearmouth, 2008).

Assessment can be a powerful educational tool for promoting learning but it depends on the kind of assessment that is used, and the manner of its use. A seminal piece of work (Assessment Reform Group, 1999) demonstrated clearly that student achievement, particularly that of lower achievers, can be raised through formative, rather than summative, assessment in the classroom. They found that improving learning through assessment depends on five, 'deceptively simple', factors: providing effective feedback, actively involving students in their own learning, modifying teaching in response to the results of assessment, recognising the influence of assessment on students' motivation and self-esteem and enabling students to assess themselves and understand what they need to do to improve (Assessment Reform Group, 1999, p. 5). The frame of reference for this research includes the view that learners have active agency in learning. They do it for themselves. Assessment that supports learning must therefore involve students so that they have information about how well they are doing to guide subsequent learning in a constructive way that shows them what they need to do, and can do, to make progress.

The shift in emphasis in the purpose of day-to-day assessment in classrooms has resulted in a focus in many places on 'Assessment for Learning' (AfL), that is, on-going day-to-day formative assessment to collect information on what children do or do not understand and the adaptation of teaching in response to this. On-going day-to-day assessments include questioning and discussions with children, observations of children while they are working; holding, analysing children's work and giving quick feedback (http://nationalstrategies. standards.dcsf.gov.uk/node/88910, accessed 14.02.11). Feedback that connects directly to specific and challenging goals related to students' prior knowledge and experience helps those students to focus more productively on new goals and next learning steps (Ministry of Education, 2005, p. 16).

CRITERION-REFERENCING

Criterion-referencing adopts a different frame of reference from norm-referencing. Whereas norm-referenced assessment ranks a learner against all other learners, criterion-referencing compares a learner's performance against identified standards of achievement. The quality of achievement is evaluated by how well the individual learner has performed in relation to specific criteria and standards that illustrate key features of learning, achievement, and quality at different stages of children's development (Dunn *et al.*, 2002). In order to enable teachers to engage in conversations that link back to and promote students' learning outcomes, some schools use authentic examples of students' work that illustrate what these criteria look like. These examples can be used by students and teachers to identify next learning steps. Teachers can compare a student's work sample with the exemplars in order to identify specific strengths and weaknesses, identify individual teaching and learning needs and prioritise new learning goals. By discussing and exemplifying a child's achievement and progress in relation to selected samples of work, parents and caregivers can be better informed about what work at a particular curriculum level looks like and how they too can better support the next learning steps.

ASSESSMENT OF BEHAVIOUR

Students' behaviour in schools does not occur in a vacuum (Watkins & Wagner, 1995, 2000). Students are members of classrooms which function as aspects of the school system within particular neighbourhoods. Students also fulfil roles within their own families and communities. Difficult behaviour which seems to relate to a particular student may be indicative of a range of contextual issues associated with society, the family, ethnic or community group, school, classroom, peer group or teacher, as well as the individual student (Wearmouth *et al.*, 2005).

Interventions designed to improve student behaviour can be centred on the child, on the environment, on the child and the environment or on the interface between the child and their environment. There are a number of ways of conceptualising the interactional relationship between the learning environment and the learner. For example, from an eco-systemic perspective Bronfenbrenner (1979) identifies four levels that influence student outcomes: *microsystem*, the immediate context of the student – school, classroom, home, neighbourhood; *mesosystem*, the links between two microsystems, for example, home–school relationships; *exosystem*, outside demands and influences in adults' lives that affect students; *macrosystem*, cultural beliefs and patterns or government or institutional policies that affect individuals' behaviour, including societal structure and organisation and prevailing value systems.

Ysseldyke and Christenson (1987, 1993) argue that it is important to assess characteristics of the classroom learning environments in which students are placed because that influence learning. They identify a number of instructional factors that can be changed to support more effective learning. They used their analysis of these features in the learning environment to design 'The Instructional Environment Scale' (TIES) as a framework for the systematic collection of data to analyse contextual barriers to students' learning. Data are gathered through classroom observation and interviews with both student and teacher on twelve components of teaching: Instructional presentation, Classroom environment, Teacher expectations, Cognitive emphasis, Motivational strategies, Relevant practice, Academic engaged time, Informed feedback, Adaptive instruction, Progress evaluation, Instructional planning and Student understanding (Ysseldyke & Christenson, 1987, p. 21).

COLLECTING EVIDENCE OF INDIVIDUAL CHILDREN'S BEHAVIOUR

Observing children and young people in the environment of the classroom or school is something that is a part of teachers' everyday practice. It is rare, however, for teachers to have the opportunity to stand back and closely observe the processes, relationships and behaviours involved in teaching and learning. For the purposes of assessment of individual students' behaviour, this process might need to be formalised. If so, it should be systematic and there should be an effective means of recording and interpreting what is seen.

One way to approach this issue is to adopt a problem-solving frame of reference to identify when the challenges presented by an individual student's behaviour require special consideration. In order to develop effective problem solving, Watkins and Wagner (1995, p. 59) pose a number of questions: What specific behaviour is causing concern? In what situations does the behaviour occur/not occur? What, specifically, happens before and after the behaviour (that is, what triggers it and what maintains it?) What skills does the person demonstrate/not demonstrate? What does the person's behaviour mean to him/her? What does the person think of him/herself, and what do others think? Who is most affected by this behaviour? The last question often turns attention from the behaviour causing concern to the way the concern is being handled by others.

Bell (1999) points out that, while direct observation of young people's behaviour is not an easy option – it requires careful organisation and practice – nonetheless it can reveal characteristics of the behaviour of groups or individuals which would have been impossible to discover by other means. Direct observation can be particularly useful to find out whether people do what they say they do, or behave in the way they claim to behave, or that other people claim they behave.

As Fisher *et al.* (2004) comment, there are a number of different formats that can be adopted. The first step is to make decisions about exactly *what* will be the focus of the observation: people, activities or events, or a combination of these. It might be important to observe an individual, a group, or a whole class in particular lessons or playground activities. If the problem-solving approach recommended by Watkins and Wagner (1995) is adopted, observations may take place in specific, pre-selected lessons or locations where individual students' behaviour has been identified as particularly problematic. Then, as Fisher *et al.* (2004) go on to note, there is a question about the time frames to be used: whether to sample what goes on during short pre-determined time periods or whether an individual student will be 'shadowed' for a longer period of time. The answers to these questions will, to a large extent, be dictated by the kinds of concerns raised in relation to the behaviour of individual students, the kinds of reflection that have already taken place in relation to the evidence already collected, and the extent to which an audit of the learning environment such as that framed by Ysseldyke and Christenson (above) has already formed part of the collection of evidence.

When conducting observations, it is usually more helpful to make notes at the time, even if systematic time sampling or event recording procedures are being implemented. These notes might be open-ended, where general points of interest are recorded, or can be focused on targeted events as and when they happen. A useful format is to write down what happened, and then to add a brief comment or interpretation later. If the observer is looking for particular events or behaviours which can be easily categorised, s/he could devise an 'observation schedule'. Systematic observation procedures might involve the construction of a grid in which instances of specified learner, peer and adult behaviours can be recorded as they occur.

FUNCTIONAL ASSESSMENT OF INDIVIDUAL BEHAVIOUR

One of the questions posed by Watkins and Wagner above relates to the gain for the individual (that is, the function that is served) by behaving in a particular way. Functional analysis can be seen as an experimental approach to behavioural assessment in which variables hypothesised to precede or to maintain the target behaviour are systematically examined in order to isolate their individual effects (Moore, 2004). Functional assessment therefore aims to discover the antecedents, setting events and consequences that cause or maintain challenging behaviours. The analysis can then be used as a means for identifying the functional relationships between particular behaviours and specific antecedent or consequent events.

One practical approach currently used in parts of the UK as well as in other areas of the world is that of 'Multi-Element Planning'. This takes account of a range of potential causes of the problems experienced by the child and factors that appear to maintain the problematic behaviour. It then focuses on strategies related to improving the learning environment and/or teaching skills that will prevent the recurrence of the problematic behaviour or provide a way of safeguarding the child, peers and staff when the behaviour does recur.

Multi-Element Planning as described by LaVigna and Donnellan (1986) has four main components. Firstly the learning environment is examined to see whether there are mismatches between the child and his/her environment (Pitchford, 2004, p. 323). Change strategies should be considered in relation to a number of contexts: interpersonal, physical and instructional. There is a deliberate attempt to teach children skills that will have a positive impact on their lives: academic or life skills that the child has not mastered; functionally equivalent skills, that is, socially acceptable skills or behaviour that will serve the same purpose for the student as that which is seen as unacceptable; coping skills designed to help students manage the difficulties in their lives, and preventative strategies. These include removing those events that act as a direct trigger to problem behaviours (Glynn, 1982). Three ways of rewarding children (LaVigna & Donnellan, 1986) are acknowledged as being effective: rewarding children for being 'good', for not being 'naughty' and for being 'naughty' less often than they were before. Reactive strategies are also included in the plan to safeguard the child, peers and/or staff when things go wrong. It is also important to consider what kind of practical and emotional help or support members of staff should be offered (Pitchford, 2004).

Three practical steps need to be taken before drawing up the plan. First should be an identification of the frequency, seriousness and the contexts in which the behavioural problems occur. Next, the problems should be prioritised. Lastly, baseline data should be collected against which progress can be assessed. All data collected should be used to support the setting of targets for the MEP, reviewing progress and establishing appropriate criteria for rewards.

The issue of ethics is a very important consideration in multi-element planning. Where teachers deliberately set out to change students' behaviour then there is always a question of how that teacher's power is exercised, what behaviour is seen as preferable and why, and in whose interest it is that the behaviour should be changed.

BIOLOGICAL AND MEDICAL ASSESSMENTS OF BEHAVIOUR

Biological and medical explanations of behaviour theorise problems as emanating from within the individuals themselves. Difficult or challenging behaviour, from a medical perspective, is the result of an underlying condition, disease or dysfunction which an individual has and which requires treatment. A behaviour problem is seen as an inherent characteristic of an individual. However, because behaviour is also located within a social context, establishing the existence of a condition or disease of 'difficult behaviour' or 'emotional disorder' as relating to the individual alone and not to the context in which it occurs is fraught with problems.

Two biologically and medically based understandings of behaviour are Attention Deficit/Hyperactivity Disorder (AD/HD) and autism.

Attention Deficit/Hyperactivity Disorder (AD/HD)

As Norwich *et al.* (2002) note, there are differences in the reported incidence of AD/HD internationally. In particular regions of the USA up to 9 per cent of children were identified as having AD/HD, whilst only 0.007 per cent were identified in the UK. In Britain and Europe, the tradition has been 'to use the diagnostic systems of the International Classification of Diseases (ICD) published by the World Health Organisation' (1992, p. 13) and to assume a 'hyperkinetic disorder'. There is a strict requirement for 'pervasiveness and persistence'. This means that behaviour which is seen largely in one context only does not constitute grounds for a diagnosis. The criteria for diagnosis in the ICD-10 manual, for example, are that the child should have demonstrated abnormality of attention and activity at home and at school or nursery, for the age and developmental level of the child. The 'directly observed abnormalities of attention or activity' must be 'excessive for the child's age and developmental level'. The child should 'not meet criteria for pervasive development disorder, mania, depressive or anxiety' the difficulties should have begun 'before the age of 6 years' should last 'at least 6 months'. The child should have a measured 'IQ above 50' (World Health Organisation, 1992).

While checklists of behaviour are an expedient way to classify adult perception of students' behaviour, behaviour assessment which is intended to lead to intervention in the context of a student's education needs to take account of a comprehensive range of factors that influence the student's behaviour in the context of school. Defining AD/HD as a mental disorder is problematic. The British Psychological Society (1996, p. 23) comments that 'The pattern of AD/HD-type behaviour might be maladaptive to environmental requirements, but it is not necessarily the result of psychological dysfunction.'

Assessment of autism

Autism is also a medical explanation of individual behaviour. 80 per cent of children with autism score below 70 on norm-referenced intelligence tests (Roth, 2002) and increasingly severe general learning difficulties are correlated with an increasing occurrence of autism (Jordan, 1999). Sheehy (2004), therefore, notes difficulty in separating out the effects of autism from those of profound difficulties in learning.

As Klin *et al.* (2000, p. 163) comment, 'There are no biological markers in the identification of autism, despite advances in neuroscience.' Hence a profile of symptoms and characteristics of autistic behaviour with agreed diagnostic criteria is used to identify autism in young people. The *International Statistical Classification of Diseases – ICD-10* (World Health Organization, 1992) is commonly used in Europe.

In the ICD-10 (World Health Organisation, 1992, F84.0), autism is described as a disorder that is 'pervasive' and 'developmental', and that is identified through 'abnormal and/or impaired development' that is evident before 3 years of age and by particular 'abnormal functioning' in social interaction, communication, and 'restricted, repetitive behaviour'. Boys are affected three to four times more often than girls. Impairments 'in reciprocal social interaction' which manifest as 'an inadequate appreciation of socio-emotional cues' are always present. Impairments in communications include a 'lack of social usage of whatever language skills are present', as well as poorly developed 'make-believe and social imitative play'. During conversations, the ability to synchronise personal responses to the utterances of others is impaired as well as the ability to respond with feeling to other people's overtures. Autism is also said to be characterised by 'restricted, repetitive, and stereotyped patterns of behaviour, interests, and activities' that are demonstrated by 'a tendency to impose rigidity and routine on a wide range of aspects of day-to-day functioning'.

Another diagnostic tool, the Autism Diagnostic Interview-Revised (ADI-R) (Le Couteur *et al.*, 2003; Rutter *et al.*, 2003), is a semi-structured interview used to assess behaviours related to autism or Autistic Spectrum Disorders. This tool is based on both the ICD-10 criteria for autism and pervasive developmental disorders and the American Psychiatric Association's *Diagnostic and Statistical Manual of Mental Disorders* (DSM-IV) (1994), which lists criteria for autism which are similar to those in the ICD-10. The ADI-R contains questions about children's early development, communication, social interaction, and patterns of behaviours. The ADI-R yields scores for current behaviours and history. A classification of autism is given when scores in all three domains of communication, social interaction, and patterns of behaviour meet or exceed the specified threshold scores, and also when behaviour patterns characteristic of autism are evident by the age of 3. Recently the DSM-5 has been introduced in the USA. A number of changes from DSM-1V have been made to the diagnostic framework:

- when people are diagnosed in future, instead of receiving a diagnosis of either 'autistic disorder', 'Asperger's disorder', 'childhood disintegrative disorder' or 'pervasive developmental disorder not otherwise specified' they will be given a diagnosis of 'autism spectrum disorder (ASD)'.
- the previous use of three areas of impairment has been reduced to two main areas:
  - social communication and interaction;
  - restricted, repetitive patterns of behaviour, interests, or activities. Sensory behaviours are included here for the first time.
- The emphasis during diagnosis will move from naming the condition to identifying needs.

Although the DSM is very influential, the main set of criteria used in the UK is the World Health Organisation's International Classification of Diseases (ICD).

ASSESSMENT OF VISUAL IMPAIRMENT

Visual Impairment (VI) is a general term that indicates a continuum of sight loss (Mason *et al.*, 1997). Total blindness is extremely rare.

A standard eye chart is used to test visual acuity. One eye is covered at a time and the vision of each eye is recorded separately, as well as both eyes together. The most common chart is the Snellen eye chart, originally devised by a Dutch Ophthalmologist, Dr. Hermann Snellen, in 1862. This chart has a series of letters or letters and numbers, with the largest at the top. As the person being tested reads down the chart, the letters gradually become smaller. Many other versions of this chart are used for people who cannot read the alphabet.

In the Snellen fraction 20/20, the top number represents the test distance, 20 feet. The lower number represents the distance that the average eye can see the letters on a particular line of the eye chart.

So, 20/20 means that the eye being tested can read a certain size letter when it is 20 feet away. If a person sees 20/40, at 20 feet from the chart s/he can read letters that a person with 20/20 vision could read from 40 feet away. Originally Snellen worked in feet but later (in 1875) he changed from using feet to metres (from 20/20 to 6/6 respectively). Currently, the 20-foot distance continues to be used in the United States, but 6 metres is used in Britain.

Although the Snellen fractions are measures of sharpness of sight in relation to identifying letters or symbols with high contrast at a specified distance, they tell us nothing about the quality of vision in general, for example, the ability to see larger objects and objects with poor contrast – or, indeed, whether vision is more or less efficient when using both eyes together (Strouse Watt, 2003).

A clinical assessment of vision usually focuses on four aspects: distance, near, field and colour vision (Mason, 2001). However, this clinical assessment identifies only what a child can or cannot see. Pupils with the same eye condition may have very different strengths and needs from each other as people. Children and young people with VI are individuals with different interests, background experiences and so on, as well as differing degrees of useful vision (Miller & Ockleford, 2005). As in other areas of special educational needs in schools, a whole range of information is needed to ensure that support for an individual is appropriate (Miller & Ockleford, 2005). This includes the views of the child and the parents/family, medical and school records as well as the clinical assessment of vision made by an ophthalmologist or other clinician.

Sight loss of any kind affects a child's ability to carry out tasks that are based on vision. Most classroom tasks depend on vision, so it is very clear that VI can have a significant impact upon learning. The kind of support that is available to visually impaired children is therefore very important.

Many people who are classed as blind have some 'functional' vision. Where a distinction is necessary for any reason, the term blind is used to refer to pupils who rely on tactile methods in their learning, for example, Braille or Tactile diagrams, and the term low vision is used with reference to children and young people who are taught through methods which rely on sight (Mason *et al.*, 1997). It is important for teachers and parents to work with the child to teach the child how to make best use of this functional vision (Davis, 2003).

AUDITORY IMPAIRMENT

A decibel (dB) is a measure of sound pressure level. Normal voice measures 60 dB at a distance of one metre, a raised voice 70 dB at one metre, and shouting 80 dB at one metre. The severity of a hearing impairment is measured in decibels of hearing loss and is ranked according to the additional intensity above a nominal threshold that a sound must be before being detected by an individual. In schools or colleges, for educational purposes, young people with hearing impairments will probably require hearing aids, adaptations to their environment and/or particular teaching strategies in order to access the curriculum.

ASSESSMENT OF HEARING

There is a variety of tests that can be used to find out how much hearing a child has. The tests used will depend on the child's age and stage of development. It is possible to test the hearing of all children from birth onwards. Screening tests are normally done first to see if it is likely that there is a hearing loss and the child needs to be referred to an audiologist. The audiologist will then perform more detailed tests to build up an accurate picture of the child's hearing.

> Since 2006, babies have been screened to test their hearing within a few days of their birth. Babies 'begin to develop language and communication from their earliest months', so early screening means that 'much can be done to positively support and encourage that development ... when early identification of deafness is combined with effective early intervention, with parents and professionals working together, language outcomes for deaf children can be similar to those for hearing children.
>
> (NDCS, 2010, p. 6)

For children of school age, hearing is usually measured with behavioural tests using pure tones. The sounds come through headphones and each time a child hears a sound they respond by moving an object, pressing a button or saying 'yes'.

Quantification of hearing loss

Hearing sensitivity varies according to the frequency of sounds. To take this into account, hearing sensitivity can be measured for a range of frequencies and plotted on an audiogram. Hearing sensitivity is indicated by the quietest sound that an animal can detect, called the hearing threshold, in other words, the quietest sound to which the person responds. The test is carried out for sounds of different frequencies.

In humans, the term hearing impairment is usually reserved for people who have relative insensitivity to sound in the speech frequencies. The severity of a hearing loss is categorised according to the increase in volume that must be made above the usual level before the listener can detect it. In profound deafness, even the loudest sounds that can be produced by an audiometer (an instrument used to measure hearing) may not be detected. Normal hearing thresholds within any given species are not the same for all frequencies. If different frequencies of sound are played at the same amplitude, some will be perceived as loud, and others quiet or even completely inaudible.

Four categories of hearing impairment are generally used: mild, moderate, severe and profound. As noted by NHS Choices (2015) (www.nhs.uk, accesssed 18.05.15):

- with 'mild deafness: 20–40 dB' a child could hear a baby crying but may be unable to hear whispered conversation. Mild deafness can sometimes make hearing speech difficult, particularly in noisy situations.
- with 'moderate deafness: 41–70 dB', a child could hear a dog barking but not a baby crying. A young person may have difficulty following speech without using a hearing aid.
- with 'severe deafness: 71–90 dB', a child would hear drums being played but not a dog barking. S/he would usually need to lip-read or use sign language, even with the use of a hearing aid.
- with 'profound deafness: >90 dB', a child might hear a large lorry but not drums being played. People who are profoundly deaf can often benefit from a cochlear implant. Other forms of communication include lip-reading and sign language.

Deaf children with the same level of deafness may experience sounds differently. About 20 per cent of primary age children suffer from conductive hearing loss caused by middle-ear problems; this reduces to 2 per cent by secondary age. As noted in Chapter 6, in some places there is a serious difference of opinion between those who believe that deaf children can be taught to speak using auditory-oral approaches, that is, assisted by hearing aids, cochlear implants, radio aids, and so on, and be integrated into mainstream society, and those who believe they should be taught through sign language. What suits the child best may depend on the degree of hearing loss, the extent of the delay in language acquisition and, of course, what the child him/herself and the family feel about his/her situation.

TAKING STUDENTS' VIEWS INTO ACCOUNT

As discussed in Chapter 1, we can look at students' learning in a number of ways. If we assume that students are active agents in their own learning we have to try to understand how they feel about difficulties in learning, behaviour, motor skills or in any other area in which they experience difficulties and what they know will support them most effectively. Otherwise there is a serious question about how we can know what will best fit what they need. This does not mean, of course, that we have to provide everything a student asks for in a school.

The assessment of students' perceptions of, and feelings about, their own behaviour depends on very finely tuned listening skills as well as suspension of judgemental responses on the part of professionals. In terms of practice it is important to recognise that 'children will make decisions about people they can talk to and trust, and those they cannot' (Gersch, 1995, p. 48).

Some pupils, of course, find it much more difficult to communicate than others. Difficulties in accessing information, communication, sensory impairment, mobility and relationship-building might make meaningful discussion with some young people problematic. For example, the communication of students with profound and multiple learning disabilities and involving reflexes, actions, sounds and facial expression needs to be carefully observed and interpreted by the various people who know those pupils the best (Porter et al., 2001). Preece (2002), working with autistic children, discusses how inflexible thought processes, lack of personal insight and dislike of change inhibit some children from participating in meaningful discussion of their ideas. For those young people who cannot express themselves verbally, but for whom pictures and symbols are meaningful and who can understand what is going on, a variety of powerful and useful tools have been developed to attempt to elicit their views. These include the use of cue cards (Lewis, 2002, p. 114) that can act 'as prompts for ideas about ... people, talk, setting (indoor/outdoor variants), feelings and consequences about the particular event under discussion ... that can convey meaning in a neutral way'. In a similar way, 'Talking Mats' (Cameron & Murphy, 2002) can enable children who experience difficulties in verbal expression to express their views by moving symbols about on mats.

ENGAGING WITH PARENTS' OR CARERS' PERSPECTIVES

In a number of different countries across the world there is a formal acceptance that parents and carers have the right to know about decisions taken in schools in relation to their children, and that they themselves are, potentially, an important source of additional support in addressing difficulties in learning and/or behaviour experienced by young people. The right of parents and/or carers to be consulted at every stage of decision-making about their children is enshrined in law across the UK (Special Educational Needs and Disability (Northern Ireland) Order, 2005; Children and Families Act, 2014 in England; 1996 Education Act, Part 1V in Wales; Education (Additional Support for Learning) (Scotland) Acts, 2004 and 2009). A number of guides for parents and carers have also been issued to support families to understand their entitlements, for example, *The Parents' Guide to Additional Support for Learning* (Enquire, 2014), which is funded by the Scottish government, and the *Special Educational Needs and Disability (SEND): A Guide for Parents and Carers* (DfE, 2014), published in England.

However, entitlement in law is not always synonymous with experience in practice. Schools have a lot of power to affect the lives of children and their families and carers through the kind of consultation arrangements, assessment and provision that they make. Embedded within the particular discourses, approaches and strategies of schools are a variety of preconceptions about the ability and right of parents, families and/or communities, from a diversity of backgrounds and cultures, to support the learning and development of their children.

The (2009) Lamb Enquiry into special educational and parental confidence in the system concluded that 'Failure to comply with statutory obligations speaks of an underlying culture where parents and carers of children with SEN can too readily be seen as the problem and as a result parents lose confidence in schools and professionals.' Lamb went on to say: 'As the system stands it often creates 'warrior parents' at odds with the school and feeling they have to fight for what should be their children's by right; conflict in place of trust' (Lamb, 2009, 1.1).

The recommendations in this report suggested a new framework for the provision of SEN and disability information that 'puts the relationship between parent and school back at the heart of the process' and 'trades adherence to a "laundry list" of rules for clear principles to guide that relationship' (Lamb, 2009, 1.4). Clearly these recommendations informed the terms of the Children and Families Act (2014) in England.

PLANNING TO MEET PUPILS' SPECIAL EDUCATIONAL NEEDS AND DISABILITIES

In order to maintain coherence and an inclusive approach, planning a curriculum to meet particular special learning needs of individual students should take place within the context of the same decision-making processes that relate to teaching and learning for all students in a school. In addition, planning to address individuals' learning needs effectively deliberately working from strengths and interests with due account taken of any formal and informal individual assessment of student learning that has taken place. This should address any statutory requirements. Students' views of themselves 'as able to learn (or not!) make for potent interactions for good or ill' (Wearmouth, 2009). When planning for students who experience difficulties in learning, we first need to know whether the student or group can, with appropriate access strategies and teaching styles, work on the same learning objectives as the rest of the class. Getting this right will depend on accurate assessment of what the student knows, understands and can do. For some students with communication and interaction needs, for students with sensory or physical impairment, for many dyslexic students and for students with behavioural, emotional and social needs it is highly likely that what is needed is adaptations to teaching styles and the use of access strategies, rather than different learning objectives.

If a student cannot work on the same objectives as the class as a whole the teacher might want to choose learning objectives that are linked to the topic on which the whole class is working, but earlier in a learning progression. Usually it will be appropriate for them to work on objectives that are similar and related to the whole class topic. However, at other times teachers will also have to consider whether individuals have other priority needs that are central to their learning, for example, a need to concentrate on some key skills such as communication, problem solving, working with others, managing their own emotions and so on.

Some students may have additional therapeutic or other needs that cannot easily be met through class activities. For these students alternative objectives may be needed to meet specific needs for identified periods of time. For example, a student might be withdrawn for a time-limited number of weeks to take part in group work to develop social, emotional and behavioural skills, or for a one-to-one literacy intervention programme. Such alternative activities are legitimate as long as they are in the context of ensuring that, over time, all students receive a broad and balanced curriculum.

Curriculum planning for any learner or group needs to incorporate an overall long-term plan based on a global view of the learner and an awareness of the context within which the plan must take effect. A longer term vision of a range of possibilities for a learner that can be shared between the learner, the parent/carer and the professionals is important to give a sense of direction to the whole planning process. From this long-term plan it is possible to draw up medium- and short-term plans.

MAKING EFFECTIVE USE OF INDIVIDUAL PLANS

The term 'Individual Education Plan' (IEP) follows the American model outlined in the 1975 special education law in the USA (Public Law 94–142), where a plan for a child perceived as having difficulties had to be drawn up in order to attract federal funds (Wearmouth,

2000). In the countries across the UK and a number of other countries also, for example, New Zealand, the individual education and/or learning plan, in some form or another, has become a major tool for planning programmes of study for individual students (NAW, 2004; DENI, 1998; Ministry of Education, 1998; Scottish Government, 2010; DfE, 2014). The Code in Scotland (Scottish Government, 2010, p. 208), for example, describes an 'Individualised Educational Programme' (IEP) as a 'written document which outlines the steps to be taken to help children and young people who require additional support needs to achieve specified learning outcomes'. Although the details, and the title of the document, may vary slightly from one country to another, overall these records are expected to contain information about the nature of the child/ young person's learning difficulties, the special educational provision to be made and strategies to be used, specific programmes, activities, materials, and/or equipment, targets to be achieved in a specified time, monitoring and assessment arrangements and review arrangements and date.

Complying with the procedures relating to individual plans can be very time-intensive. It is important therefore for schools to develop ways of working that keep this pressure to a minimum whilst developing systems for ensuring that the learning programme is carried out, monitored and evaluated.

TARGET SETTING

Individual plans, profiles or records can only be as effective as the rigour of the thinking underlying their design. Similar issues arise in relation to target setting for individual plans, programmes and profiles to those relating to target setting within the national context. The strength of targets may be that they provide a focus for the combined efforts of all those concerned to support a learner's progress and highlight the need to link planning and provision. However, some areas lend themselves to this approach more easily than others, but there are specific areas of the curriculum where it may be problematic to conceptualise measurable targets. These areas involve, for example, behaviour, the emotions and creativity.

Setting measurable targets is closely associated with behavioural approaches. A school and a national curriculum can be seen as a ladder of progression which children are expected to climb, with specific assessment learning goals at each rung. An inherent difficulty in this view, however, is that not all children learn the same way, so setting targets which follow in a similar sequence for all students is not necessarily appropriate. Dockrell and McShane (1993) highlight problems associated with this approach and note that there may be a number of ways in which a child can acquire mastery, rather than a single hierarchy that is common to all children. There is a possibility that too much reliance on task components can lead to rigid and prescriptive teaching which takes no account of what the individual learner brings to any particular task or the specific strategies that the individual child uses (1993).

STATUTORY ASSESSMENT OF INDIVIDUAL NEEDS

Chapter 2 (pp. 76–8) describes the process of identifying and assessing needs that are particularly severe to the extent that they require special provision that is mandatory.

PLANNING FOR DIFFERENTIATION

Differentiation of lesson activities, tasks and resources needs to take account of the full range of learning needs among children in the classroom and any requirements on individual education plans. This includes current reading levels, consideration of possible visual and auditory difficulties, interest level of the poems that are used, considerations of student grouping in the classroom, prior experiences of students, the potential range of applications of ICT that might support learning, and so on. Resources include the human as well as the material. In a primary classroom, discussion and preparation with teaching assistants and any other adults prior to the sequence of lessons is vital. If we focus on the needs of those pupils who experience difficulties in language and cognition, it might seem sensible to use Bruner's three modes of representation, enactive, iconic and symbolic, as a general framework for curriculum differentiation. Some students still need to learn by doing and require concrete objects to work with; others need recognisable representations of reality in the form of, for example, pictures; others still can benefit from using symbolic representations and abstract reasoning. This offers a clear justification for stating that good use of practical resources can make lessons interactive and motivational for children.

SUMMARY

Assessment should be viewed as a tool that supports learning and not simply as a politically expedient solution to perceived concerns about standards and ways to make schools accountable to parents, families and society as a whole (Assessment Reform Group, 1999). A constructive and positive approach to assessment begins with an evaluation of the learning environment and considerations of how to modify it to enhance behaviour and learning. The approach then continues if necessary with a greater focus on understanding the individual student as behaving 'normally' and actively engaged in making sense of the situation in which s/he finds him/herself. Such an approach is more likely to empower students to take an active part in the management of their own behaviour.

The awareness of learning and ability of learners to direct it for themselves is of increasing importance in the context of encouraging lifelong learning. Assessment can therefore serve to either reinforce or undermine the motivation to strive for future achievement. Particular forms of assessment may assist, or alternatively may damage, students' sense of their own ability to learn and achieve well in comparison with their peers. Assessment therefore must aim to build on students' experiences and identities and not marginalise or destroy them (Wearmouth, 2009). Assessment that is on-going, continuous and formative and provides teachers with formal and informal opportunities to notice what is happening during learning activities, recognise where the learning of individuals and groups of students is going and how they as the teacher can help take that learning further is likely to lead to positive learning gains (Assessment Reform Group, 1999). This process begins by ensuring students receive appropriate learning goals and are engaged in interactive conversations throughout their learning activities.

NOTES

1   Child or young person in England.
2   Or disability in England.

8

THE WIDER CHILDREN'S WORKFORCE ASSOCIATED WITH SPECIAL EDUCATIONAL NEEDS PROVISION

INTRODUCTION

The probability that a student and his or her family will be involved with other agencies in addition to the school often depends on the complexity and severity of the difficulty, with more complex and severe difficulties (as well as some medical conditions associated with learning problems) generally being identified before school age. The difficulties experienced by particular students vary and it may be impossible for families or schools to sort out the complex interaction of factors which produce or result in a learning difficulty without the involvement of others. For teachers, parents and families, knowing when and how to interact with the vast array of professionals, inside and outside the school, who may become involved with a particular child is very important to the student's welfare and progress, albeit confusing and time-consuming on occasions. This chapter will first outline the range of people who might be expected to have an interest in supporting children who experience some sort of difficulty, and their likely roles: the special educational needs co-ordinator, teaching assistants, parents and families, outside agencies, and so on.

It will go on to discuss challenges in relation to this kind of partnership work – with examples of what can happen in practice.

This discussion will include issues of planning as well as what might be considered examples of good practice.

IN-CLASS SUPPORT ARRANGEMENTS

The use of support staff in the classroom to assist students who experience some kind of difficulty in learning or physical disability is common practice in many schools these days. The 'core' team in the classroom is usually the class teacher and one or more teaching assistants (TAs) who, overwhelmingly, tend to be female. The responsibility for student–adult interactions in classrooms, together with oversight of support staff's work with individual students, legally belongs to teachers. TAs, for example, cannot, legally, be in loco parentis (in the place of a parent) in the same way as a teacher can. Funding in-class support is an expensive option for schools. It was always inevitable, therefore, that the effectiveness of this kind of provision would come under great scrutiny as demands for accountability in education have grown.

Teaching assistants (TAs) and other support staff – 'paraprofessionals' – are part of a large workforce in schools. The rapid expansion in numbers of TAs has shifted the focus of TAs' work from simply preparing resources, general assistance, clearing up, student welfare, and so on, to duties much more clearly focused on student learning and achievement (Wearmouth, 2009). A second adult in the classroom can, as Lorenz (1998) comments, increase the child/adult ratio, make time to listen to students and their point of view and thus increase the amount of positive attention available to students. S/he can also be responsible for giving regular praise and encouragement to particular students while the class teacher takes responsibility for the learning programme, intervene early where misbehaviour is developing and nip problems in the bud, and give individual children space to calm down without disrupting the class. New TA roles have been introduced, for example, 'learning mentors' in some schools.

Most schools employ assistants in classrooms but their roles vary. They may, or may not, have some formal training. Infant and primary teachers may well also have the help of a Nursery Nurse, who may be trained in language and number skills and in social and moral education, or a qualified classroom assistant, at least for some of the time. Special Support Assistants/ Special Attachment Welfare Assistants/Special Individual Teachers may be employed in some schools to support children on Statements of SEN or Education, Health and Care Plans arising from the relevant Special Needs Code of Practice. SITs are trained teachers allocated to individual children. Special Teacher Assistants are trained to work alongside teachers in classrooms, focusing on key curriculum areas such as mathematics and English. In some schools, individual governors are assigned to different classes and make visits to familiarise themselves with classroom life and routines. In many schools, parents come in to assist teachers in classrooms. Schools should have clear policies for parental involvement and may have a teacher with responsibility for partnership with parents.

EFFECTIVE USE OF SUPPORT STAFF IN CLASSROOMS

Ideally partnerships between teachers and support staff should be built on a foundation of mutual respect and trust and a common understanding of how to address the difficulties in learning that some students might face. Having said this, positive relationships are not created automatically. They often develop out of accommodations made by all parties as they negotiate their ways of working and establish their working relationships. The potential for clashes inherent in a situation where, traditionally and conventionally, one professional has been seen to be in control by him/herself is clear. If the adults are not in close agreement, or do not get on, students will play one off against another. Students often have a strong sense of where power and control lies in the classroom and of fairness.

Cremin *et al.* (2003) comment that having teaching assistants in a classroom does not necessarily lead to improved learning and behaviour for students. Balshaw's (1991) description of LSAs, for example, as potentially being 'overgrown students', 'piggy in the middle', 'spies in the classroom' or 'dogsbodies' illustrates how things can go seriously wrong and an implied lack of respect that is unhealthy for everyone. Situations where LSAs are treated like children are likely to result in low status for those LSAs among the students. LSAs can find themselves in a 'go-between' role if the teacher assumes that responsibility for the learning and behaviour of particular students lies with them. For example, where work expected of the student is far too difficult, easy or otherwise inappropriate, and there is no direct communication or discussion between student and teacher, the LSAs may find themselves shuttling to and fro, overburdened with messages and tasks and unsupported. Either students or teachers can feel themselves spied upon if there is little trust in classroom relationships, or where the LSAs cannot maintain an appropriate sense of balance in their responsibilities to teachers and individual students. A report (Blatchford *et al.*, 2009) indicated that, for classroom assistants to be effective, teachers need training to manage support staff in their lessons, and assistants need training for their pedagogical roles.

The Ofsted review team (2010) found that when a child was identified as having special educational needs of a serious nature this usually led to the allocation of further additional resources from within and outside the school, but that the additional provision was often making up for poor whole-class teaching or pastoral support. Even for students identified as having the most severe degree of need during the process of statutory assessment, the statutory provision that was made as a result often did not meet their needs effectively and did not lead to significantly better outcomes for the child or young person, either because it was not appropriate or not of good quality or both.

Effective use of staff and their skills can often depend on how the team is organised. Cremin *et al.* (2003) describe 'room management', an approach that emphasises the need for clarity of roles among adults; roles that are defined by looking first at the roles that teachers usually carry out on their own and then determining which of these it is appropriate for others to perform. They also discuss 'zoning', that is, dividing the classroom into learning zones where the teacher takes responsibility for the learning and activities of students in one zone, and the TA for the rest. A systematic literature review (Alborz *et al.*, 2009) concluded that TAs can help pupils with literature and language problems to make significant learning gains but that they need to be trained and supported to do so. 'Sensitive' TA support can facilitate pupil engagement in learning and social activities with teacher and peers, but these TAs need to be skilled at encouraging interaction and aware when pupils need to undertake self-directed actions. TAs can also promote social and emotional adjustment but they are less successful in therapeutic tasks for children with emotional and behavioural problems. For teachers, use of TAs can allow them to engage pupils in more creative and practical activities and class-related workload can be reduced, but management workload can be increased.

ISSUES IN INTER-AGENCY COLLABORATION

The concept of 'special educational needs' covers a wide area that may go well beyond school and the conventional realm of 'education' into, sometimes, health and welfare. In the past it has often been quite difficult for schools to work closely with outside agencies to protect the welfare of individual students seen by teachers as at risk of injury or abuse. In terms of child welfare, there is a long history of problems in inter-agency work in, for example, the exchange of information between agencies and of disputes over responsibility for offering particular services, sometimes with duplication of interventions by different agencies working on the same case (Roaf & Lloyd, 1995). The three primary care agencies, Education, Health and Social Services, have tended to operate to different legislative frameworks with different priorities and definitions of what constitutes a need. Lack of clear structure to determine responsibilities in inter-agency working could also generate considerable tension, especially when resources were under pressure. The loser has been the client and his or her parents or carer. Roaf and Lloyd (1995) quote the frustration of one young person's parents.

> He was offending while truanting from school. ... In the end we felt like tennis balls because Education said it was a social problem and Social Services said it was an education problem, and we were just going backwards and forwards from one to another.
>
> (Roaf & Lloyd, 1995, in Wearmouth, 2000, p. 192)

Ofsted inspectors (2010) found poor evaluation by a wide range of public agencies of the quality of the additional support provided for children and young people. Too often, the agencies focused simply on whether a service was or was not being provided rather than whether it was effective. In particular, it was not enough for pupils to have a statement of special educational needs. The statement itself did not mean that their current needs were being met, but merely that they were likely to receive the service prescribed by their original statement.

System failures is illustrated, most notably, in recent years, in the case of the tragic death of Victoria Climbié, a child known to be at risk by both educational and social services. In 2003, alongside the formal response to the report into the death, the Government published a Green Paper, *Every Child Matters*, followed by the Children Act (2004), which gave legal force to five interdependent outcomes (DfES, 2004). The clear failure in the system re-stated the need for closer co-operation between agencies which exist to support children in difficulties and their families or carers. The 'Every Child Matters' (ECM) agenda has sought to resolve these difficulties by unifying the range of children's services. All local education authorities combined with other services to become local authorities (LAs). One important implication for all teachers, particularly classroom teachers, is to listen carefully to what students say and how they behave, and work closely with, and under the guidance of, the teacher(s) designated to oversee the safety and well-being of the students in the school.

As part of this agenda a Common Assessment Framework (CAF) for use across the children's workforce has been developed to provide a shared framework for enabling decisions 'about how best to meet [children's] needs, in terms of both what the family can do and also what services could be provided (CWDC, 2009, para. 1.11). As a result of the common assessment discussion, concerns about the child might be resolved, or particular actions for the professional undertaking the CAF and his/her service might be agreed with a date for review and monitoring progress. Alternatively, actions might be identified for other agencies. This involves sharing the assessment with these agencies, subject to the appropriate consent of the child or young person/family, and forming a team around the child (TAC) to support the child or young person. The actions needed would be agreed with the other agencies and a plan and responsibilities for delivering the actions recorded on the CAF form (CWDC, 2009).

Clearly, in the attempt to ensure the 'joined-up thinking' that is required by the 2004 Children Act and the ECM agenda in schools there is a potential overlap between assessment associated with provision for special educational needs and that carried out for the CAF. However, the CAF is not intended to replace other statutory assessments, but to complement or be integrated with them. The CAF is also not intended for assessment of a child where there is any suggestion of harm. Guidance given by the CWDC (2009, para. 1.4) states 'The CAF is not for a child or young person about whom you have concerns that they might be suffering, or may be at risk of suffering, harm. In such instances, you should follow your Local Safeguarding Children Board (LSCB) safeguarding procedures without delay'.

EARLY IMPACT

So far there are mixed reports of the effectiveness of integrated children's services in addressing children's needs. In a study of fourteen local authorities (Kinder *et al.*, 2008) children, young people and parents reported a range of improvements in outcomes: getting on well with school work, feeling safer and feeling happier. Practitioners, however, raised a number of concerns, including workload implications, a reported lack of sign-up from some agencies, for example, schools and health, issues around communication and leadership, loss of professional identity and distinctiveness and resource issues and different service priorities that could inhibit the embedding of integrated children's services in some instances.

In 2009, Laming confirmed that significant problems remained in the 'day-to-day reality of working across organisational boundaries and cultures, sharing information to protect children' (para. 1.6). There were training issues still to be resolved and data systems to be improved (para. 1.5). Ultimately children's safety depends on individual staff having the time and the skill 'to understand the child or young person and their family circumstances'. Laming also feels that 'Staff across frontline services ... need to be able to notice signs of distress in children of all ages, but particularly amongst very young children who are not able to voice concerns and for whom bedwetting, head-banging and other signs may well be a cry for help' (para. 3.1).

INTER-AGENCY COLLABORATION AND STATUTORY ASSESSMENT OF SEND

Across the UK statutory assessment of children and young people's special educational needs and disabilities and/or additional support needs requires effective inter-agency collaboration in order to ensure that they are supported with the special/additional provision that they need to engage with the school or college curriculum and make good progress. In Scotland the individual plan that results from statutory assessment is termed 'a co-ordinated support plan':

> a number of children and young people have additional support needs arising from complex or multiple factors which require a high degree of co-ordination of support from education authorities and other agencies in order that their needs can be met. This support is co-ordinated through the provision of a co-ordinated support plan under the Act.
>
> (Scottish Government, 2010, p. 74, § 1)

To achieve the level of effective inter-agency collaboration that is required the Code in Scotland (2010, p. 30, § 8) reads:

> Education authorities need to play their part in ensuring that there is effective communication, collaboration and integrated assessment, planning, action and review when other agencies are involved.

In England the new Education, Health and Care plans introduced by the Children and Families Act, 2014, by definition also require a similar degree of collaboration, however problematic the history of such collaboration may have been in previous years. In England also there is the issue of the continuation of the CAF process, which, in some ways, appears to duplicate the EHC assessment process. The relationship between the CAF process and that of EHCs does not seem to be entirely clear at the time of writing (March, 2015). However, some LAs have published documents that differentiate between the two, for example, Hertfordshire:

> CAF is a separate early intervention. The EHC plan and arrangements are for those children and young people with complex needs. With the new EHC plan arrangements, the CAF will continue to be used where appropriate.
>
> (Hertfordshire Special Educational Needs and Disability Pathfinder, n/d)

In Devon LA, the parent partnership service advises that assessment carried out through the CAF might be incorporated into plans for children whose needs are not so severe that they require statutory assessment:

> For children who do not meet the level of need required for a statutory assessment, parents and carers may be offered a plan that is non-statutory, but that still identifies their child's needs and the support that will be put in place. This might incorporate other assessments that are carried out through education, health and social care, such as the current Common Assessment Framework.
>
> (Devon Parent Partnership Service, n/d,
> www.parentpartnershipdevon.org.uk, accessed 18.05.15)

SUMMARY

There are two particular areas in schools where work with other professionals is important: classroom learning and child protection. Funding in-class support for students is an expensive option for schools and recent research has shown that this is not always effective. In the classroom there are a number of different ways of conceptualising the role of support teachers which indicate the need to consider very carefully the aim of this kind of provision. Two useful systems for organising classrooms so that adults and students are all aware of who has responsibility for what are room management and zoning (Cremin *et al.*, 2003). Even so, adults will need to be very clear about what is expected of them.

Policies related to the *Every Child Matters* agenda have not been entirely successful in resolving in-agency working. The 'single most important factor' identified by Wilson and Charlton (1997) underpinning successful inter-agency work remains the existence of a clear inter-agency structure where a policy and planning group with members drawn from all the agencies supported a multi-agency, multi-disciplinary team. An effective networking system provided feedback about gaps in provision, identified needs and resources and facilitated the free flow of information among a wide range of practitioners.

REFERENCES

Adams, C. & Lloyd, J. (2007) 'The effects of speech and language therapy intervention on children with pragmatic language impairments in mainstream school', *British Journal of Special Education*, 34(4), pp. 226–233

Adult Literacy and Basic Skills Unit (1992) *The ALBSU Standards for Basic Skills Students and Trainees*, London: Adult Literacy and Basic Skills Unit

Aitken, S. (2000) 'Understanding deafblindness', in S. Aitken, M. Buultjens, C. Clark, J.T. Eyre & L. Pease (eds) *Teaching Children Who Are Deafblind*, London: David Fulton Publishers

Aitken, S. & Millar, S. (2002) *Listening to Children with Communication Support Needs*, Glasgow: Sense Scotland

Alborz, A., Pearson, D., Farrell, P. & Howes, A. (2009) *The Impact of Adult Support Staff on Pupils and Mainstream Schools: A Systematic Review of Evidence*, London: Institute of Education, EPPI Centre

American Psychiatric Association (1994) *Diagnostic and Statistical Manual of Mental Disorders* (DSM-IV), Arlington, VA: American Psychiatric Association

Anthony, G. & Walshaw, M. (2007) *Effective Pedagogy in Mathematics/Pāngarau: Best Evidence Synthesis Iteration*, Wellington: Ministry of Education

Armstrong, D. (1994) *Power and Partnership in Education: Parents, Children and Special Educational Needs*, London: Routledge

Asch, S.E. (1952) *Social Psychology*, Englewood Cliffs, NJ, Prentice-Hall

Asch, S.E. (1955) 'Opinions and social pressures', *Scientific American*, 193, pp. 31–35

Asch, S.E. (1958, 3rd edn) 'Effects of group pressure upon modification and distortion of judgements' in E.E. Maccoby, T.M. Newcomb & E.L. Hartley (eds) *Readings in Social Psychology*, New York: Holt, Rinehart and Winston

Asperger, H. [1944] (1991) Translated as 'Autistic psychopathy in childhood', in U. Frith (ed.) *Autism and Asperger Syndrome*, Cambridge: Cambridge University Press, pp. 37–92

Assessment Reform Group (1999) *Assessment for Learning: Beyond the Black Box*, Cambridge: University of Cambridge School of Education

Atkinson, R.L., Atkinson, R.C., Smith, E.E. & Bem, D.J. (1993, 11th edn) *Introduction to Psychology*, Fort Worth, TX: Harcourt Brace College Publishers

ATL (1996). *Bullying at Work: A Guide for Teachers*, London: Association of Teachers and Lecturers

Audit Commission/HMI (1992) *Getting in on the Act: Provision for Pupils with Special Educational Needs*, London: HMSO

Autism Education Trust/Centre for Research in Autistic Education (CRAE) (2011) *What Is Good Practice in Autism Education?*, London: Autism Education Trust/CRAE

Baer, D.M., Wolf, M.M. & Risley, T.R. (1968) 'Some current dimensions of applied behavior analysis', *Journal of Applied Behavior Analysis*, 1, pp. 91–97

Bakker, D.J. (1990) *Neuropsychological Treatment of Dyslexia*, New York: Oxford University Press

Balshaw, M. (1991) *Help in the Classroom*, London: David Fulton

Bandura, A. (1969). *Principles of Behavior Modification*, New York: Holt, Rinehart & Winston

Barron, S. (1992) *There's a Boy in Here: Emerging from the Bonds of Autism*, London: Simon & Schuster

Beaman, A.L., Barnes, P.J., Klenz, B. & McQuirk, B. (1978) 'Increasing helping rates through information dissemination: teaching pays', *Personality and Social Psychology Bulletin*, 4, pp. 406–411

Beattie, R. (2006) 'The oral methods and spoken language acquisition', in P. Spencer & M. Marschak (eds) *Advances in the Spoken Language Development of Deaf and Hard-of-hearing Children*, New York: Oxford University Press

Bell, D. (ed.) (1967) *An Experiment in Education: The History of Worcester College for the Blind, 1866–1966*, London: Hutchinson

Bell, E. (1999) 'The negotiation of a working role in organisational ethnography', *International Journal of Social Research Methodology*, 2(1), pp. 17–37

Benn, C. & Chitty, C. (1996) *Thirty Years On: Is Comprehensive Education Alive and Well or Struggling to Survive*, London: David Fulton

Bennathan, M. (2000, 2nd edn) 'Children at risk of failure in primary schools', in M. Bennathan & M. Boxall (eds) *Effective Intervention in Primary Schools: Nurture Groups*, London, David Fulton, pp. 1–18

Bennett, R. (1992) 'Discipline in schools: the report of the Committee of Enquiry chaired by Lord Elton', in K. Wheldall (ed.) *Discipline in Schools: Psychological Perspectives on the Elton Report*, London, Routledge

Berryman, M. & Glynn, T. (2001) 'Hei Awhina Matua: strategies for bicultural partnership in overcoming behavioural and learning difficulties', Wellington: Specialist Education Service

Bird, G. & Thomas, S. (2002) 'Providing effective speech and language therapy for children with Down syndrome in mainstream settings: a case example', *Down Syndrome News and Update*, 2(1), pp. 30–31

Bishop, D.V.M. (2000) 'Pragmatic language impairment: a correlate of SLI, a distinct subgroup, or part of the autistic continuum?', in D.V.M. Bishop & L. Leonard (eds) *Speech and Language Impairments in Children: Causes, Characteristics, Intervention and Outcome*, Hove: Psychology Press

Bishop, D.V.M. & Adams, C. (1989) 'Conversational characteristics of children with semantic-pragmatic disorder. II: what features lead to a judgement of inappropriacy?', *British Journal of Disorders of Communication*, (24), pp. 241–263

Black, D. (1998) 'Coping with loss: bereavement in childhood', *British Medical Journal*, 316 (7135): pp. 931–936

Black, D. & Urbanowicz, M.A. (1987) 'Family intervention with bereaved children', *Journal of Child Psychology and Psychiatry*, 28, pp. 467–476

Blatchford, P., Bassett, P., Brown, P., Martin, C., Russell, A. & Webster, R. (2009) *Deployment and impact of support staff (DISS) project*, London: London University Institute of Education.

Borthwick, A. & Harcourt-Heath, M. (2007) 'Calculation strategies used by Year 5 children', *Proceedings of the British Society for Research into Learning Mathematics*, 27(1), pp. 12–23

Botting, N. & Conti-Ramsden, G. (1999) 'Pragmatic language impairment without autism: the children in question', *Autism*, 3, pp. 371–396

Bowers, T. (1996) 'Putting back the "E" in EBD', *Emotional and Behavioural Difficulties*, 1(1), pp. 8–13

Bowlby, J. (1944) 'Fourty-four juvenile thieves: their character and home life', *International Journal of Psychoanalysis*, 25, pp. 19–52

Bowlby, J. (1952) 'A two-year-old goes to hospital', *Proceedings of the Royal Society of Medicine*, 46, pp. 425–427

Boxall, M. (2002) *Nurture Groups in School: Principles and Practice*, London: Paul Chapman

Bradley, L. & Bryant, P.E. (1983) 'Categorising sounds and learning to read: a causal connection', *Nature*, 301, pp. 419–421

Brandon, S. (1961) 'An epidemiological study of maladjustment in childhood', unpublished MD thesis, University of Durham

British Psychological Society (BPS) (1996) *Attention Deficit Hyperactivity Disorder (ADHD): A Psychological Response to an Evolving Concept*, Leicester: BPS

British Psychological Society (BPS) (1999) *Dyslexia, Literacy and Psychological Assessment*, Leicester: BPS

British Society of Audiology (1988) *Audiometric Descriptors for Pure-tone Audiograms*, London: British Society of Audiology

Bronfenbrenner, U. (1979) *The Ecology of Human Development: Experiments by Nature and Design*, Cambridge, MA: Harvard University Press

Bruner, J. (1966) *Toward a Theory of Instruction*, Cambridge, MA: Harvard University Press

Bruner, J. (1996) *The Culture of Education*, Boston, MA: Harvard University Press

Burman, D., Nunes, T. & Evans, D. (2006) 'Writing profiles of deaf children taught through British Sign Language', *Deafness and Education International*, 9, pp. 2–23

Buzan, T. (2000) *The Mind Map Book*, London: Penguin

Cameron, L. & Murphy, J. (2002) 'Enabling young people with a learning disability to make choices at a time of transition', *British Journal of Learning Disabilities*, 30, pp. 105–112

Campion, J. (1985) *The Child in Context: Family Systems Theory in Educational Psychology*, London: Methuen

Canter, L. & Canter, M. (1992) *Assertive Discipline: positive behaviour management for today's classroom*, Santa Monica, CA: Lee Canter and Associates

Cathcart, B. (2005) 'School's out', *Independent* [newspaper], 23 January, http://www.independent.co.uk/life-style/health-and-families/health-news/schools-out-6154276.html, accessed 26.05.15

Chazan, M., Laing, A. & Davies, D. (1994) *Emotional and Behavioural Difficulties in Middle Childhood*, London: Falmer Press

Children's Workforce Development Council, (2009) *The Common Assessment Framework for Children and Young People: A Guide for Practitioners*, London: CWDC

Chitty, C. & Dunford, J.E. (1999) *State Schools: New Labour and the Conservative Legacy*, London: Woburn Press

Clark, C., Dyson, A., Millward, A. & Skidmore, D. (1997) *New Directions in Special Needs*, London: Cassell

Clay, M.M. (1993) *Reading Recovery*. Auckland: Heinemann

Clay, M.M. (1998) *An Observation Survey of Early Literacy Achievement*, Auckland: Heinemann

Cole, B.A. (2005) 'Mission impossible? Special educational needs, inclusion and the re-conceptualization of the role of the SENCO in England and Wales', *European Journal of Special Needs Education*, 20(3), pp. 287–307

Cole, T. (1989) 'Apart or a part? Integration and the growth of British special education', Milton Keynes: Open University Press

Cole, T. (1990) 'The history of special education: social control or humanitarian progress?', *British Journal of Special Education*, 17(3), pp. 101–107

Cooper, P. (1999) 'Changing perceptions of EBD: maladjustment, EBD and beyond', *Emotional and Behavioural Difficulties*, 4(1), pp. 301–321

Cooper, P. & Upton, G. (1991) 'Controlling the urge to control: an ecosystemic approach to behaviour in schools', *Support for Learning*, 6(1), pp. 22–26

Corbett, J. (1996) *Bad Mouthing: The Language of Special Needs*, London: Falmer Press

Cornwall, J. (2000) 'Might is right? A discussion of the ethics and practicalities of control and restraint in education', *Emotional and Behavioural Difficulties*, 5(4), pp. 19–25

Cornwall, J. (2004) 'Pressure, stress and children's behaviour at school', in J. Wearmouth, R.C. Richmond, T. Glynn & M. Berryman (eds) *Understanding Pupil Behaviour in Schools: A Diversity of Approaches*, London: Fulton, ch. 20

Council of Europe (1966) *European Convention on Human Rights (Rome, 1950) and its Five Protocols*, Strasbourg: Council of Europe

Cremin, H., Thomas, G. & Vincett, K. (2003) 'Learning zones: an evaluation of three models for improving learning through teacher/teaching assistant teamwork', *Support for Learning*, 18(4), pp. 154–161

Davis, P. (2003) *Including Children with a Visual Impairment in Mainstream Schools: A Practical Guide*, London: Fulton

de Shazer, S. (1985) *Keys to Solution in Brief Therapy*, New York: Norton

de Shazer, S. (1988) *Investigating Solutions in Brief Therapy*, New York: Norton

de Shazer, S., Dolan, Y., Korman, H., McCollum, E., Trepper, T. & Berg, I.K. (2007) *More than Miracles: The State of the Art of Solutions-focused Brief Therapy*, New York: Haworth

Department for Education (DfE) (1994) *The Code of Practice for the Identification and Assessment of Special Educational Needs*, London: DfE

Department for Education (DfE) (2013) *Use of Reasonable Force: Advice for Headteachers, Staff and Governing Bodies*, London: DfE

Department for Education (DfE) (2014) *Special Educational Needs and Disability Code of Practice: 0 to 25 Years*, London: DfE

Department for Education and Employment (DfEE) (1997) *Excellence for All Children*, London: DfEE

Department of Education and Science (DES) (1978) *Warnock Report: Special Educational Needs. Report of the Committee of Enquiry into the Education of Handicapped Children and Young People, Cmnd 7212*, London: HMSO

Department of Education and Science (DES) (1989) *Discipline in Schools: Report of the Committee of Enquiry Chaired by Lord Elton* (Elton Report), London: HMSO

Department for Education and Skills (DfES) (2001) *Special Educational Needs Code of Practice*, London: DfES

Department for Education and Skills (DfES) (2002) *National Statistics*, London: DfES

Department of Education Northern Ireland (DENI) (1998) *Code of Practice on the Identification and Assessment of Special Educational Needs*, Bangor: DENI

Department of Education Northern Ireland (DENI) (2005) *Supplement to the Code of Practice on the Identification and Assessment of Special Educational Needs*, Bangor: DENI

Devon Parent Partnership Service (n/d) *Look Out for EHPCs Near You*, www.parentpartnershipdevon.org.uk, accessed 21.05.15

Dockrell, J. & McShane, J. (1993) *Children's Learning Difficulties: A Cognitive Approach*, Oxford: Blackwell

Donaldson M. (1984) *Children's Minds*, London: Fontana

Douglas, G. & McLinden, M. (2005) 'Visual impairment', in B. Norwich & A. Lewis (eds) *Special Teaching for Special Children? Pedagogies for Inclusion*, Maidenhead: Open University Press, ch. 3

Douglas, J.W.B. (1964) *The Home and the School*, St Albans: Panther

Dowling, E. & Osbourne, E. (eds) (1985) *The Family and the School*: London, Routledge & Kegan Paul

Down, J.L.H. (1866). 'Observations on an ethnic classification of idiots', Clinical Lecture Reports, London Hospital 3:259–262. http://www.neonatology.org/classics/down.html, accessed 21.05.15

Duke, N.K. & Pearson, P.D. (2002) 'Effective practices for developing reading comprehension', in A.E. Farstrup & S.J. Samuels (eds) *What Research Has to Say about Reading*, Newark, NJ: International Reading Association

Dumortier, D. (2004) *From Another Planet: Autism from Within*, London: Paul Chapman

Dunckley, I. (1999) *Managing Extreme Behaviour in Schools*, Wellington: Specialist Education Services

Dunn, L., Parry, S. & Morgan, C. (2002) 'Seeking quality in criterion referenced assessment', Learning Communities and Assessment Cultures Conference, University of Northumbria, 28–30 August

Dwivedi, K. & Gupta, A. (2000) '"Keeping cool": anger management through group work', *Support for Learning*, 15(2), pp. 76–81

Dykens, E.M. & Kasari, C. (1997) 'Maladaptive behavior in children with Prader–Willi syndrome, Down syndrome, and nonspecific mental retardation', *American Journal on Mental Retardation*, 102(3), pp. 228–237

Dyson, A. (1997) 'Social and educational disadvantage: reconnecting special needs education', *British Journal of Special Education*, 24(4), pp. 152–157

Eden, G.F., Van Meter, J.W., Rumsey, J.M., Maisog, J.M., Woods, R.P. & Zeffrio, T.A. (1996) 'Abnormal processing of visual motion in dyslexia revealed by functional brain imaging,' *Nature*, 382, pp. 66–69

Education Department (1898) *Report of the Departmental Committee on Defective and Epileptic Children (Sharpe Report)*, London: HMSO

Enquire (2014) *The Parents' Guide to Additional Support for Learning*, Edinburgh: Enquire

Everatt, J. (2002) 'Visual processes', in G. Reid & J. Wearmouth (eds) *Dyslexia and Literacy: Research and Practice*, Chichester: Wiley

Fabbro F., Pesenti S., Facoetti A., Bonanomi M., Libera L. & Lorusso M. (2001) 'Callosal transfer in different subtypes of developmental dyslexia', *Cortex*, 37, pp. 65–73

Farrington, D.P. (1993) 'Understanding and preventing bullying', in M. Tonry (ed.) *Crime and Justice. A Review of Research,* Chicago: University of Chicago Press

Fawcett, A.J. (2002) 'Dyslexia and literacy: key areas for research', in G. Reid & J. Wearmouth (eds) *Dyslexia and Literacy: Research and Practice*, Chichester: Wiley

Fawcett, A.J., & Nicholson, R.I. (2001) 'Dyslexia: the role of the cerebellum,' in A.J. Fawcett (ed.) *Dyslexia: Theory and Practice*, London: Whurr

Fawcett, A.J., Nicolson, R.I. & Dean, P. (1996) 'Impaired performance of children with dyslexia on a range of cerebellar tasks', *Annals of Dyslexia*, 46, pp. 259–283

Field, E.M. (1999) *Bully Busting*, Lane Cove: Finch Publishing Pty

Field, T.M. (1979) 'Games parents play with normal and high-risk infants', *Child Psychiatry and Human Development*, 10, pp. 41–48

Finch, A.J., Nicolson, R.I. & Fawcett, A.J. (2002) 'Evidence for an anatomical difference within the cerebella of dyslexic brains', *Cortex*, 38, pp. 529–539

Fisch H., Hyun G., Golden R., Hensle T.W., Olsson C.A. & Liberson G.L. (2003) 'The influence of paternal age on down syndrome,' *Journal of Urology*, 169(6), pp. 2275–2278

Fisher, G., Richmond, R. & Wearmouth, J. (2004) *E804 Managing Behaviour in Schools: Study Guide Part 4*, Milton Keynes: Open University Press

Florian, L. & Hegarty, J. (2004) (eds) *ICT and Special Educational Needs: A Tool for Inclusion*, Maidenhead: Open University Press

Ford, J., Mongon, D. & Whelan, M. (1982) *Special Education and Social Control*, London: Routledge

Fraivillig, J., Murphy, L. & Fuson, K. (1999) 'Advancing children's mathematical thinking in everyday mathematics classrooms', *Journal for Research in Mathematics Education*, 30(2), pp. 148–170

Freeman S.B., Taft L.F., Dooley K.J., Allran K., Sherman S.L., Hassold T.J., Khoury M.J. & Saker D.M. (1998) 'Population-based study of congenital heart defects in Down syndrome' *American Journal of Medical Genetics*, 80(3), pp. 213–217

Fulcher, G. (1989) *Disabling Policies: A Comparative Approach to Educational Policy and Disabilities*, London: Falmer Press

Furlong. V.J. (1985) *The Deviant Pupil: Sociological Perspectives*, Milton Keynes: Open University Press

Furlong, V. (1991) 'Disaffected pupils: reconstructing the sociological perspective', *British Journal of Sociology of Education*, 12(3), pp. 293–307

Galloway, D.M. & Goodwin, C. (1987) *The Education of Disturbing Children: Pupils with Learning and Adjustment Difficulties*, London: Longman

Galloway, D.M., Armstrong, D. & Tomlinson, S. (1994) *The Assessment of Special Educational Needs: Whose Problem?*, Harlow: Longman

Gamlin, R. (1935) *Modern School Hygiene*, London: James Nisbet

Gee, J. (2000) 'New people in new worlds: networks, the new capitalism and schools', in B. Cope & M. Kalantzis (eds) *Multiliteracies: Literacy Learning and the Design of Social Futures*, London: Routledge

Gersch, I. (1995) 'Involving the child', in *Schools' Special Educational Needs Policies Pack*, London: National Children's Bureau

Glynn, T. (1982) 'Antecedent control of behaviour in educational contexts', *Educational Psychology*, 2, pp. 215–229

Glynn, T. & Bishop, R. (1995) 'Cultural issues in educational research: a New Zealand perspective', *He Pūkengo Kōrero*, 1(1), pp. 37–43

Goldberg, L.R. & Richberg, C.M. (2004) 'Minimal hearing impairment: major myths with more than minimal implications', *Communication Disorders Quarterly*, 24, pp. 152–160

Gordon, A (1961) 'Mongolism (correspondence)', The Lancet, 1 (7180), p 775

Grandin, T. (1996) *Emergence: Labelled Autistic*, New York: Warner Books

Grauberg, E. (2002) *Elementary Mathematics and Language Difficulties*, London: Whurr

Gray, P., Miller, A. & Noakes, J. (1996) *Challenging Behaviour in Schools*, London: Routledge

Greeno, J.G. (1998) 'The situativity of knowing, learning, and research', *American Psychologist*, 53(1), pp. 5–26

Gregory, E. (1996) *Making Sense of a New World*, London: Paul Chapman

Gross, J. (1996) 'The weight of the evidence', *Support for Learning*, 11(1), pp. 3–8

Hage, C. & Leybaert, J. (2006) 'The effect of cued speech on the development of spoken language', in P. Spencer & M. Marschak (eds) *Advances in the Spoken Language Development of Deaf and Hard-of-hearing Children*, New York: Oxford University Press

Hanko, G. (1994) 'Discouraged children: when praise does not help', *British Journal of Special Education*, 21(4), pp. 166–168

Hargreaves, D.H. (1967) *Social Relations in a Secondary School*, London: Routledge

Harris, M. & Moreno, C. (2006) 'Speech reading and learning to read: a comparison of 8-year-old profoundly deaf children with good and poor reading ability', *Journal of Deaf Studies and Deaf Education*, 11, pp. 189–201

Harris, S. (1976) 'Rational-emotive education and the human development program: a guidance study', *Elementary School Guidance and Counselling*, 10, pp. 113–122

Harris-Hendriks, J. & Figueroa, J. (1995) *Black in White: The Caribbean Child in the UK*, London: Pitman

Hart, S. (1995) 'Differentiation by task or differentiation by outcome?', in National Children's Bureau, *Schools' Special Educational Needs Policies Pack*, London: NCB

Hatcher, J. & Snowling, M. (2002) 'The phonological representations hypothesis of dyslexia', in G. Reid & J. Wearmouth (eds) *Dyslexia and Literacy: Research and Practice*, Chichester: Wiley

Hertfordshire Special Educational Needs and Disability Pathfinder (n/d) *Local Networks and the Local Offer*, http://www.hertsdirect.org/docs/pdf/s/faqs.pdf, accessed 21.05.15

Hiebert, J., Carpenter, T., Fennema, E., Fuson, K.C., Wearne, D., Murray, H., Olivier, A. & Human, P. (1997) *Making Sense: Teaching and Learning Mathematics with Understanding*, Portsmouth, NH: Heinemann

Higashida, N. (2013) *The Reason I Jump,* London: Hodder and Stoughton

Holmes, J. (1993) *John Bowlby and Attachment Theory*, London: Routledge

Howard-Jones, N. (1979) 'On the diagnostic term "Down's disease"', *Medical History*, 23(1), pp. 102–104

Irlen, H. (1991) *Reading by the Colors*, New York: Avery

Jordan, R. (1999) *Autistic Spectrum Disorders an Introductory Handbook for Practitioners,* London: David Fulton

Jordan, R. & Powell, S. (1995) *Teaching and Understanding Children with Autism*, Chichester: Wiley

Jordan, R., Jones, G. & Murray, D. (1998) *Educational Interventions for Children with Autism: A Literature Review of Recent and Current Research,* London: HMSO

Kanner, L. (1943) 'Autistic disturbances of affective contact', *Nervous Child*, 2, pp. 217–250

Kinder, K., Lord, P. & Wilkin, A. (2008) *Implementing Integrated Children's Services, Part 1: Managers' Views on Early Impact*, Slough: National Foundation for Educational Research (NFER)

Klin, A., Sparrow, S., Marans, W.D., Carter, A., & Volkmar, F.R. (2000) 'Assessment issues in children and adolescents with Asperger syndrome', in A. Klin, F.R. Volkmar & S. Sparrow (eds) *Asperger Syndrome,* New York: Guilford Press

Lamb, B. (2009) *Report to the Secretary of State on the Lamb Inquiry Review of SEN and Disability Information*, London: DCSF

Lamb, B (2010) *Improving Parental Confidence in the Special Educational Needs System: An Implementation Plan*, London: DCSF

Lampert, M. (1990) 'When the problem is not the question and the solution is not the answer: mathematical knowing and teaching', *American Educational Research Journal*, 27(1), pp. 29–63

Lave, J. (1993) 'The practice of learning', in S. Chaiklin & J. Lave (eds) *Understanding Practice: Perspectives on Activity and Context*, Cambridge: Cambridge University Press

Lave, J. & Wenger, E. (1998) *Communities of Practice: Learning, Meaning, and Identity*, Cambridge: Cambridge University Press

LaVigna, G.W. & Donnellan, A.M. (1986) *Alternatives to Punishment: Solving Behavior Problems with Non-aversive Strategies*, New York: Irvington

Law, J., Lindsay, G., Peacey, N., Gascoigne, M., Soloff, N., Radford, J. & Band, S. (2002) 'Consultation as a model for providing speech and language therapy in schools: a panacea or one step too far?', *Child Language Teaching and Therapy*, 18, pp. 145–163

Le Couteur, A., Lord, C. & Rutter, M. (2003) *Autism Diagnostic Interview-Revised (ADI-R)*, Los Angeles: Western Psychological Services

Leadbetter, J. & Leadbetter, P. (1993) *Special Children: Meeting the Challenge in the Primary School*, London: Cassell

Leinonen, E. & Letts, C. (1997) 'Why pragmatic impairment? A case study in the comprehension of inferential meaning', *European Journal of Disorders of Communication*, 32, pp. 35–51

Leinonen, E., Letts, C. & Smith, R. (2000) *Children's Pragmatic Communication Difficulties*, London: Whurr

Lennox, D. (1991) *See Me After School*, London: David Fulton

Levine, M. (1999) 'Rethinking bystander non-intervention', *Human Relations*, 52(9), pp. 1133–1155

Lewis, A. (2002) 'Accessing through research interviews the views of children with difficulties in learning', *Support for Learning*, 17(3), pp. 110–116

Lewis, A. & Norwich, B. (2000) *Mapping a Pedagogy for Learning Difficulties*, report submitted to the British Educational Research Association (BERA), February, London: BERA

Lewis, S. (1996) 'The reading achievement of a group of severely and profoundly hearing-impaired school leavers educated within a natural aural approach', *Journal of the British Association of Teachers of the Deaf*, 20, pp. 1–7

Licht, R. (1994) 'Differences in word recognition between P- and L-type reading disability', in R. Licht & G. Spyer (eds) *The balance model of dyslexia*, Assen: Van Gorcum

Lifton, R.J. (2000) *The Nazi Doctors: Medical Killing and the Psychology of Genocide*, New York: Basic Books

Lord, C., Rutter, M. & Le Couteur, A. (1994) 'Autism diagnostic interview – revised: a revised version of a diagnostic interview for caregivers of individuals with possible pervasive developmental disorders', *Journal of Autism and Developmental Disorders*, 24, pp. 659–685

Lorenz, K. (1969) *On Aggression*, London: Methuen

Lorenz, S. (1998) *Effective In-class Support*, London: David Fulton

Lunzer, E.A. & Gardner, W.K. (1979) *The Effective Use of Reading*, London: Heinemann Educational

Macfarlane, A. (1997) 'The Hikairo rationale: teaching students with emotional and behavioural difficulties: a bicultural approach', *Waikato Journal of Education*, 3, pp. 135–168

Macfarlane, A. (2000a) 'Māori perspectives on development', in L. Bird & W. Drewery (eds) *Human Development in Aotearoa: A Journey through Life*, Auckland: McGraw-Hill

Macfarlane, A. (2000b, 2nd edn) 'The value of Māori ecologies in special education', in D. Fraser, R. Moltzen, R. & K. Ryba (eds) *Learners with Special Needs in Aotearoa New Zealand*, Palmerston North: Dunmore Press

Mair, M. (1988) 'Psychology as storytelling', *International Journal of Personal Construct Psychology*, 1, pp. 125–132

Maslow, A. (1943) 'A theory of human motivation', *Psychological Review*, 50(4), pp. 370–396

Mason, H. (1997) 'Assessment of vision', in H. Mason, S. McCall, C. Arter, M. McLinden & J. Stone (eds) *Visual Impairment: Access to Education for Children and Young People,* London: Fulton, ch. 6

Mason, H. (2001) *Visual Impairment*, Tamworth: NASEN

Mason, H., McCall, S., Arter, C., McLinden, M. & Stone, J. (1997) *Visual Impairment: Access to Education for Children and Young People,* London: Fulton

McDermott, R.P. (1999) 'On becoming labelled: the story of Adam', in P. Murphy (ed.) *Learners, Learning and Assessment*, London, Paul Chapman

McLeod, J. (1998, 2nd edn) *An Introduction to Counselling*, Buckingham: Open University Press

McNaughton, S. (2002) *Meeting of Minds*, Wellington: Learning Media

Mehan, H. (1996) 'The politics of representation', in S. Chaiklin & J. Lave (eds) *Understanding Practice: Perspectives on Activity and Context*, Cambridge: Cambridge University Press

Meichenbaum, D. & Turk, D. (1976) 'The cognitive-behavioural management of anxiety, anger and pain', in P.O. Davidson (ed.) *The Behavioural Management of Anxiety, Anger and Pain*, New York: Brunner/Mazel

Mencap (undated) *About Profound and Multiple Learning Disabilities*, London: Mencap

Mental Deficiency Committee (1929) *Report of the Mental Deficiency Committee (Wood Report)*, London: HMSO

Merrett, F. (1985) *Encouragement Works Better than Punishment: The Application of Behavioural Methods in Schools*, Birmingham: Positive Products

Milgram, S. (1963) 'Behavioural study of obedience', *Journal of Abnormal and Social Psychology*, 67, pp. 371–378

Milgram, S. (1974) *Obedience to Authority: An Experimental View*, New York: Harper and Row

Miller, O. & Ockleford, A (2005) *Visual Needs*, London: Continuum

Ministry of Education (New Zealand) (2005) *Effective Literacy Practice*, Wellington: Learning Media

Ministry of Education (MoE) (1945) *The Nation's Schools*, London: MoE

Minuchin, S. (1974) *Families and Family Therapy*, Cambridge, MA: Harvard University Press

Moeller, M.P., Tomblin, J.B., Yoshinaga-Itano, C., Connor, C. & Jerger, S. (2007) 'Current state of knowledge: language and literacy of children with hearing impairment', *Ear and Hearing*, 28, pp. 740–753

Moore, D. (2004) 'Behaviour in context: functional assessment of disruptive behaviour in classrooms', in J. Wearmouth, R. Richmond & T. Glynn (eds) *Addressing Pupil Behaviour: Responses at District, School and Individual Levels*, London: David Fulton

Moores, D. (2001) *Educating the Deaf*, Boston: Houghton Mifflin

Moores, D. (2008) 'Research in Bi-Bi instruction', *American Annals of the Deaf*, 153, pp. 3–4

Morris, J.K., Wald, N.J., Mutton, D.E. & Alberman, E. (2003) 'Comparison of models of maternal age-specific risk for Down syndrome live births', *Prenatal Diagnosis*, 23(3), pp. 252–258

Morris, M. & Smith, P. (2008) *Educational Provision for Blind and Partially Sighted Children and Young People in Britain: 2007*, London: RNIB

Moseley, D.V. (1992) 'Visual and linguistic determinants of reading fluency in dyslexics', in R. Groner (ed.) *Reading and Reading Disorders: International Perspectives*, Oxford: Elsevier

Mosley, J. (1996) *Quality Circle Time in the Primary Classroom: Your Essential Guide to Enhancing Self-esteem, Self-discipline and Positive Relationships*, Cambridge: LDA

Murphy, S. (2002) 'Literacy assessment and the politics of identity', in J. Soler, J. Wearmouth & G. Reid (eds) *Contextualising Difficulties in Literacy Development: Exploring Politics, Culture, Ethnicity and Ethics*, London: Routledge, pp. 87–101

National Assembly of Wales (NAW) (2004) *Special Educational Needs Code of Practice*, Cardiff: NAW.

National Autistic Society (2015a) 'Position statement: causes of autism', http://www.autism.org.uk/News-and-events/Media-Centre/Position-statements/Causes-of-autism.aspx, accessed 21.05.15

National Autistic Society (2015b) 'What is Asperger syndrome?', http://www.autism.org.uk/About-autism/Autism-and-Asperger-syndrome-an-introduction/What-is-Asperger-syndrome.aspx, accessed 21.05.15

National Council for Educational Technology (NCET) (1995) *Access Technology: Making the Right Choice*, Coventry: NCET

National Deaf Children's Society (NDCS) (2008) *Acoustics Toolkit*, London: NDCS

National Deaf Children's Society (NDCS) (2010) *Communicating with Your Deaf Child*, London: NDCS

National Institute of Neorological Disorders and Stroke (2005) *Tourette Syndrome Fact Sheet*, Bethesda, MD: NINDS

Neale, M.D. (1999, 3rd edn) *The Neale Analysis of Reading Ability*, London: GL Assessment

Nicolson, R.I. & Fawcett, A.J. (1994) 'Reaction times and dyslexia', *Quarterly Journal of Experimental Psychology*, 47A, pp. 29–48

Nicolson, R.I. & Fawcett, A.J. (1999) 'Developmental dyslexia: the role of the cerebellum', *Dyslexia*, pp. 155–177

Nind, M. (1999) 'Intensive interaction: a useful approach?', *British Journal of Special Education*, 26(2), pp. 96–102

Nisbett, R.E., Caputo, G.C., Legant, P. & Marecek, J. (1973) 'Behavior as seen by the actor and as seen by the observer', *Journal of Personality and Social Psychology*, 27(2), pp. 154–164

Norbury, C.F. & Bishop, D.V.M. (2003) 'Narrative skills in children with communication impairments', *International Journal of Language and Communication Impairments*, 38, pp. 287–313

Norwich, B., Cooper, P. & Maras, P. (2002) 'Attentional and activity difficulties: findings from a national study', *Support for Learning*, 17(4), pp. 182–186

Nunes, T., Bryant, P. & Bindman, M. (1997) 'Morphological spelling strategies: developmental stages and processes', *Developmental Psychology*, 33, pp. 637–649

O'Connor, M.C. (1998) 'Language socialisation in the mathematics classroom: discourse practices and mathematical thinking', in M. Lampert & M. Blunk (eds) *Talking Mathematics in School: Studies of Teaching and Learning*, Cambridge: Cambridge University Press, pp. 17–55

Office for Standards in Education (Ofsted) (2001) *Improving Attendance and Behaviour in Secondary Schools*, London: Ofsted

Office for Standards in Education (Ofsted) (2010) *The Special Educational Needs and Disability Review*, London: Ofsted

Oliphant, J. (2006) 'Empowerment and debilitation in the educational experience of the blind in nineteenth-century England and Scotland', *History of Education*, 35(1), pp. 47–68

Olweus, D. (1993) *Bullying at School: What We Know and What We Can Do*, Oxford: Blackwell

Olweus, D. (1999) 'Sweden', in P.K. Smith, Y. Morita, J. Junger-Tas, D. Olweus, R. Catalano & P. Slee (eds) *The Nature of School Bullying: A Cross-national Perspective*, London: Routledge

Open University (2000) Audio interview, in *E831 Professional Development for Special Educational Needs Co-ordinators*, Milton Keynes: Open University

Open University (2005), Study Topic 7: 'Needs, rights and opportunities', in *E111 Supporting Learning in Primary Schools*, Milton Keynes: Open University

Padden, C. & Gunsals, D. (2003) 'How the alphabet came to be used in a sign language', *Sign Language Studies*, 4, pp. 1–13

Park, K. (2003) 'A voice and a choice', *Special Children*, 153, Feb./March, www.education-quest.com, accessed 21.05.15

Parkes, C.M. (1986) *Bereavement: Studies of Grief in Adult Life*, Harmondsworth: Penguin

Paveley, S. (2002) 'Inclusion and the web: strategies to improve access', in C. Abbott (ed.) *Special Educational Needs and the Internet: Issues for the Inclusive Classroom*, London: RoutledgeFalmer

Piacenti, J., Woods, D.W., Scahill, L., Wilhelm, S., Peterson, A.L., Chang, S., Ginsburg, G.S., Deckersbach, T., Dziura, J., Levi-Pearl, S. & Walkup, J. (2010) 'Behavior therapy for children with Tourette disorder', *Journal of the American Medical Association*, 303(19), pp. 1929–1937

Piaget, J. (1954) *Construction of Reality in the Child*, New York: Basic Books

Piaget, J. (1964) 'Cognitive development in children', *Journal of Research in Science Teaching*, 2(3) pp. 176–186

Piaget, J. (1969) *The Child's Conception of Time*, London: RKP

Pickersgill, M. & Gregory, S. (1998) 'Sign bilingualism: a model', London: LASER

Pickles, P. (2001) 'Therapeutic provision in mainstream curricula', in J. Wearmouth (ed.) *Special Educational Provision in the Context of Inclusion: Policy & Practice in Schools*, London: Fulton, pp. 291–304

Pitchford, M. (2004) 'An introduction to multi-element planning for primary aged children', in J. Wearmouth, R.C. Richmond & T. Glynn (eds) *Addressing Pupils' Behaviour: Responses at District, School and Individual Levels*, London: Fulton, pp. 310–327

Pohlschmidt, M. & Meadowcroft, R. (2010) *Muscle Disease: The Impact. Incidence and Prevalence of Neuromuscular Conditions in the UK*, London: Muscular Dystrophy Campaign

Pollard, A. (2002) *Reflective Teaching: Effective and Evidence-informed Professional Practice*, London: Continuum

Porter, J. Ouvry, C., Morgan, M. & Downs, C. (2001) 'Interpreting the communication of people with profound and multiple learning difficulties', *British Journal of Learning Disabilities*, 29(1), pp. 12–16

Poulou, M. & Norwich, B. (2002) 'Cognitive, emotional and behavioural responses to students with emotional and behavioural difficulties: a model of decision-making', *British Educational Research Journal*, 28(1), pp. 111–138

Preece, D. (2002) 'Consultation with children with autistic spectrum disorders about their experience of short-term residential care', *British Journal of Learning Disabilities*, 30(3), pp. 97–104

Primary National Strategy (PNS) (2005) *Speaking Listening Learning: Working with Children Who Have Special Educational Needs* (Ref 1235/2005), London: QCA

Pumfrey, P.D. (1996) *Specific Developmental Dyslexia: Basics to Back. Fifteenth Vernon–Wall Lecture*, Leicester: British Psychological Society

Randall, P.E. (1991) *The Prevention of School-based Bullying*, Hull: University of Hull

Rapin, I. & Allen, D. (1983) 'Developmental language disorders: neuropsychological considerations', in U. Kirk (ed.) *Neuropsychology of Language, Reading and Spelling*, New York: Academic Press

Ravenette, A.T. (1984) 'The recycling of maladjustment', *Association of Educational Psychologists Journal*, 6(3), pp. 18–27

Restorative Practices Development Team (2003) *Restorative Practices for Schools*, Hamilton, NZ: University of Waikato

Rice, M. & Brooks, G. (2004) *Developmental Dyslexia in Adults: A Research Review*, London: NRDC

Riddick B., Wolfe J. & Lumsdon D. (2002) *Dyslexia: A Practical Guide for Teachers and Parents*, London: David Fulton

Rigby, K. (1997) 'What children tell us about bullying in schools', *Children Australia*, 22(2), pp. 28–34

Rigby, K. (2002) *New Perspectives on Bullying*, London: Jessica Kingsley

Roaf, C. & Lloyd, C. (1995) 'Multi-agency work with young people in difficulty', *Social Care Research Findings*, 68, June, York: Joseph Rowntree Foundation

Robertson, J. & Bakker, D.J. (2002) 'The balance model of reading and dyslexia', in G. Reid & J. Wearmouth (eds) *Dyslexia and Literacy: Research and Practice*, Chichester: Wiley

Rogers J. (2007) 'Cardinal number and its representation: skills, concepts and contexts', *Early Childhood Education and Care*, 178(2), pp. 211–225

Rogers, B. (2013) 'Communicating with children in the classroom', in T. Cole, H. Daniels & J. Visser (eds) *The Routledge International Companion to Emotional and Behavioural Difficulties*, London: Routledge, pp. 237–245

Rogers, B. (1994) 'Teaching positive behaviour in behaviourally disordered students in primary schools', *Support for Learning*, 9(4), pp. 166–170

Rogers, W. (1994a) *The Language of Discipline*, Plymouth: Northcote House.

Rogers, W. (1994b) *Behaviour Recovery: A Whole School Approach for Behaviourally Disordered Children*, Melbourne: Australian Council for Educational Research

Rogoff, B. (1990) *Apprenticeship in Thinking: Cognitive Development in Social Context*, New York: Oxford University Press

Rose, J. (2009) *Identifying and Teaching Children and Young People with Dyslexia and Literacy Difficulties*, London: DCFS

Rosenheim, E. & Reicher, R. (1985) 'Informing children about a parent's terminal illness', *Journal of Child Psychology and Psychiatry*, 26, pp. 995–998

Rosenthal, R. & Jacobson, L. (1968) *Pygmalion in the Classroom*, New York: Holt, Rinehart and Winston

Roth, I. (2002) 'The autistic spectrum: from theory to practice', in N. Brace & H. Westcott (eds) *Applying Psychology*, Milton Keynes: Open University, pp. 243–315

Royal National Institute for the Blind (RNIB) (2015) *Invention of Braille,* http://www.rnib.org.uk/braille-and-other-tactile-codes-portal-braille-past-present-and-future/invention-braille, accessed 21.05.15

Royal National Institute for the Deaf (RNID), (2004) *Inclusion Strategies*, London: RNID

Rutter, M. (1966) *Children of Sick Parents*, Oxford: Oxford University Press

Rutter, M. (2005) 'Incidence of autism spectrum disorders: changes over time and their meaning', *Acta Paediatrica*, 94, pp. 2–15

Rutter, M., Le Couteur, A. & Lord, C. (2003) *ADI-R: The Autism Diagnostic Interview-Revised*, Los Angeles, CA: Western Psychological Services

Rutter, M., Tizard, J. & Whitmore, K. (1970) *Education, Health and Behaviour*, London: Longman

Rutter, M., Maughan, B., Mortimore, P. & Ouston, J. (1979) *Fifteen Thousand Hours: Secondary Schools and Their Effects on Children*, London: Open Books

Salmon, P. (1995) *Psychology in the Classroom*, London: Cassell

Sarbin, T. (1986) *Narrative Psychology: The Storied Nature of Human Conduct*, New York: Praeger

Schweigert, F.J. (1999) 'Moral behaviour in victim offender conferencing', *Criminal Justice Ethics*, summer/fall, pp. 29–40

Scottish Executive (2004) Education (Additional Support for Learning) (Scotland) Act (2004), Edinburgh: Scottish Government

Scottish Government (2010) *Supporting Children's Learning Code of Practice*, Edinburgh: Scottish Government

Scottish Government (2014) *Planning Improvements for Disabled Pupils' Access to Education*, Edinburgh: Scottish Government

Selikowitz, M. (2008) *Down Syndrome*, Oxford: Oxford University Press

Shapiro, S. & Cole, L. (1994) *Behaviour Change in the Classroom: Self-management Interventions*, New York: Guilford Press

Sharron, H. (1995) 'Behaviour drugs: headteachers speak out, *Special Children*, April, pp. 10–13

Sheehy, K. (2004) 'Approaches to autism', in J. Wearmouth, R.C. Richmond & T. Glynn (eds) *Addressing Pupils' Behaviour: Responses at District, School and Individual Levels*, London: Fulton, pp. 338–356

Singleton, C. (1994) 'Computer applications in the identification and remediation of dyslexia,' in D. Wray (ed.) *Literacy and Computers: Insights from Research*, Widnes: United Kingdom Reading Association

Skinner, B.F. (1938) *The Behaviour of Organisms*, New York: Appleton Century Crofts

Skinner, B.F. (1953). *Science and Human Behavior*, New York: Macmillan.

Slack, J. (2010) 'Our children don't fail due to racism, says black academic', 23 September, *Mail Online*, http://www.dailymail.co.uk/news/article-1314433/Our-children-dont-fail-racism-says-black-academic.html, accessed 21.05.15

Slee, P.T. (1995) 'Peer victimization and its relationship to depression among Australian primary school students', *Personality and Individual Differences*, 18(1), pp. 57–62

Smedley, M. (1990) 'Semantic-pragmatic language disorders: a description with some practical suggestions for teachers', *Child Language Teaching and Therapy*, 5, pp. 174–190

Smith, P.K. & Sharp, S. (1994) *School Bullying: Insights and Perspectives*, London: Routledge

Snowling, M.J. (2000, 2nd edn) *Dyslexia*, Oxford: Blackwell

Spencer, P. & Marschak, M. (2010) Evidence-based Practice in Educating Deaf and Hard-of-hearing Students, Oxford: Oxford University Press

Spencer, P. & Marschak, M. (eds) (2006) *Advances in the Spoken Language Development of Deaf and Hard-of-hearing Children*, New York: Oxford University Press

Sproson, B. (2004) 'Some do and some don't: teacher effectiveness in managing behaviour', in J. Wearmouth, T. Glynn, R.C. Richmond & M. Berryman (eds) *Inclusion and Behaviour Management in Schools*, London: David Fulton, ch. 17

Stanovich, K. (2000) *Progress in Understanding Reading: Scientific Foundations and New Frontiers*, London: Guilford Press

Strouse Watt, W. (2003) *How Visual Acuity Is Measured*, http://www.mdsupport.org/library/acuity.html, accessed 21.05.15

Summerfield, A./Department for Education and Science (DES) (1968) *Psychologists in the Education Services: Report of the Working Party (the Summerfield Report)*, London: HMS

Sutton, J., Smith, P.K. & Swettenham, J. (1999) 'Social cognition and bullying: social inadequacy or skilled manipulation', *British Journal of Developmental Psychology*, 17, pp. 435–450

Tate, R., Smeeth, L., Evans, J., & Fletcher, A. (2005) *The Prevalence of Visual Impairment in the UK: A Review of the Literature*, www.rnib.org.uk/xpedio/groups/public/documents/PublicWebsite/public_prevalencereport.doc, accesssed 21.05.15

Taylor, K. (2007) 'The participation of children with multi-sensory impairment in person-centred planning', *British Journal of Special Education*, 34(4), pp. 204–211

TEACCH (1998) Treatment and Education of Autistic and Related Communication Handicapped Children, http://www.teacch.com/, accessed 21.05.15

Tew, M. (1998) 'Circle time: a much neglected resource in secondary schools', *Pastoral Care*, September, pp. 18–27

Tomlinson, S. (1988) 'Why Johnny can't read: critical theory and special education', *European Journal of Special Needs Education*, 3(1), pp. 45–58

Topping, K. (2001) *Thinking, Reading, Writing,* London: Continuum

Trevarthen, C., Aitken, K., Papoudi, D. & Robarts, J. (1998, 2nd edn) *Children with Autism: Diagnosis and Intervention to Meet Their Needs*, London: Jessica Kingsley Publishers

Underwood, J.E.A. (1955) *Report of the Committee on Maladjusted Children*, London: HMSO

Vygotsky, L.S. (1962) *Thought and Language*, Cambridge, MA: MIT Press

Watkins, C. & Wagner, P. (1995) 'School behaviour and special educational needs: what's the link?', in National Children's Bureau, *Discussion Papers 1: Schools' Special Educational Needs Policies Pack*, London: NCB

Watkins, C. & Wagner, P. (2000) *Improving School Behaviour*, London: Paul Chapman

Wearmouth, J (1986) 'Self-concept and learning experience of pupils with moderate learning difficulties', unpublished Masters thesis, Institute of Education, London University

Wearmouth, J. (1997) 'Prisoners' perspectives on what constitutes a 'good' education', paper presented to the British Psychological Society Annual Conference (Education Section), autumn, Warwicks, England

Wearmouth, J. (1999) 'Another one flew over: 'Maladjusted' Jack's perception of his label', *British Journal of Special Education*, 26(1), pp. 15–23

Wearmouth, J. (2000) *Co-ordinating Special Educational Provision: Meeting the Challenges in Schools*, London: Hodder

Wearmouth, J. (2003) 'Investigating the "problem space" in special educational provision in mainstream schools', unpublished PhD manuscript, Open University

Wearmouth, J. (2004) 'Learning from "James": lessons about policy and practice for literacy difficulties in schools' special educational provision', *British Journal of Special Education*, 31(2), pp. 60–67

Wearmouth, J. (2008) 'Testing, assessment and literacy: a view from England', *Curriculum Perspectives*, 28(3), pp. 77–81

Wearmouth, J. (2009) *A Beginning Teacher's Guide to Special Educational Needs*, Buckingham: Open University Press

Wearmouth, J., Glynn, T. & Berryman, M. (2005) *Perspectives on Student Behaviour in Schools: Exploring Theory and Developing Practice*, London: Routledge

Wearmouth, J., McKinney, R. & Glynn, T. (2007) 'Restorative justice; two examples from New Zealand schools', *British Journal of Special Education*, 34(4), pp. 196–203

Weavers, J. (2003) 'Dyslexia and mathematics', in M. Thomson (ed.) *Dyslexia Included*, London: Fulton, pp. 33–45

Weller, R.A., Weller, E.B., Fristad, M.A., Bowes, J.M. (1991) 'Depression in recently bereaved prepubertal children', *American Journal of Psychiatry*, 148, pp. 1536–1540

Wilde, J. (1994) 'The effects of the let's get rational board game on rational thinking, depression and self-acceptance in adolescents', *Journal of Rational-Emotive and Cognitive-Behavior Therapy*, 12, pp. 189–196

Wilde, J. (1995) *Anger Management in Schools: Alternatives to Student Violence*, Lancaster, PA: Technomic Publishing Co.

Wilde, J. (2001) 'Interventions for children with anger problems', *Journal of Rational–Emotive and Cognitive-Behavior Therapy*, 19(3), pp. 191–197

Wilkins, M. & Ertmer, D.J. (2002) 'Introducing young children who are deaf or hard of hearing to spoken language', *Language, Speech and Hearing Services in Schools*, 33, pp. 196–204

Wilkins, A.J., Evans, B.J.W., Brown, J.A., Busby, A.E., Wingfield, A.E., Jeanes, R.L. & Bald, J. (1994) 'Double-masked placebo-controlled trial of precision spectral filters in children who use coloured overlays', *Ophthalmic and Physiological Optics*, 14, pp. 365–370

Wilkinson, E. (1947) *The New Secondary Education*, London: HMSO.

Wilson, A. & Charlton, K. (1997) *Making Partnerships Work: A Practical Guide for the Public, Private, Voluntary and Community Sectors*, York: Joseph Rowntree Foundation

Wing, L. (1996) *The Autistic Spectrum: A Guide for Parents and Professionals*, London: Constable.

Wing, L. & Gould, J. (1979) 'Severe impairments of social interaction and associated abnormalities in children: epidemiology and classification', *Journal of Autism and Developmental Disorders*, 9, pp. 11–29

Wood, D., Bruner, J. & Ross, G. (1976) 'The role of tutoring in problem solving', *Journal of Child Psychology and Psychiatry*, 17, pp. 89–100

Wood, K.C., Smith, H. & Grossniklaus, D. (2001) 'Piaget's stages of cognitive development', in Ii M. Orey (ed.) *Emerging Perspectives on Learning, Teaching, and Technology*, Athens, GA: University of Georgia

World Health Organisation (WHO) (1992) *The International Statistical Classification of Diseases, ICD-10,* Geneva: WHO

World Health Organisation (2010) *Deafness and Hearing Impairment, Fact Sheet* no. 300, Geneva: WHO

Wray, D. (2002) 'Metacognition and literacy', in G. Reid & J. Wearmouth (eds) *Dyslexia and Literacy: Research and Practice*, Chichester: Wiley

Yoder, P.J. (1990) 'The theoretical and empirical basis of early amelioration of developmental disabilities: implications for future research', *Journal of Early Intervention*, 14, pp. 27–42

Yoshinaga-Itano, C. (2003) 'From screening to early identification and intervention: discovering predictors to successful outcomes for children with significant hearing loss', *Journal of Deaf Studies and Deaf Education*, 8, pp. 11–30

Ysseldyke, J.E. & Christenson, S.L. (1987) *The Instructional Environment Scale (TIES)*, Austin, TX: Pro-Ed

Ysseldyke, J.E. & Christenson, S.L. (1993) *TIES-II: The Instructional Environment System – II*, Longmont, CO: Sopris West

Yurdakul, NS, Ugurlu, S. & Maden, A. (2006) 'Strabismus in Down syndrome', 43(1), pp. 27–30

Zimbardo, P.G. (1970) 'The human choice: individuation, reason and order versus deindividuation, impulse and chaos', in W.J. Arnold & D. Levine (eds) *Nebraska Symposium on Motivation*, 16, Lincoln, NE: University of Nebraska Press

INDEX